THE MAKING
OF THE
NEW JAPAN

THE MAKING
OF THE
NEW JAPAN

Reclaiming the
Political Mainstream

Yasuhiro Nakasone

Translated and annotated by
Lesley Connors

Routledge
Taylor & Francis Group

LONDON AND NEW YORK

First Published in 1999
by Routledge
Published 2014 by Routledge

2 Park Square, Milton Park, Abingdon, Oxfordshire OX14 4RN

711 Third Avenue, New York, NY 10017

First issued in paperback 2014

Routledge is an imprint of the Taylor & Francis Group, an informa business

Transferred to Digital Printing 2010

This translation © 1999 Lesley Connors

Designed and Typeset in LucidaBright by LaserScript Ltd, Mitcham, Surrey

British Library Cataloguing in Publication Data
A catalogue record of this book is available from the British Library

Library of Congress Cataloguing in Publication Data
A catalogue record for this book has been requested

ISBN 978-0-700-71246-5 (hbk)
ISBN 978-1-138-86322-4 (pbk)

Publisher's Note
The publisher has gone to great lengths to ensure the quality of this reprint
but points out that some imperfections in the original may be apparent.

Seiji to Jinsei

CONTENTS

Contents

ACKNOWLEDGEMENTS

The translation has benefited from the advice and criticism of friends, family and colleagues in both the United Kingdom and Japan, and specifically from the opportunity to spend several weeks at the Institute for International Policy Studies in Tokyo; a visit which was facilitated by the Daiwa Anglo-Japanese Foundation and by the School of Oriental and African Studies.

I would particularly like to acknowledge the support of Professor Yui Tsunehiko of Bunkyo Women's University, who was extremely supportive throughout the early stages of the process of translation, and of Mr Saito Akira, International Editor of the Yomiuri Shimbun, who reviewed the final manuscript. I would also like to thank Mr Takiguchi Susumu, Vice-President of the British Haiku Society for his sympathetic translation of the haiku. Mr Jin-emon Konishi, President of Nippon Zoki Pharmaceutical Company kindly provided financial support toward the preparation of the book.

I hope that any remaining flaws, for which I am wholly responsible, will not spoil the readers appreciation of these fascinating memoirs.

Lesley Connors, SOAS, University of London

CHAPTER ONE

THE CHILD IS FATHER OF THE MAN

My mother and my father, the timber merchant

In the middle of the garden where I was born and brought up was a big Japanese pine. The pine was the symbol of the Nakasone family, which was involved in the forestry industry, running lumber mills and selling timber.

It appears that my family moved to what was then Satomimura, and is now Harunamachi, about three hundred and fifty years ago at about the time that Takeda Shingen advanced from the area around Saku to Kōzuke in order to attack the Naganos in Minowa castle in northern Takasaki. It seems that they were natives of that area and were descended from vassals of the Takedas.[1]

I have a Nakasone family genealogy passed on by a cousin[2] who lived in Satomimura. Concerning Yoshikiyo, the second son of Shinra Saburō [Minamoto no Yoshimitsu], it states, 'Kainokami, servant of Takeda Akino, died aged seventy-five on 23 July, in the year 1149.' Tsunayoshi, the eleventh generation after Yoshimitsu, took the name Nakasone Jūrō and the record states, 'Died in battle on 9 January, 1417 at Sagamigawa.' Sixteen generations after Tsunayoshi came my father, Matsugoro.

Before the Tokugawa period, such stories were customary and many are apocryphal. However in the case of this particular genealogy, the entries from the time of Nakasone Sōuemon Mitsunaga, who was alive from the Sengoku period to the time of the third Tokugawa Shogun, Iemitsu, were reasonably accurate and detailed. It tells us that Mitsunaga migrated to Kōzuke province, Usui county, Satomimura, in 1590. Even today, in the main family house in what was Satomimura, there is a flower-shaped stone rhombus monument to Takeda and in the graveyard nearby there is still a group of a hundred and sixty-nine tombstones of the

Nakasone family. Mortuary tablets have been enshrined in the main house since the year 1629 to the present day.

According to the records in the register of deaths at the family temple of Kōmyoji, the Nakasone family split, three generations before my father's time, at the time of Kichizaemon, into the Kichizaemon line and the Jouemon line. Both families dealt in silk and silkworms, as was common in this area, and both ran pawnshops and apparently competed for control of the neighbourhood. In each family there was one three hundred year old cryptomeria tree, but one fell shortly before the Pacific War as a result of hollowing while the other was apparently requisitioned by the army toward the end of the war.

My father was educated at Takasaki Middle School.[3] He left middle school in 1908 when my grandfather, the first Matsugoro, died suddenly and he inherited the family business. At the same time my father changed his name from Kan'ichi, to Matsugoro II. In 1912 he moved to Takasaki city and began a timber business which flourished as a result of the boom caused by the first world war. It was this which formed the basis of his future fortune.

My father was a firm, honest man who was rather taciturn. In fact, I was afraid of him as a child. However, he had a good head for business and a feel for the way the world was changing. He was also enthusiastic about rationalisation and the use of technology. During the slump of the late twenties and early thirties, for example, he equipped himself with an imported saw machine and a six-wheeled truck, both of which were rare at that time. According to village records, there was, among the Nakasone ancestors in the middle ages, before the Edo period, one Nakasone Shingo Muneyoshi who was a senior disciple of the great mathematician, Seki Takakazu, and who studied at the Yamaga Ryū school of martial arts. This rationalism and modernism was in my father's blood too.

My mother, Yuku, was the eldest daughter of the Nakamura family, who were wealthy farmers and merchants with four rice granaries. Her father was also the post office chief, and the story has it that her name came from the first and last syllables of *yubinkyoku*, the Japanese for post office.[4] She was educated at Kyōai Girls School, a mission school in Maebashi.

I was born on May 27, 1918, at 35 Suehirocho, Takasaki City, Gunma Prefecture, the second son of six children with one older brother, one older sister, two younger brothers and one younger sister. The last two died young so, effectively, there were four of us. The name Yasuhiro was chosen from among several put forward at

The house in Takasaki where I was born

the request of my father by the chief priest of the Takasaki shrine, Takai Tōichi. Later, when people asked me with what characters it was written, I would boast: 'It's the *yasu* of the *Shōgun* Tokugawa Ieyasu and the first character of K̲ō̲bō Daishi, the great literary figure, which is also read *hiro*'. At the risk of sounding self-satisfied, it is my philosophy that such auto-suggestion is not a bad thing in life.

Around the side of the house where I was born was a fast-running canal about five meters wide. In autumn, ranks of big white radishes hung to dry from the edge of the eaves cast their shadow on the smooth surface of the water. It was my mother's job to prepare the pickles and as a child I used to enjoy helping her. After many busy days the twenty gallon barrels of pickles would be lined up in the dim shed and winter would not be long arriving.

Jōshū winters bring tumbleweed and dry winds which blow round and round in a hulling motion. It would happen that I would open my eyes one morning and, without warning, there would be snow on the distant mountain ranges and I would know that winter had arrived.

3

The mountains bring change, they create a boundary of a single night. On days when the cloud is low and freezing, people stop short, surprised by the tumbleweed that grazes their cheeks. Powdery snow blows in from the peaks of Mt. Akagi and is scattered like flowers across the fields of the north.

In my memory my mother is standing at her work, her kimono sleeves tied securely with a cord, her apron fastened tight. Perhaps as her son I should not say so, but my mother was strikingly beautiful and I was secretly proud of her. I used to pray to myself that she would never become a withered old woman.

There were always ten or more people, maids and workers, in our house, and I still remember the dull glint of silver as my mother, unbeknownst to my father, slipped a fifty sen silver coin to a new errand boy as he did the cleaning. When one of the workers caught something contagious and was admitted to the hated isolation hospital, my mother slept there and nursed him. It was perhaps the influence of the mission school that meant that she treated everyone

My first birthday with my older brother Kichitaro and older sister Shōko

equally and would invite even the peddler and the masseuse for dinner. Without fail, when I came home from primary school, there would be such people there and I would have to kneel and formally greet them.

When I was small my mother would teach me hymns as we bathed together. She was such a gentle person but she was also strong. When my father was ill with stomach problems during a labour dispute at our factory in the early 1930s for example, she sent him to a hot spring and met and negotiated with the workers' group herself and didn't give an inch. But there was another, softer, side to her. When I was in grade three of primary school, an essay I had written about my experiences of a seaside school was selected for a Kōzuke Newspaper concourse. I had written, 'I build sand castles by the sea and the bullying waves break on the shore, one after another they destroy them. Next time I will build them stronger, I won't be beaten.' My mother carried this cutting in the sash of her kimono and would take it out and read it even when I was at high school and at university.

When my mother died, my father felt obliged to try to supply the care and affection she had always given my younger brother and me. But I was at university and was embarrassed in front of my friends by my country-bumpkin father who had not even attended high school. It was an immature vanity that made me act that way. I didn't appreciate my father's strengths until I myself had to learn that, to make my way as a politician, I had to be able to bow my head and get on with people. An official seems important when he is firmly planted in the seat of power and making judgements, but when he has left office and you see him around the town he cuts a poor figure. From behind he seems particularly dubious.

My timber merchant father was warm hearted and skilful with people to an extent that I did not appreciate. His business was formed and developed on the basis of these emotional ties. Even from behind my father cut an authoritative figure. At the time I did not understand the greatness of the man in the street. During my first election campaign, unknown to me, my father tramped around in wellington boots, visiting mountain families along the borders of Jōshū, Shinshū and Echigo and calling at the homes of his steady customers, soliciting votes at each house. According to a letter from Satō Kamozō, who lived in the mountains of Agatsuma county, he was sitting in the *kotatsu*, the low, heated table where everyone gathers in the winter months, and having a drink one blustery, snowy night when there was a knock on the door. He wrote that when he opened the door, my father, 'Seemed to roll in on to the dirt floor with the wind and the snow.' My father never mentioned a word of this during his lifetime and now it is too late to feel sorry or make amends.

Meditations on nature in Jōshū

People called me 'Yatchan'.[5] My elder brother, Kichitaro, was naughty and my mother called him '*tobase*', meaning rash or easily elated, but in contrast, though I say it myself, I was a quiet, easy child.

My younger brother, Ryōsuke, was prone to gastritis caused by nerves. When I was in primary school my pulmonary lymph glands would swell to the size of a pigeon egg and I was forever having x-rays. My parents were so worried about our health that they took us in the summer holidays to Hiraiso in Ibaraki prefecture and sea bathing in places like Kawarago or the Kamo River in Chiba prefecture or to Tateyama or Kitajō to strengthen our bodies. We were woken up early every morning at the beach in Hiraiso and sent to gather the glue plants that wash up on the shore there. I'm told that I was the most assiduous collector.

The timber yard was our usual playground. We kicked stones in the fields behind and caught silver carp and mud fish in the streams, but I remember that when the thunder clouds bubbled up like devils over Mt. Haruna, we felt as though we might be snatched away, and would fly home shivering.

In November we would gather together the casual workers and hold a banquet in honour of Ebisu, the God of merchants, on the second floor of the house. The guests would make pretend business talk about the sea bream and the herring roe dishes lined up in the *tokonoma*[6], saying, 'Lets shake hands on 50,000 *ryō*.' or 'I'll give you 30,000.' and each time, they would clap their hands in unison. They would do this to encourage good business conditions. I would be there in the lowest seat clapping along with my brothers and sisters.

I attended Takasaki North primary school. The school had almost 1,500 pupils, and a big lotus tree in centre of the garden which still stands today. I was taken by my father to the entrance ceremony, dressed in formal wear of *haori hakama*, and I took off my hat and greeted the teacher on duty, Ochiai Tatsuji. The teacher patted my head and said, 'This is a good child. He will grow up to be like Saigo Takamori'.[7] The comment made a profound impression on me.

When you are a child it is easy to believe that women are sacred. Maybe it is because Japan, in terms of its roots, is a matriarchal

6

Takasaki middle school period. With my elder sister, Shōko, my mother, Yuku, and my younger brother, Yōsuke.

society, or maybe it is the influence of the Sun Goddess and founder of Japan, Amaterasu Ōmikami. When you are talking of women teachers this is even more true. As a result, until I was in the third grade of primary school I was convinced that women teachers didn't do things like use the lavatory. However a friend in my class disagreed and a big debate ensued which was settled one break time when we watched the teacher's lavatory and lo and behold a woman teacher emerged. For the first time the difference between dreams and reality was brought home to me.

For the first three years of school my marks were middling: I was especially poor at gymnastics, drawing and singing, and this seems to have been passed on to my children and grandchildren who are all hopeless at games and art. Then something happened and from the fourth grade my marks began to improve till by the fifth and sixth grades I was top, and head of year. The head of year had to write the day's diary each day before leaving school so I would stay and help the pupils responsible for cleaning. This made me popular in class.

I have one particular memory from primary school that even now weighs heavily on my heart. It was in the sixth grade when we were set mock exam questions in the supplementary study room for the middle school exam. The answers were on the last page of the question paper. There was just one arithmetic question that I was completely stuck on, and in the end I stole a surreptitious glance at the answers. This cheating has continued to torture me.

I came second in the Takasaki Middle School exam and got in. There were a good many people whose grades were good but who failed the exam. You need ability to pass exams, but the boundary between success and failure can be the thickness of one sheet of paper depending on whether what you are good at comes up or not and whether your mind is working well at that particular time. Thirty percent of it is luck. I seem to have been blessed with luck in exams. At the end of the fourth year of middle school I was accepted into what, under the old educational system, used to be the Shizuoka High School. The exams for Tokyo University, the higher civil service and a short service commission in the navy also went without a hitch.

The Manchurian Incident occurred in 1931 during my first year at middle school. I was made uneasy by the strange atmosphere and I remember discussing it with a friend in my class called Mogi Saburō. I led an ordinary existence, I was a normal middle school kid, a stolid mediator sort if anything. In the lower grades I wore my elder brother's hand-me-downs, faded like a beggar's bag, but though I was a little ashamed, I couldn't tell my mother. I was especially good at maths and English and helped the others in my year whenever they asked. I was head of year throughout. I once beat eight people in a class *kendō* competition. I seemed to know intuitively how to take the initiative and take the gauntlet or mask.

Our teacher, Mr Furuhata, told us about the distinguished botanist Dr Makino Tomitarō and I remember being deeply impressed by the story of his efforts at self-education. From the ethics teacher, an old man, and a scholar of Chinese classics with fine whiskers, Mr Ikari, we learned about positive assertion and universal ethics. I used to apply myself diligently to experiments and my science teacher, Mr Nagasawa, seeing how I studied, told me, 'You are patient; you should become a researcher.' I learned spoken English from a teacher called Kurihara who had worked as a purser on the Pacific Ocean Line and when I went to US for first time in 1950, during the occupation, people commented on the shades of New York in my speech and asked where I had learned to speak English. This was down to Mr Kurihara.

If I close my eyes and think about that time, I can conjure up various faces. There is something called the Thirty-five club, a class club of the thirty-fifth graduating year which left Takasaki Middle School in March 1936. The members are all over seventy but some of them still ski, some are helping to compile village records, some travel abroad with their wives, others are influential men with municipal responsibilities while yet others are teachers in private schools looking after less able children. Strangely, they have all turned into devoted husbands. On one occasion during the occupation when the 'War-dead Memorial Club' had gathered for a drink, someone made a suggestion. Since our dead comrades would surely have wanted to see them, we should watch some pornographic films. We watched them in the main hall of a temple and, late that night, a part of the temple burned down. My friends were good, guileless people and laughed at this 'punishment from Buddha'. A man who grows old calmly, without haste, without rush, without greed, is a thing of beauty.

At that time we kept homing pigeons and it was my job to look after them. In the mornings I would set the birds free to fly in circles in the sky and when the time was up I would blow on a whistle to call them back. I used to scatter soy beans or maize in the centre of the côte to get them back in. Mating pairs are affectionate. They puff themselves up and trill and press together and kiss. When I saw them, my face would flush.

There was a girl, a student at the nearby Prefectural Girl's High School, who used to open the corridor window and watch me training the pigeons. In order to pick up my school bag and go to Takasaki Middle School when the training was finished, I had to pass in front of the main gate of the Girl's school. Walking alone, in the midst of a large crowd of girls on their way to school, was hard. Sometimes I would even take a long detour to avoid the school. I was very naive when I think of it. Normally it would be the girl who would avert her face, but there were a lot of them and only one of me and they would all look. I didn't have the courage to look back. I realised then that women have a lot of nerve when they have strength in numbers.

On the subject of women, my older sister Hatsuko went to Jissen Women's College, now Jissen Women's University, and would come home with records and novels and fashionable clothes. My older sister was the sole source of so-called Tokyo, urban, flamboyant culture in our house. It was thanks to her that I tasted this culture, but I never went from having anti-centralist, conservative feelings to idolising Tokyo. It was mother nature in Jōshū that raised me.

In fact, they used to say, 'If Yatchan isn't around he'll be on the roof.' I would climb up on to the veranda where the clothes were hung to dry on the second floor of the timber store and watch the sky and the mountains through the changing seasons: Mount Akagi, Haruna, Myōgi, Asama and Tanigawa. Their features wrapped the Jōshū plain like a folding screen.

From my seat on the orange box that I'd carried up to the veranda I would watch the clouds weave a brocade of autumnal tints. Beyond them, the evening sun fell on Mt. Asama with its shoulders, trailing white wisps of smoke, a majestic sight, especially in autumn, when the air was clear. The azure would gradually grow to a deeper and deeper purple. Then, before long, the stars would come out and I would be startled by the depths of the darkness enveloping me. Coming to myself, I would climb down from the roof. At those times I felt as though I ruled the universe. Perhaps when human beings are alone, it is their nature to respond to the call from the ends of the firmament and to aspire to outstanding grandeur.

I had only read a smattering of the collected works of the Meiji and Taisho periods, of writings by Kunigita Doppō, Tayama Katai and Natsume Sōseki, and there is no doubt that it was this, the natural environment of Jōshū that I used to watch so long ago from the roof platform where the clothes were hung to dry, that had the bigger influence on my spiritual life.

Fall-back position: success at Shizuoka High

I entered what used to be Shizuoka High School in April 1935. A cherry tree with many branches blossomed by the moat of Sunpu Castle and the sacred slopes of Mt. Fuji sparkled with white snow.

In the fourth year of middle school we did mocks for the old high school exams. As far as high schools were concerned, there was Mito, Urawa or Shizuoka to choose from and a lot of people went from Takasaki Middle School to Shizuoka High. At the time Nakasone Shigeo, a member of the main branch of the Nakasone family, was already studying science there and I was strongly encouraged to go to Shizuoka too. It had the sea and tangerines and strawberries, things we didn't have in Gunma, and from windy Jōshū, it looked like heaven. Also, it was said that the townspeople took good care of Shizuoka High School students and that, although there was only one old style high school, there was a total of five public and private girl's schools including the prefectural women's teaching college, so the ratio of boys to girls was good.

Family photo with my father, Matsugoro, 1935

In the exam for Shizuoka High I scored in the seventies for English translation, Japanese and Mathematics, but in the English aural I couldn't understand the accent of the examiner and failed dismally. Just when I felt that I had failed and that it couldn't be helped and would serve as a practice run, a notice came saying that I had passed into the Department of Liberal Arts, Class C in which the principal language studied was French. At that time, the more able students did German and English and French was rated a fall-back position. I hesitated because I too wanted to do German and English. I could have stayed for a fifth year in middle school and reapplied for high school but my decision to go was the right choice in terms of my later life.

Shigeo also pressed me to take up the place because a lot of students in Class C had either taken four years or had repeated a year, so that he believed it to be a broad-minded group with greater ability in the real world than those who specialised in German or English. And that was indeed how it was. French culture tends to reject drones and to foster interesting dilettantes.

Student life in the Department of Liberal Arts, Class C, eased my adjustment to post-war Japanese culture and society. After the war was lost German was no longer spoken but French was useful. I could quote Pascal in French at summits and surprise President Mitterand.

11

I could also make a speech to the Canadian parliament using both French and English as required by law. Mitterand flattered me saying, 'Every time we meet, your French is improved.' Perhaps it tickled his French pride that I had read Les Pensées, Pascal's Thoughts: An Apology for Christianity. All this was due to the fact that I had entered the fall-back position Department of Liberal Arts Class C. You really never know where happiness will lie in life.

1

Gathering rain clouds from the north
Are interrupted by Mt. Fuji's peak.
Emerald in the south
Is the Sea of Suruga
Such a wonderful world
Inspires our studies

2

Enlightened Zen priest Hakuin
Ambitious King Nagamasa,
The noble presence of such great men!
Let us look up to them and make progress.
Japan's future
Is waiting for us.

As the second verse of the school song suggests, high school was the ideal place to cultivate internationally-minded Japanese through the teaching of philosophy and culture. At that time school life revolved around the dormitories, the sports clubs and reading. I threw myself into all these things and joined the field and track club, specialising in middle distance. However I damaged my lower back doing shot-put. The pain became severe and I gave up track and joined the shooting club run by Shigeo.

Coming, as I did, from the fourth grade of a country middle school, I had something of an inferiority complex initially and felt nervous when I came to live with bright pupils from the First and Fourth Tokyo Middle Schools. When we had speeches in the all dormitory socials, they would be quoting from *Chūō Kōron, Bungei Shunju, Kaizō* and other journals popular among intellectuals. I was impatient to catch up with them and others like them as fast as possible.

In my second year I was chosen as cooking monitor for the dormitory. In fact, I was an unwilling nominee, but once I was chosen, and I was responsible for the health of a group of extremely active young men who were using a lot of energy, my serious side came out

Together with dormitory Friends at Shizuoko High School

and I made a study of nutrition and calorie counts and exercised my ingenuity on menus. Unusually for those days there was a self-service system operating in the dining room. They have the same system now in golf clubs and so on where you can just sign a voucher and help yourself to fruit or confectioneries. The fact that the balance agreed, was a measure of the honesty of the students at Shizuoka High School.

Once I forgot to include the Saturday night meal in the menu plan and didn't realise it till the same day. Too late I thought, 'Now I've had it.' There is no resentment so fearsome as that about food. An idea of last resort came to me. I laid out pickled radish, horse radish, red radish, sliced vegetables preserved in soy sauce, all the pickles I had, and put up a sign in large letters saying, 'Saturday; pickle night.' Some people were not overly happy with it, but I got round them by asking if it wasn't that bad for a change occasionally.

Nobody wanted to do what was seen as a menial job and become a kitchen worker, so I got in touch with the dormitory superintendents of the local girls' schools and, on the pretext of studying menus together, arranged permission to visit the girl's dormitories where boys were normally forbidden. Once this was granted competition to join the kitchen staff became fierce.

Dilettante period

There was graffiti in the lavatory that read:

> *Tying the cords of my 'sarumata' pants*
> *A single thought fills my mind:*
> *How lonely I am!*

... and a collection of writings in the dormitory which included the following:

> *Our mortal days being what they are,*
> *Admire he who dances at the edges of life,*
> *Planning everything for that life,*
> *And burning with love for life,*
> *An artist of life!*

Nights in the dormitory were long: we would debate in the darkness about human nature. Life consisted of shouting and roughhousing in the corridors; rubbing shoulders, dressed only in loin-cloths and high wooden *geta*. There was no violence but the older students would scold the lower years. There were swimming competitions between the five dormitories, and drumming, drinking and dormitory song festivals where we would dance rondos.

I was appointed chief editor for the dormitory magazine which was being prepared for the fifteenth anniversary of the founding of the dormitory. I visited people like Kabashima Chiharu (second graduating year), who had distinguished himself as a government official in the Ministry of Commerce and Industry, and Kashiwamura Nobuo (sixth graduating year), who later became Director of the National Police Agency to quiz them about a variety of things.

The most difficult problem I had was what historical perspective to bring to the task of compilation. Many of the students were drawn to Marxism and there were arguments within the editorial committee and at the inter-dormitory socials. I myself rejected ideology and just wanted to set out the facts correctly and make a judgement on that basis. It was accepted that we would confer on the method of evaluation when the time came. It was work that required quiet effort but I did it seriously.

Dormitory life had a proud tradition of self-government: it was an important three years when a student was free to indulge himself but at the same time was acquiring the foundations of his character. It was where one handed down to the younger students the spiritual climate of folklore, grew as a person, and fostered one's own will power and all-round education. Nevertheless when the third year students were taking their university entrance exams, many chose to leave the dormitory and go into lodgings. It is a fact that rough-housing and socials are not conducive to studying for exams. However, the thirteen people in my year loved the dormitory and, even at the cost of studying, we pledged ourselves to defend dormitory self-government from the efforts of both the Ministry of Education, and of the school, to strengthen regulations. We played the game to the end, staying three full years (1935–38) in the dormitory.

We formed a club called 'Aishinkai', The Friends. When we graduated from high school we all went on to study at a number of different places but when the family of one of our number fell into sudden financial difficulty, and could not raise the money for school fees, we each sent on five yen a month and with this and the money he earned in part-time work, our friend was able to graduate from university. This was putting into practice the Imperial Rescript on Education, the principle of '*Hōyū aishinji*' – friends should believe in each other.

I was blessed with many and various good friends both older and younger from that time. These included Miyazawa Jirō, Yamazaki Tei'ichi, Koyama Gorō, and Uchiyama Shin'ichi who later set up my support group the Gyōshūkai and supported me in a way that was consistent with the spirit of the old high school system.

Of course the lectures led me into worlds I knew nothing of and made me feel I was truly in high school. Mr Kinomiya's discussion of Himiko, in Japanese history, Mr Tanaka's Greek and Indian philoso-phy, Mr Hiratsuka's world history, Mr Sawaguchi's lectures on the Chinese classic, *The Book of Songs*, all were fresh and all stimulated my love of learning. I learned French from Mr Nagai, Mr Okada, and from a M. Jean Pierre Hauchecorne and English from Mr Sasagi, Mr Inamura and Mr Cassidy.

Mr Cassidy was Canadian with a nasal voice that was hard to understand. He was an unkind teacher and in exasperation one snowy day, when there was no fuel despite the cold, we threw our text books in to the stove and Mr Cassidy got angry and went back to Canada. Our behaviour was inexcusable. The maths lectures given by Mr Kido were so difficult to understand that I gave up trying and for the exam I memorised the solution to just one formula. It had nothing to do with the question but I wrote it anyway and left the rest of the paper blank. Even so they still let me pass.

When I visited France as Prime Minister in 1985 it was reported in the French press how I went to see M. Hauchecorne in Provence, in the South of France, and presented him with the Third Order of the Sacred Treasure. The French government were also conferring the Legion of Honour on him, and Vice Foreign Minister Ross, a former ambassador to Japan who was travelling with me, brought it along.

But discussion with friends and private reading were in fact more of a focus than the actual lessons in high school. I enjoyed the history of philosophy and steeped myself in Ōrui Noboru, Sakaguchi Takashi, Hegel, Ranke, Nishida Kitarō and Kuwaki Genyoku. At the same time I also read a lot written by famous authors like Kawai Eijirō, Abe Yoshishige, Watsuji Tetsurō and Abe Jirō. Among novelists I liked Akutagawa Ryūnosuke and Yokomitsu Riichi and among writers of *haiku*, Mizuhara Shūōshi, Yamaguchi Seishi, Murakami Kijō and Iida Dakotsu. I scored high marks in history and was told by Mr. Hiratsuka that I should go to Tokyo University and study European history under Professor Imai Toshiki.

I went to a lot of films. I was addicted to the French films of Julien Duvivier and the German films of Willy Horst. Jean Gaban in 'Pepe Le Moko', scenes from 'Club de Femmes', 'Un Carnet de Bal', 'Le Paquebot Tenacity' and 'Foreign Legion', beautiful actresses like Francoise Rosay and Danielle Darrieux .... 'Travels in Winter' by the German singer Fische, the chanson, 'Dead leaves' of Yves Montand, I learned them all in the original.

It was a period of dilettantism in my life. A classmate and I travelled, penniless, from the Izu Peninsula to Oshima. After the fashion of Kawabata Yasunari's 'The Izu Dancer' (*Izu no Odoriko*)[8] we crossed from Shuzenji to Amagi and found our way at last to Rendaiji. We had planned to stay at my friend's house, but instead, his family treated us to a room at a hot spring. It was a beautiful early autumn moonlit night.

A beautiful young maid, tall and slender, brought us *sake*, and after dinner, we all arranged to go together to a shrine nearby dedicated to Yoshida Shōin. As we started off along the narrow miscanthus-lined path through the wood toward the shrine, the bright moonlight lit the white nape of the girl's neck as she walked before us. It was as if she were bewitched. A shiver ran through me; I could not take my eyes from the nape of her neck. My friend felt the same. Phrases like 'He will do by you as you do by him', floated into my mind and I feared we had incurred Yoshida Shōin's anger. My heart raced, but in the end nothing happened.

In Oshima we were put up in a church belonging to some new religion. A crowd of believers was singing and dancing and others were laying hands on the bodies of the sick. We looked on from a corner, our heads in our hands, and scoffed at how unscientific it all was, and yet a part of me felt how wonderful it would be to be able to forget everything, to dance along with them and become intoxicated by it.

Gradually everything became more difficult. The spirit of the old high school system was a mixture of well-roundedness and aloofness. One might have thought that the students would feel driven to counter the mounting social oppression and the attempts to control and erode the self-government of the dormitories. But after the Marco Polo Bridge Incident in May 1937, the sound of army boots marched unchecked across the history of Japan.

This is a verse from a dormitory song I wrote that was chosen for the tenth anniversary celebration of dormitory self-government at that time.

> Stars have fallen; men have gone,
> Heaven and earth of five continents are tragic,
> Dark is the setting sun: who's responsible?
> Stars have fallen; men have gone.

The era ebbed away with the mournful evening echoes of the temple bells at Rinzaiji.

My mother becomes a star

From 1938 to 1940, I commuted to Tokyo Imperial University (now Tokyo University) in Hongō, from lodgings at the Fushūkan by Dangozaka. The owner of the lodgings was a widow from Kushiro by the name of Komatsu Eiko. Komatsu Shinroku, who in later years became a literary critic, was her younger brother and at that time lived with her.

It was a time when the cold current of state nationalism was merging with the traditional warm current of liberalism. At the university, the right wing faction of Minoda Muneki was mobilising the students to denounce liberal professors. In the school of economics a group of teachers known as the reform faction clashed with Kawai Eijirō and Yamada Fumio and others. Hiraga Yuzuru, the president, who was a world authority on the design of warships, blamed both sides for the quarrel and sacked the professors from both factions.

Let me recall the professorial camps as they were then. I was enchanted by the orderly systems and the sincerity of Wagatsuma, who taught civil law, and was drawn to the Kantian personalism and buoyant character of Ono, who taught criminal law. I sympathised too with Oka, who taught European political history in a manner full of pure, latent energy. Miyazawa, who taught constitutional law, was clever and his informal talks were interesting. Yet, perhaps because he was keeping a low profile as a means of self-protection given the political circumstances, he didn't talk about Articles One to Three of the Constitution, dealing with the Emperor, and I was left with a feeling of suspicion.

Yasui, who taught international law, was so prim that I heckled from the back of the hall. At that time he was writing journal articles in defence of the Great East Asia Co-prosperity Sphere, but after the war he made a sudden conversion and played the peace apostle. In contrast Mr Kamikawa, who taught diplomatic history, was consistent in his beliefs and after the war resisted the occupation policies of the omnipotent General MacArthur and advocated the independent enactment of a constitution. I also learned economics with Maide, but he made little impression on me. His colleagues had been driven out by Hiraga's purge and, though it was his first lecture as head of the school of economics, he did not speak of the university or the current situation, but amazed me by beginning his lecture with the words 'As for Schumpeter ...'. I had my doubts about Marxist economics and was not convinced by the so-called modern school of economics based on equilibrium theory.

I was acquainted with the social power theories of the Kyoto Imperial University professor, Takada Yasuma, and answered a question on them in my higher civil-service exams. However, the person whose pupil I became, and who had the greatest impact on me, was Professor Yabe Teiji. I was drawn to his learning, and by the dashing way he taught politics, dressed in his double breasted suit with his handkerchief peeping from his breast pocket.

I believe that Yabe Teiji's academic approach of harmonising traditional Japanese character with modern political science was a Japanese form of the *Gemeinschaft* theories of Tenius. He was extremely critical of Nazi Germany but was also of the opinion that the British and American brand of individualistic liberalism did not suit the Japanese character either, and he propounded a particular unified political science. As advisor to prime minister Konoe Fumimaro, Yabe was asked to work over the fundamental plans for the Imperial Rule Assistance Association [*Taiseiyokusankai*], the non-party, government association. However, the body Konoe actually formed was a totalitarian structure, completely different from Yabe's proposals and Yabe's resentment at this is recorded in *The Yabe Diaries.*

At any rate, the predominant ethos of liberal democracy in Tokyo Imperial University at that time had not yet been eroded and I believe both staff and students were supportive of it. However, struck broadside by the independent actions of the army, the ship of state drifted. I was worried by this but also doubtful whether Japan, under pressure internationally and isolated, would achieve the individualistic liberalism of England and America.

If at that time I had been asked, 'Are you a liberal?' [*jiyūshugisha*] I could not have answered in the affirmative. If I had been asked, 'Are you a state nationalist?' [*kokkashugisha*], I would have answered, 'No.' Had I been asked, 'Are you a nationalist in the cultural sense?' [*nashionarisuto*] , I would have been at a loss how to answer. However, influenced as I was by Kant, I was strongly opposed to the organistic philosophies of Communism and Nazism which regarded men as tools. In short, you could call it a belief in personal cultural identity.

I had doubts about the way both left and right-wing students were conducting themselves and was myself both too prudent and too timid to enter the ring armed with just one 'ism'. I stayed awake at night worrying about Japan's future, but when I thought about my own long term future I thought of my father and mother's hopes and my own desire to succeed as a bureaucrat. I intended to go out into society and play my cards boldly. I think, to be honest, I probably hovered on the edges of a 'common-sense, establishment reformism'.

March 10, 1940 was a day of such sorrow that I couldn't forget it even if I wished. It was in during my second year term exams that a telephone call came from my father in Takasaki to my lodgings late at night. His breathless voice told me 'Yuku is seriously ill'. I hurried to Ueno Station but the last train had already left and by the time that I returned home by the first train next day, my mother had already breathed her last. I wanted to know why I hadn't been told earlier and railed, in my desperation, at my father. My mother had caught pneumonia as she saw off a group of soldiers leaving for the front the week before. She had continued to have a fever but insisted that we children were in the midst of exams and shouldn't be worried with the news. I was told that my mother had called my father to her bedside and asked him to visit the Takasaki shrines and temples in her place to pray for the children's success in their exams as she always did. My father got on his bicycle and did as she had asked. When my mother learned this she was very happy but that night her condition deteriorated.

When I heard this I cried aloud. I guessed at how much our doting mother had wanted to see us by her sickbed. She wrote without fail once or twice a week and when the vacations drew close she would write, 'Hurry back home. I can't wait to see you.' My mother, the wife of a timber merchant, who entrusted her hopes to her children; my mother who would visit my lodgings in Tokyo bearing lily-of-the-valley pot-plants bought at the department store; my mother who, when winter came, sent me *chanchanko,* padded sleeveless kimono, with thick silk lining ... I clung to her body.

My mother's funeral took place and I returned to Tokyo but wherever I was, in the library or in my lodgings the vision of my mother would come and go before me, and study was impossible. My academic results suffered of course. I had no desire to sit the higher civil-service exam. I went back to Takasaki and did nothing for a month or more until one day a shiver ran through me as though I had been struck by lightening, and words came to me that pierced my heart. 'Why did your mother die without letting you know she was ill? Wasn't it so as not to disturb your studies. So what do you think you are doing?'

From that point on I changed. I took my seat as soon as the library opened and when I got back to my lodgings at 8.00pm I would work again until 11.00. I went to the bath house only every other day and I went to bed at midnight. But I had left it too late and couldn't finish the required reading which amounted to more than ten books. I paid the price. The question in civil law on rival claims, was discussed in a book I had not read. I regretted it bitterly but it was too late. Drawing on the knowledge of the law that I had, I tried my best to come up with an independent theory of competition in rights of claim and wrote an answer. I had no confidence, but notification came that I had passed. Still, I thought 'Well I'll be bottom and won't get into the Ministry of Home Affairs, or the Finance Ministry, but probably only the Ministry of Overseas Development.' Nevertheless, the interview went well and when nervously I opened the ranking lists at the Cabinet Legislation Bureau I was administrative class eight. For a moment I thought, 'This is a mistake.' and I thought how terrible it would be if I checked at the window and they revised it. Then I put the list into my breast pocket and without saying anything went home to Takasaki where I offered up the papers at my mother's grave.

Without my mother's death I would not have worked so whole-heartedly and I would not have passed. My mother's unreserved love, in death, formed the basis of my life. Even now when I look up at the stars I feel that my mother is watching me from one of them. There are many vicissitudes in life. At times of particular adversity what consistently protects me is my mother up in heaven.

———————

CHAPTER TWO

NAVAL PAYMASTER SUB-LIEUTENANT

'Two years active service':
the spirit of the navy

'Why do you want to join the Ministry of Home Affairs?'

'Because the Ministry of Home Affairs will make the best use of someone with my abilities.'

'What would you do if we didn't make good use of you?'

'I would resign and assail the ministry from outside.'

The man asking the questions in the interview for the Ministry of Home Affairs was the head of personnel affairs, Machimura Kingo. When I come to think of it I was an exceptionally self-assertive candidate, but that year they were said to be turning away those they found fitted the common mould and I was one of the ones they took. This was the period when Prime Minister Konoe Fumimaro's Imperial Rule Assistance Association was formed, a time when Hazama Shigeru, the former administrative vice-minister for Home Affairs had become director of the Secretariat and older colleagues were in strategic positions everywhere. The Ministry of Home Affairs was in high spirits and was overwhelmed by applicants.

By the time I joined the Ministry of Home Affairs in April 1941, Hiranuma was minister, Kayaba Gunzō was administrative vice-minister, Yamazaki Iwao was Chief of the Metropolitan Police, Furui Yoshimi was head of Personnel, Nadao Hirokichi was head of Finance and Mizuchi Tōru was head of Archives and Documents. There were fifty entrants in my year. A lot of them, very talented men, rose to positions of authority and became director of the National Personnel Authority, director of the Police Agency, administrative vice-minister of Home Affairs, Welfare, Defence and so on. A good many of them joined the Ministry of Home Affairs because they were drawn by the personal magnetism of Machimura.

Shortly after I joined the Ministry in Tokyo, I entered the Naval Paymaster's School near the approach to Kachidoki Bridge in Tsukiji. I had been accepted whilst I was at Tokyo University. After a simple physical exam I was appointed immediately as naval paymaster sub-lieutenant and a student of the sixth graduating year. There were one hundred and ten of us in that intake, twenty-two were to die in the war.

Straight away, I took off the suit that I'd worn as and when I pleased until then, folded it in a wrapping cloth and put on the number two whites so that I looked, but only looked, the part of the naval officer. As I walked down the corridor, the sailors saluted me. Since I hadn't yet learned how to salute, I was at a loss what to do. Taking the plunge I returned an army-style salute and made do with that. Rather than the clothes making the man, it would be closer to the mark to say in this case that the clothes made a monkey of the man.

When the induction ceremony was over we went to the palace for registration and then waited upon the Chief of the Naval General Staff, Prince Fushimi Hiroyasu. When we got back to the school we changed into khaki work uniform and the first thing we learned was words. 'You' and 'I', normally '*kimi*' and '*boku*', became '*kisama*' and '*ore*'. At first it sounded stilted but habit is a fearsome thing and before we knew it we had become accustomed to it. These words mould men into members of a community which shares a common destiny.

Then there were manners. From the way you used your chopsticks to the way you folded your shirt and took care of your shoes, everything was done in a prescribed manner. They were most particular about dress. There were full length mirrors at the end of the corridor and on the landing and we would stop in front of them to adjust our uniform and our hats or to practice our salute. We took the stairs at double time and when, five minutes before meals, the order went out, 'Wash hands,' we did it all together. It was like teaching kindergarten children. First we memorised the words, 'A sailor is smart, far-sighted, methodical and of unyielding spirit.' I had a bit of trouble with 'smart' and 'far-sighted', but when I tasted the high-speed turn drills and the life aboard a small warship I understood their meaning.

Whether you were passing through the narrow side doors in the warship's bulkheads or aiming a gun, if you didn't act immediately, and at the same time forecast what would happen next, you were too

Appointment as naval paymaster
sub-lieutenant

late. In life ashore there is more leeway. In the navy there is the order, 'Five minutes to go'. 'Five minutes to all hands muster', 'Five minutes to inspection', 'Five minutes to hoisting of the flag', all meant complete your preparations to shift to the next action.

Because for some time we were forbidden to go out, and communications from the outside were not allowed in, we naturally applied ourselves to studying the eccentricities of our comrades. We came to know who kept dozing off in class, who hurried to be first at the canteen, even who had the biggest wedding tackle. He was given the nickname 'three splashes' because of the sound he made when he climbed into the bathtub.

It was not long before the 'bun slapping-incident' occurred. In June, colleagues from the Ministry of Home Affairs came to pay a call and brought buns with them. The seven of us who had come from the Ministry munched away in the meeting room, talking in loud voices and laughing. Early the following morning the call for all hands to muster went out. Our instructor, Tanaka, shouted, 'Last night, people were eating buns and making a noise without permission. In this school there is no private eating except in special circumstances. It leads to slackness. Everybody stand legs apart, take off glasses, clench your teeth.' Then he slapped everyone's face.

We went round and apologised to everyone for what we had brought on them but this was where everybody learned how to take a slap. We were confined to barracks on Sundays for some time and made to do early morning long-distance rowing in a cutter with oars that were unbelievably bulky and heavy. As we rowed in the back streets in Ginza, or perhaps it was Tsukiji, in any case, streets that are now spanned by expressways, we saw a girl in a red kimono under-slip blown open at her breast by the wind push back the rain shutters and gaze absent-mindedly down at the canal. We looked at each other in distress and rowed on furiously.

After the Washington Treaty on disarmament in 1922 there was a dramatic reduction in the recruitment of naval officers with the result that, immediately before the Pacific War, there was a shortage of officers between the ranks of sub-lieutenant and lieutenant commander. The two year active service system for the paymaster's department was set up as a result. The political situation was tense and the numbers of naval vessels was strengthened in a shipbuilding race. However there were no junior class officers, particularly first lieutenants, to put on them. It takes ten to fifteen years to train an officer. So the Navy Ministry came up with a plan to employ graduate reservist students in large numbers as combatant officers. They employed university graduates on a fixed period of duty as short-term active service trainees in the paymaster's department. This way they could ensure a good supply of junior officers and also, if they were not needed, they could transfer them to the reserves and be rid of them, bringing them back in as necessary.

This system was popular. In the army, starting as a private first class, you had to polish the shoes of the superior ranking officers, but in the naval paymaster's department you became a sub-lieutenant as soon as you joined the accounting school. The navy, with this special treatment, caught very good people in its net and undermined the army, or so the army criticism went.

There were roughly nine hundred applications for the thirty-five places for students in the first round of recruitment in May 1938; twenty-six applicants for every place. When I applied, the odds were fifteen to one. Toward the end of the war one thousand, four hundred and seventy five were employed in a year and by the 12th intake, the total had risen to three thousand five hundred and fifty-five. Four hundred and eight, twelve percent of these, died in the war.

The Imperial Navy was defeated and extinguished but its spirit survived among the post-war leaders in all spheres. From the mid 1960s to the mid 1970s, fully half of the administrative vice-ministers[1] were graduates of the two year active service program. During my own administration my aims were administrative reform and the internationalisation of Japan. I pushed these policies in a fairly bold manner and the officials in each ministry who were former two year active service people gave me their support. It was colleagues such as these, who embodied the naval spirit, who became the motive power for bodies like the Provisional Commission for Administrative Reform and the Tax Commission during my cabinets in the mid to late eighties. I pride myself that it will be some time before another prime minister is blessed with advisors such as these.

Dispute aboard the warship Aoba on the opening of hostilities

When I graduated from the naval accounting school in August 1941 I was ordered to join the cruiser Aoba, the flagship of the First Fleet, Sixth Squadron. My year mates from the Ministry of Home Affairs, Hayakawa Takashi and Ōmura Jōji, were on number three ship, Kako, and number four ship, Furutaka. The day I arrived at my post on the Aoba, I ended up causing trouble straight away. When I entered the gun room[2], a senior midshipman called Yoshimura Gorō was sitting above me in the seating order at the dining table. He was a gifted graduate of the Naval Academy and had been told, in confidence, of his imminent promotion to the rank of sub-lieutenant and that he would become head of the officer's room and gun captain. In the navy, a commissioned officer takes precedence over an officer of similar rank in the paymaster's section or the medical section, and the latter takes orders from him even when the commissioned officer is appointed later. However, at this point I was already a sub-lieutenant. I took it up with him directly telling him I had something to say and asking him to come with me, but he rejected this proposal from a new entrant. I thought perhaps my words had been a little abrupt so I asked him again to meet me in the gun room and that was where our negotiations took place. I said to him, 'We are only temporary but even though this is not our usual occupation, we have a strong determination to do our best for the country just like you. In the naval accounting school we were taught that a sub-lieutenant sits above an acting sub-lieutenant You haven't been officially announced as sub-lieutenant yet so I want you to act in accordance with military law.'

These were rough words from a newcomer but I had reason on my side. The acting sub-lieutenant changed seats reluctantly and for some time the job of gun captain continued to be done by a senior lieutenant, a leading signalman by the name of Hoshino Saburō.

In fact I had another reason for taking such drastic action. When I first opened the door of the gun room I was initially shocked and then angry. On the bookshelves in the gun room were tossed low-brow recreational magazines such as *Kōdan Club* and Yoshikawa Eiji's book, *Miyamoto Musashi*, and nothing at all educational or that contributed to a knowledge of naval and military affairs or to culture. These officers, graduates of the Naval Academy, were men of ability, destined to become admirals and ministers. I was worried about where they were going, these young men who in their youth never studied and read only worthless magazines and I came to wonder if having worked so hard at my studies I could just give in silently to the current fashion among some in the navy who rested on the laurels of their service epaulettes. Hayakawa and Ōmura, who were expert fencers, used their skills to vent their anger by beating the officers of

Having a good time with my fellow officers before leaving port

27

the naval academy and the engineering schools during military arts training.

Coincidentally the critical negotiations taking place in Washington between Japan and America were having a rough passage and Japan was poised to plunge into the abyss. Round about then, the quarrelsome atmosphere within the Sixth squadron, which was undergoing intensive training in night raids at sea, suddenly blew over. As for the magazines, when I watched the young officers training day and night, every day of the week, without a break, I came to feel they were not being unreasonable.

'Whale to starboard. All free hands permission to look.' The buzzer sounded. Officers and men rushed up the gangway ladders from the turbid air at the bottom of the warship. Five hundred meters ahead, to starboard of the vanguard destroyer, crossing the swell of the late autumnal open sea off Tosa a single whale was about to sound. The blue of the sky, the white caps of the waves and the deep green of the whale burned themselves on the eyes of officers and men. Chests were bared. Lungs exhausted by relentless training and a haste that did not even admit of sleep drew in the salty air. Hands reached out to the mellow autumn sun. It was 15 October 1941.

'Leading signalman, I'm sorry about last night.' I recognised the leading signalman beside the gangway, letting the wind blow in his field cap. 'Oh it's you. No, no that's all right.' The leading signalman replied lightly. The previous evening during a brief rest period after supper I had been talking with him about what was happening in the negotiations between Japan and America and, before long, this had developed into an argument between graduates of the Naval Academy and graduates of the Accounting School about the pros and cons of war.

> *Leading signalman Hoshino:* War between Japan and America is inevitable so if negotiations continue as they are, we'll be giving them time to prepare and Japan will end up dead, like a beggar, at the side of the road.

> *Paymaster sub-lieutenant Nakasone:* But do you think in the end we will win? Do you think the people want war?

> *Hoshino:* If we are going to die by the road anyway, is there any choice but to give it a try, sink or swim? Do you know what Japan's oil stocks are now?

Nakasone: No, of course I don't know what the oil stocks are, but it's simple-minded views like, 'we're going to end up dead by the roadside' that are the problem. Didn't we put up with the Triple Intervention in the Meiji period even though so much blood had flowed?[3] We still don't know how the war is going world-wide and on top of that, the people are tired from the China Incident and they've no desire for war.

Acting sub-lieutenant: You're wrong; if we do it, the nation will be with us.

Nakasone: That's just a sense of obligation. They might follow for a year or so but a long-term war is out of the question.

Acting sub-lieutenant: If they do it then the leaders must be confident of success. All we have to do is obey orders and be prepared to die.

Nakasone: If war once starts then of course that's right but it shouldn't be just the leaders who make the calculations about starting a war. Osaka merchants know more about our own strength and the strength of other nations and about the war situation around the world.

Hoshino: No, You people are just scared. We have enough newly-built Zero fighters in Japan and you've seen how we are for warships and aircraft carriers.

Nakasone: How can you say we are scared? We two year active service personnel are military men too. You people were brought up on 'War, war,' and you're addicted to it. This narrow view that we'll end up dead by the roadside if things go on as they are is proof of it. You have to think about war in terms of history, science and politics. Right now Japan should watch the war situation around the world and preserve her military power, then when the rest of the world has gone as far as it can we should use our casting vote. On no account should we go to war.

The argument was broken off by the signal to prepare to leave port. In order to carry out night attack training, the Aoba was to leave Saiki Bay and head south through the Bungo Straits and across the South Kyushu Sea to cruise around the open sea off Tosa. I thought of the previous day when I had seen, for the first time, the gallant figure of the newly-built giant aircraft carrier Shōkaku and the battleship Yamato at anchor in Saiki Bay. I had been bathed in the cheers of the officers and men of the combined fleet. Beside them the old battleships, Mutsu and Nagato, looked like destroyers. When I come to think of it, the same argument must have been going on in Tokyo between Konoe and Tōjō.

29

Thirty years later I became Director of the Defence Agency and made my first pilgrimage to the office of the Inspector General, Self Defense Forces, Yokosuka region. On that occasion the commanding officer of the Self Defense Force was leading signalman Hoshino, formerly of the Aoba, while the chief staff officer of the Inspector General's Office was acting sub-lieutenant Yoshimura with whom I had argued about seating precedence.

It was at about the time of this exchange that censorship of seamen's letters began. It was necessary to conceal all movements of ships and I read all the letters for official secrets, even letters to wives or lovers at home, and all without the knowledge of the seamen. As a bachelor I was moved by what love between man and wife was like, but I was tormented by a sense of sin. War is inhuman.

Before long an order was delivered to the Aoba which was in Saiki Bay with three months of provisions and ammunition. It read, 'Paymaster sub-lieutenant Nakasone to take up his post at Kure Chinju navy base as soon as possible.' The job that awaited me was that of leading paymaster to the construction corps. When I asked what the construction corps was, the senior staff officer explained with a grave countenance, 'It is a unit which occupies enemy airfields and has responsibility for maintaining them for use by our own planes.' I was told there would be roughly two thousand drafted workers and naval engineers under me. I thought, 'It's war at last,' and my body burned.

I braced myself and asked where we would be going, but I was told that it would be a military secret until we set sail on November 29th, barely ten days away. I spoke up and told the chief of staff, 'It costs money to move a big unit. You have to pay the workers wages and make preparations too for military scrip to supply materials on the ground. I can't make preparations under those conditions.' He looked perplexed, then he stared at me sternly and saying, 'These are military secrets, you should die before you leak them to another person,' he ran a pen over a slip of paper near to hand and pushed it at me. It said 'Philippines, three months worth, Indonesia three months worth.' Then straightaway, he set fire to it.

The next day I went to the accounting office and got 700,000 yen's worth of military scrip in pesos and guilders, the equivalent in today's terms of several billions of yen. I immediately placed a special order for seven wooden boxes about the size of coffins, packed the military scrip inside and installed it in the office of the chief of construction, hidden behind mosquito nets. At night I laid rain shutters on top of the boxes and spread a blanket and slept on top of them. There were two guards with fixed bayonets keeping night watch. It was the first and last time I slept on top of a money box with guards in attendance; it was not comfortable and my body ached and creaked.

Then for ten days I literally worked without thought for food or rest. I divided the provisions, materials, ammunition, bombs and the vast quantities of fuel for use in the Zeros and other fighters out between the three transport ships. I went on the Taitō Maru with the naval engineers, Yabe, the officer commanding the unit, naval surgeon lieutenant Taira, assistant engineers, non-commissioned officers and half the drafted workers totalling 1,162 men. Another 1,160 starting with the engineer, Miyaji, went aboard the Tenryu Maru. Military stores filled the Tonan Maru.

At that time there were a lot of female workers at the naval construction base in Kure. On the go all the time, getting ready to leave without even the time to shave, I seemed to make an impression on the women. Later, when I was posted to Indonesia, I got my first care package and it was full of things from the women workers and typists in Kure. Among them was a long love letter that spoke endlessly of the stirrings of love. There was also a book called 'Little Finger' which was popular at the time. It was an immature love story, but I was pure and innocent and I burned the lot thinking that letters from the opposite sex would just get in the way of me carrying out my duties in the field of war. Now I think what a waste it was.

The construction corps puts up a brave fight

Among the people I can't forget there is one man of whom I have sentimental memories, let's call him 'Y'. 'Y' was what you might call 'a man's man'.

The ten days of preparation flew by and the transport fleet left Japan on 29 November 1941. I ran aboard at the last minute carrying a trunk in each hand. The trunks were crammed full with the personal histories of two thousand workers.

In the early winter darkness, some of the men waved toward the retreating lights of the homeland, others sang. I was alone in the wardroom. I sank into the sofa and gave myself up to the throbbing of the engines. I felt, 'I have done my duty to Japan'. Suddenly my eyes grew hot and the tears flowed. They were not sentimental tears, but the tears of happiness that a man can shed only when he has put his all into something and finished it successfully. Without drying my eyes, I muttered, 'Now all we have to do is make the assault.'

My real work would begin when we left port. By the time I reached my post I had to have organised two thousand workers and formulated a command structure. There were doctors and there were literary men; young men and old. They were like a band of wandering *samurai*. For me, who had just reached twenty years of age, to put such wild old hands in order was extremely difficult.

Finally, after considering this and that, I decided to fight fire with fire and to take advantage of the influence of a ruffian with a record. Right away I got out the personal histories and gathered eighty-odd likely candidates on deck. The one I chose from among them was 'Y'. He had eight offences on his record. Across his forehead was a cut and on his back a vivid, full-body tattoo. But when I took him to the wardroom even he could not keep the bewilderment and suspicion from his face.

I broke the ice by telling him, 'I'm from Jōshū province, home to Chūji Kunisada,[4] but I'm just out of school and I know nothing about the navy. I'm banking on you; will you follow me as a loyal henchman? You've caused the Emperor nothing but trouble so far: wouldn't you like to make amends?' 'Y' seemed to be moved by my frankness and accepted. 'Right then, I'm your man.'

I had the guards bring a big bottle of rice wine[5] and sitting cross-legged I poured the sake into cups till it overflowed and offered it to him so that we could exchange cups. With his right hand 'Y' restrained me saying, 'No. At times like this the boss empties his cup first.' I drank it down in one and refilled it. He took the cup and raising it reverently to his head he suddenly drew back three paces and made the formal greeting that began, 'My home province is ... .' and with a flourish drank it dry.

I was stumped. I hadn't learned this etiquette in school so I didn't know the ropes. But it didn't matter, our gruff introductions continued nevertheless. Viewed from outside I'm sure it seemed like some big joke, but we were in earnest. Group leader 'Y' was born.

I appointed an Osaka man called Iwata as messenger. Iwata ran a picture story show and I thought that a voice with that sort of training would be just right for a messenger. I made the youngest lathe worker, an eighteen year old called Sasagi, guard. Being young he carried himself easily and was agile. Whenever we made an assault landing he would keep about twenty metres in front of me. Even when I told him there were land mines and to keep back, he wouldn't listen. He was determined to risk his own life in my place.

It would be only a slight exaggeration to say that even the rank and file who make up the independent town firemen have their own particular talents, and by putting them all in the right place our unit somehow got by. Their patriotism was simple and innocent.

In the early dawn of 20 December the fleet hurried into Davao on the island of Mindanao. Wasting no time we landed men, machinery and materials and began building an airfield. Then, early on the morning of 25 December, the distant sky began to reverberate and black spots, like rat droppings, fell one after another from a formation of American army B17s. Soon the surrounding wharf and coconut groves were exploding with a deafening noise. It was my first time under air attack and I was struck with terror. When I looked at 'Y' he was sitting, cross-legged as always and wearing a twisted headband, on top of a hatch on the transport ship. It wouldn't have done for me to run. I girded my loins and sat cross-legged beside him. 'Y' stared up at the enemy planes and shouted, 'You sons of bitches.'

Thereafter the air raids were a regular event. The most dangerous time was when we were cooking rice, because the smoke and flames from the cooking fires made a good target. 'Y' must have been tired from his labours during the day but on his own initiative he watched out for the fires at night. There was a distribution of drink once a week but he never touched a drop and instead passed it on to the older men. Privately I learned to respect and admire him.

On 7 January 1942, the seventeenth year of Showa, a squadron of medium range naval attack planes sortied from the 1,200 metre runway we had so enthusiastically repaired and extended, and a cheer went up from the watching workers. On 24 January, we were lying in open sea off Balikupapan on the island of Borneo with the Sakaguchi army corps in readiness for a surprise landing when the ship suffered an attack from a Dutch destroyer. The enemy rained bombs on us. Moreover because they had got into the middle of a convoy of ten or more ships, our convoy escort of light cruisers and destroyers on the outside could not return fire for fear of hitting our own side. There were three friendly transports about us then suddenly the fire blazed and they sank instantly.

We fought desperately to help the army officers and men in the water as they swam toward us clutching the bodies of their fallen comrades. Right then the enemy destroyer sped by a hundred meters from our eyes, firing its secondary battery and its machine guns at random. Our hull floated into the light from the enemy searchlights. Instantly enemy bullets hit number four hatch and fingers of smoke and flame swirled. When I ran there it was like terrible pictures of hell. There were men with their arms blown off, bodies without heads and the smell of blood and battle.

The shout went up that the group leader had been hit. Into the torch-light came the blood-soaked figure of 'Y', breathing heavily and borne on the back of a comrade. His feet, held on by a single layer of skin, flapped. When 'Y' caught sight of me his features stiffened immediately and he murmured incoherently, his bushy eyebrows twitching in his distorted face. 'Chief Paymaster, I'm sorry.' I shouted at him to take courage and gave directions for him to be carried to the emergency infirmary. Then I was taken up with fighting fires.

As day broke, the time to land drew close. In accordance with the earlier plan, I was on the first push ashore. I went ashore at the southern side of Manggar airfield in Balikupapan worrying what sort of condition 'Y' was in. I heard later that he had scolded a wounded patient in the infirmary who was crying aloud with pain saying, 'Don't be bloody stupid: look at my wound', and that he died telling the military surgeon to 'Look to the youngsters first'.

In a unit of two thousand there were all classes of men, all sorts of people whom you would never have met in an entire lifetime had you not been in a wartime military environment. Among them were men who were mean or unfair. But they too wanted to do their best for the country and they worked hard. In extreme conditions where life and death were side by side their human dignity was evident. On 27 January we piled up firewood on top of a sheet of metal on the beach and cremated twenty three bodies, including that of 'Y'.

> *Bear this iron sheet overhead to burn*
> *The bodies of fallen comrades*
> *On a summer beach.*

The secret of shooting the crocodile

War is terrible, but even in such extreme conditions people look for fun. Indeed, I'm sure that even trivial pleasures survive as vivid memories just because conditions are extreme. One such concerned food supplies, another, crocodile shooting.

Our construction corps was not a front line fighting unit and a lot of the workers were conscripts. Moreover, we were a new construction corps with neither connections nor experience, and, to make matters worse, they had a new paymaster sub-lieutenant in charge on the ground, so food supplies were short and hunger caused dissatisfaction. In this respect we suffered more than the Sakaguchi army corps with whom we were travelling. So I thought out a plan to get to Balikupapan first and, in the confusion of landing, to steal a march on the army and take the foodstuffs that had been left in the warehouses and markets.

We landed in the northern part of the town near the airport and the army landed in the south. As soon as we landed I took thirty men armed and on bicycles and we rushed to a town about ten kilometres away. The enemy had more or less pulled back and so, keeping an eye out for land mines and snipers, we hurried as fast as we could to beat the army to it. As we set off I directed three big boats to make for the wharf in the town.

Eventually we came to a town smouldering with the smoke of war and when we looked around we found a general store still locked up. When we forced our way in we found daily necessities and foodstuffs untouched. Straight away I stuck huge sheets of paper all around the entrance and in the nearby streets saying, 'Under naval control, Yabe Navy Corps', posted guards and set about moving the stuff. Our objective was the three big boats waiting at the wharf.

Before long the army arrived too and staff officer Yano of the Sakaguchi Army Corps came and protested that central arrangements had given control of the airport to the navy and that of the town to the army and he asked me to pull out immediately. This was where I took a stand to resolve the unhappiness in my unit. I told him, 'We lower-ranking officers don't know anything of difficult issues like central arrangements. I will make enquiries, please bear with me.' When he asked how long that would take, I replied. 'There is no telephone so it might take about thirty to forty minutes, but if I can confirm that arrangement I will pull out straight away'. Of course we worked like hell during that time to move the stuff from inside and an hour later we withdrew from an empty shop.

Even so, that amount could not be expected to satisfy two thousand drafted workers. Soon, however, these efforts at plunder, which had brought me into conflict with the army and put my life at risk, were known to everyone and even people I didn't know would say, 'Well done,' or 'Thank you chief paymaster.' The lucky ones in the draw got their very first taste of scotch whisky or Bordeaux wine.

Next came the crocodile shoot. One day, when work on the airport was well advanced, I was taking a truck to the town when on the way we came across a crocodile, lying sprawled on a sandbar in the middle of the river on our route. I stopped the truck and found the road was closed and it was forbidden to sound the horn. I pulled out the gun I had captured in the Philippines, and kneeled to shoot. People at their wits end with the road closure poured out of army, navy and civilian vehicles in great numbers shouting 'What's happening, what's happening?' The voices of those who knew what was going on could be heard saying, 'It's no job for someone with a short term commission' and, 'The best he can hope for when he misses is to just be laughed at.'

Indeed it is very difficult to kill a crocodile Even if you hit it, if you get it in the back or stomach, it will escape into the river. You have to pierce the motive centre of its brain with one shot. The crocodile was asleep facing me so its head was even harder to hit. Cautiously I changed to a prone position. There was about 150 metres between the crocodile and me. Inadvertently I had become the Nasuno Yoichi[6] of Balikupapan.

Praying silently to Hachiman, the god of war, I held my breath and squeezed the trigger. Along with the resounding report, a strong recoil hit my shoulder. With a prayer in my heart, I looked at my target. It was a splendid hit. The huge crocodile was thrusting violently at the ground with its jaws and spinning round and round on its back like a top. The applause grew. Then the messenger, Iwata, who had brought a manila rope from the truck, ran at full speed toward the crocodile. As we looked on in blank amazement, he plunged into the river and came up on the sandbar. Iwata pulled his wooden sword from his waist and struck the writhing crocodile a blow to the tail. 'Watch out Iwata, get his head.' Perhaps my shouts reached him for he turned to the crocodile's head and began striking out blindly with his sword. In the end, the tough wooden sword broke into three and the brave crocodile stopped moving.

The trophy was a big animal 2.8 metres long. We loaded it on to the truck and took it back and recruited men from among the 2,000 workers who were confident they could skin it. As might be expected there was an abundance of talent among the construction corps and three names were put forward. That night we ate crocodile sukiyaki to our hearts content. It had a slight odour but it was more tender than chicken and more deliciously chewy than fish. Thereafter I had the unmerited accolade of 'Sub-lieutenant Nakasone the marksman.'

The wooden sword used by Iwata had been given to us by a local village chief because of mistake on our part. Unwittingly, we had used the local Islamic prayer hall as a military store. It was a rough-hewn building and we did not realise it was sacred. The next day, the village chief came fearfully to ask us if we would just vacate that particular building. When I heard the reason, I was appalled. When I was a student and learned that the Kwantung Army had built a branch shrine of Ise Jingu in Manchuguo (what is now Northeast China) and had named it a sacred shrine of Manchuria and insisted that the local people worship there, I was outraged. Ise Shrine is what it is precisely because it belongs to the Japanese. To force it on to foreigners is incredibly presumptuous. The dark premonitions I had felt about Manchuria were graphically resuscitated.

I immediately begged his pardon and gave him tobacco to take back by way of apology. Straight away I gave directions for the materials to be moved and the place of worship returned to its former condition and I stayed there while it was done. In appreciation of this, the village chief presented me with a wooden sword made locally of ironwood. Then, as now, freedom of religious belief and the protection of human rights were of immutable importance.

Singing the Seiwa dormitory song

On 25 March 1942, the order was received for the second construction corps to merge with the 102nd. naval building section in Surabaya, Java. At the same time, I was transferred to the Takao naval building section in Taiwan. Subsequently, the naval building section was re-designated as the equipment section. The Takao equipment section had been started in 1937 when it was decided to build the Takao naval port as a southern base of operations. This was designated strategic place 'F' in the plan to build a naval port of about 10,000 hectares, stretching from the Kotobuki mountain range in the north of Takao harbour to the coast. The orders were to have it ready by 1945, with facilities comparable to the military port of Sasebo.

When war broke out, naval air corps were hurriedly set up in each area to make the Taiwanese islands into 'an unsinkable aircraft carrier' and orders were given to provide fuel depots to handle the oil coming in from the south, so they were in the midst of the confusion of a rush job. When I arrived in the middle of April, the breakwaters, sea walls and workshops were making steady progress and facilities for a Police Headquarters and housing for essential personnel were underway.

We were building a naval port and a port town, centered on a main road 60 metres in width and 1,400 metres in length. The breakwater that formed the outer harbour where the squadron would anchor was intended to be a huge structure extending to 7,500 metres, 3,500 meters on the beach line and with a water depth of thirteen metres, but very little of the construction was finished when the war ended.

The man who took technical responsibility for the actual construction work was Captain Ueno Chōzaburō. Captain Ueno was responsible for building Tokyo harbour off Harumi and when, after the war, he was asked to build a steel complex in Chiba and a petrochemical complex in Mizushima, Ōkayama, he brought in the whole clan of technicians and assistants who had worked on Tokyo harbour. He was not only a physically big man but a boss with heart.

Working under Chief Ueno I had sole responsibility for helping the senior officer, paymaster lieutenant commander Kakunami, to collect and manage materials, order and supervise the construction works, handle cash, the education of the workers and so on. Chief Ueno and Lieutenant Commander Kakinami trusted me and left me to get on with the job. I only found out after the war was over that Gotoda Masaharu was in army headquarters in Taiwan and that there was a battle over materials going on with him.

Taiwan was under the rule of a governor general who was a navy man and the regional governors made navy men welcome and made disparaging comparisons between them and the 'army men'. The timber yards in the areas of forestry production were all under the command of the equipment section and we went to the experimental forests of all the Imperial Universities and had them send timber. Toward the end we were using bamboo of various kinds in place of wood to construct barracks and there were innovative plans by the equipment section to use the flexibility of bamboo for arch shaped shelters.

Round about the middle of 1943, a cement dug-out hut about six foot square came empty in the woods near the equipment corps and I moved my bunk in there and lived alone. There was no electricity so I used acetylene. I hung a mosquito net to catch the lizards falling from the ceiling, and put up a bamboo stockade to try to keep out the poisonous snakes. Inside the stockade I kept two ducks. It was like making a hermit's cell and the word went around that I was eccentric, but in this relentless war, I was driven by my love of solitude. There was neither dwelling nor light within about four or five hundred metres. At night I would sit there and copy out the *Sansuikyō* sutras of Dōgen or be absorbed in reading the Buddhist scriptures or struggling with *haiku*. And of course I lit incense and prayed for the souls of those who had died in the war.

When the typhoons struck without warning, my house often seemed about to blow away, and when the air raid siren sounded and I would pull on my army boots and run out, the ducks would come rubbing their cheeks against my knee as if to say, 'don't go'. They too seemed to know when something was out of the ordinary. My love of solitude was inborn, and has found expression throughout my life: in my meditations on the drying veranda when I was in middle school to my contemplation in my mountain retreat in Hinode and Zenshōan.

New young officers were sent to help me when my work load became too heavy. Among the personnel in the Paymaster's Department were Kobayashi Yoshinobu and Kajikasawa Kenzo. Shigematsu Makoto was one of the technical officers. I became gun captain by special order of Captain Ueno. The new officers were not taught as such, rather they learned by watching what went on each day.

The combined numbers of the volunteers corps and public service squads grew rapidly until they vastly exceeded what navy regulations allowed for. But on paper, numbers were based on the official figures. Consequently, the naval surgeon had to cope with an extreme shortage of drugs. There was in particular a lack of quinine to treat malaria. When I learned of this sorry state of affairs, I raised the issue at a conference of higher officials. Chief Ueno listened sympathetically to the chief surgeon's explanation, then asked what was to be done. I thought it over for a moment and replied, 'Let's lose it in the category of general work expenses.' Thereafter there was a tacit understanding and measures were taken to resolve the problem. An officer in the paymaster's office showed us how to do it; he laughed and asked, 'Shall we say that you have dug a length of tunnel'? As soon as we had the funds, the chief nursing officer went all round Taiwan. He found four or five pharmacies where they were disposing of their inventory because they were withdrawing and so this was a timely opportunity to do business, but the stock was a mixed bag and even included herb medicines and gynaecological medicines. Afterwards when supplies at home dried up, they came in very useful.

By the summer of 1944 we were under aerial bombardment as the Americans sortied from southern China. As autumn deepened we came under wide-scale bombing. By good fortune, the equipment section escaped destruction but the Okayama base and the fuel depots were totally destroyed. The recovery of the soldiers' bodies was carried out quickly but many Taiwanese workers were left where they had fallen for lack of personnel to help. I thought it wrong that the navy should treat the Taiwanese differently from the Japanese even in death and I asked to be allowed to go to the Okayama base to recover the bodies. But Captain Ueno refused, saying that there would be another air raid and that I would be needed in the headquarters of the equipment section. Reluctantly I sent a truck with an experienced naval engineer in charge. This was the only time that Ueno and I did not see eye to eye.

At this time the senior officer at the airforce base fell, and engineer Tominaka Saburo assumed command of the naval anti-aircraft gunners. Tominaka was a handsome, friendly man who did not hesitate to speak his mind to his superiors and everybody loved him for his purity of character. As captain of the Tokyo University tennis club he had taught me how to play. Tominaka had just married a girl from home and was in the first flushes of wedded bliss. He told me, 'Marriage is a karmic relation so if, when you meet, you think, "this is it", then go for it.' What he meant was that arranged marriages where desire grows with repeated meeting are inappropriate and won't work out well.

The preceding April I had gone to Taipei to recruit female workers. The business of the equipment section had grown and the number of conscripts with it. Consequently, there was a shortage of office staff and we were falling behind with the construction work, so I obtained permission from headquarters to employ a women's volunteer corps. I went immediately to the First and Second Girls High Schools in Taipei. I had them all gather in the assembly hall and spoke to them about the work, the pay and what the dormitories were like and entreated them to apply. The high school girls in Taipei only knew soldiers and so, in my sailor's uniform, I was a novelty and applications poured in. Our sights were set on single, female high school graduates between the ages of eighteen and twenty-three and we employed altogether, in two rounds, seventy-seven people.

The female volunteers arrived in Takao on 5 May, and settled down in the dormitory that had been prepared for them with the home economics teacher, Miss Kanemura and the language teacher Miss

Takada. The dormitory's name was *Seiwa* or Serenity. Sometimes the young officers of the paymasters office or the medical corps would present educational lectures and I gave one on Japanese culture. It was not an easy job to make the dormitory into a place of culture and at the same to uphold military regulations and discipline, but the girls liked singing and I asked Miss Kanemura to write the lyrics and music for a dormitory song. Everyone liked the dormitory song and the girls often sang it in chorus. We never had them sing military songs. European ballads like 'The Orange Flower', and Japanese songs like 'We are Children of the Sea', 'Red Shoes' and 'Coconuts', were popular. I will never forget one particular face; that of Miss Kanemura, the small, graceful dormitory superintendent, smartly turned out in her work pants.

This was a total war that drew in even such sweet young girls. War is cruel and it can lead to barbarities. When the war is over and we come to investigate these barbarities there is always going to be a problem with the protagonists' claims about their motives and the way things developed. But what lies engraved in my heart, immutable and forever, are my memories of the drafted workers and the girl volunteers who suffered with us in Taiwan, the construction workers who landed by my side in the face of the enemy, and the wagering of the lives of the young.

Following Captain Hamada

In November 1944 I became paymaster lieutenant to the navy armaments department third section at Yokosuka naval station. The section chief there was Captain Hamada Sukeo. There were more than ten officers, ranging from captain to lieutenant commander, within the section, for whom lieutenant and sub-lieutenant pay-masters on short-term active service acted as personal aides. My direct superior was Captain Hayashi Takayoshi. In addition to his other duties he was responsible for the southern political affairs section. This meant that I too was involved in the administration of the southern occupied territories.

The war situation was already critical. Emergency increases in aircraft production, the securing of oil supplies from the south and the strengthening of naval escorts to effect this had become our top priority. Naval General Staff projections of likely damage to transport vessels for the first and second years of the war were 800,000 to 1,000,000 tons and 600,000 to 800,000 tons respectively. In fact, in the first year of the war 1,650,000 tons and in the second year 1,500,000 tons, that is, two and a half times the tonnage forecast, were lost. As our war potential fell, the damage mounted further.

As for production of aircraft, setbacks in the recovery of scrap iron and in securing supplies of aluminium fuelled fierce competition between the army and navy over the allotment of materials. In February 1944, production plans had been agreed of 27,120 aircraft for the army and 22,500 for the navy but these were impractical, empty theories, just castles in the air, and no more than ten percent of these projected aircraft were built.

Not long after, the Armaments Department, Third Section changed its spots and became the Bureau of Military Affairs, Third Section, but the fights with the army over allocation of materials continued; it was all just tinkering. Around this time there were subtle changes in the political situation, the Tōjō cabinet fell and the Koiso cabinet was formed. The mood of the senior officers grew turbulent as they realised the hopelessness of the situation they were in.

On the register of short-term active service personnel acting as aides at that time were paymaster Lieutenant-Commander Ikeda Masao [later of Mikimoto Pearls], paymaster Lieutenant-Commander Nakano Hideo [Ministry of Commerce and Industry], paymaster Lieutenant Hayakawa Takashi [Ministry of Welfare], paymaster Lieutenant Akazawa Shōichi [Ministry of Commerce and Industry], paymaster Lieutenant Andō Yoshio [Tokyo University], paymaster Lieutenant Yoshikuni Jirō [Ministry of Finance], paymaster Lieutenant Kakinuma Kōichirō [Ministry of Finance], paymaster Lieutenant Amino Makoto [Ministry of Commerce and Industry], paymaster Lieutenant Inoue Ichirō [Mitsubishi Mining], paymaster Lieutenant Chikaraishi Koyata [Bank of Tokyo] and paymaster Sub-lieutenant Arai Tatsuo [Asia Oil].

Because Captain Hamada took note of what we regular graduate officers thought even though officer graduates of the naval academy and the Naval Staff College were dominant, he became the subject of malicious gossip. Captains and commanders in the section accused him of being soft on the young non-professional officers instead of favouring the experts who had graduated from Naval Staff College as he should in a time of emergency. They also accused him of treating the lowest and highest ranks alike. In fact he was tired of the advice he got from bureaucratic captains and commanders with their narrow fields of vision and he listened closely to our more objective opinions. Captain Hamada was close to Rear Admiral Takagi Sōkichi, chief of the investigation section, and I believe was one of the faction seeking to end the war.

Akazawa, one of our group, was in charge of matters relating to the south, and he asked to be allowed to make an on-the-spot inspection in the occupied territories. However, permission was not readily forthcoming. There was strong resistance to such special treatment being afforded to two year active service personnel. Then suddenly one day Captain Hamada called in Akazawa and surprised him by saying, 'Your written orders have arrived so get on with it.' Akazawa was surprised because he had been aware of the opposition and had more or less given up hope. It turned out that Captain Hamada wanted to send this young, fresh officer from the paymaster's section south to look into the faults of the occupation administration. He had been to see the head of personnel any number of times and finally had taken two bottles of *sake* to the senior adjutant.

At year end, Captain Hamada used up his special job allowance and bonus to buy *sake* and New Year things and he gave presents to the short-term personnel and to the copyists and typists exactly as he did to the permanent staff. To give presents without regard to rank was completely contrary to customary naval practice. It seems that Captain Hamada got the *sake* by soliciting his old friend from his time at the Asia Development Board, Ōhira Masayoshi, director of the Tokyo National Tax Bureau Customs Department and later, prime minister.

Right about the time when Lieutenant Seki and the others died in the first *kamikaze* special attack force, I visited the governor of the communication bureau, Ogata Taketora, with my colleague, Hayaka-wa. Seeing the noble sacrifice made by an officer no older than ourselves we could not contain ourselves and we appealed to him to send Tokutomi Sōhō as an envoy to the front line to express the public's emotion and gratitude to the young officers of the special attack forces, and to use the opportunity to arouse the people's concern and increase production of aircraft. We suggested that he could take amulets from temples and shrines across the country and stick prayers for success in war on the planes, and we offered to go with him ourselves if necessary. Ogata thanked us and said he would look into it. We went home happy that he would do it.

A few days later we were sent for by Captain Kurihara of the Navy Ministry press section. When we reported we were sent to Captain Isshiki. Without warning we were made to stand to attention and were beaten for ignoring naval discipline and moreover for visiting a superior officer in another department. Captain Kurihara also shouted at us saying, 'The navy has its own methods. You are just two year recruits, don't get above yourselves.'

We thought it best to keep quiet and so we kept our heads down and got on with our work. Two or three days later chief of section Hamada called, 'Hey Nakasone.' Glancing quickly at me over his glasses he said simply, 'When you're going to do what you want, just let me know first.'

When the war was over we set up the so-called Hamada School to repay our debts to section chief Hamada and we assembled every year. Late in life, when he was a genial old man, he would tell us stories. He told us, for example, about the time when, having graduated second from the Naval Academy, he went with a training squadron to Europe and took up with a beautiful young Italian girl with whom he continued to keep in touch by letter. It continued even though they both married, and when he went on holiday to Europe after the war, he went and had tea with the old lady she had become. Our meetings took place until Captain Hamada passed away in 1986. The fine relationship between the chief of the Naval Affairs Third Section and the young short-term active service officers in the paymaster's section, was born of the war and humanism. To this day we remember Captain Hamada as a virtuous man and consider it an honour to have served under him.

Ochiai *sensei*, the teacher
I can't forget

On 11th Feb 1945, I married Kobayashi Tsutako. On a visit back to Japan during the time I was working in Takao in Taiwan, I had been entrusted with some letters and dried mullet roe by my successor, paymaster Sub-lieutenant Kobayashi Yoshiharu. My delivery of these to his house in Mejiro in Tokyo was the beginning of our relationship: Tsutako was my colleague's younger sister.

Kobayashi Giichiro, Tsutako's father, was a doctor of science who had been a geological surveyor in China and Southeast Asia before the war and who, after the war, excavated hot springs in Japan. Her mother, Tamako, was a woman's activist who worked as a member of the Imperial Rule Assistance Association Research Committee with Hani Setsuko and Oku Mumeo and she was involved in the fight to secure suffrage for women. Tamako also worked with Ichikawa Fusae, Yoshioka Yayoi, Kubushiro Ochimi, Inoue Hideko and Yamada Waka

44

in marriage discussions and in supporting students. She had close connections in the political world with people like Hatoyama Ichiro and Uehara Etsujiro and with bureaucrats like Kumagai Kenichi in the Ministry of Home Affairs and, given my position at the Ministry, she took a liking to me. Tsutako's mother, who was also a representative for the Greater Japan Mother's Union, had me marked out.

At the time, Tsutako was working in the administrative section of the Great East Asia Department China Bureau. I shocked her by crying when we went to see the film *Rikugun,* [The Army] together. But it was then, gripped by a premonition of the tragic destiny that lay in store for Japan, that I became aware of my desire to live and die together with this woman, and I decided to marry. The words of my friend from my time in Takao, were a major factor in my decision. Tominaka Saburo, had said that when marriage is first mooted, it is important to make up your mind intuitively, without hesitating. His words had stayed with me. My father and older brother in Takasaki accepted my decision saying, 'If its right for you than it should be all right' and it all went smoothly.

With my marriage, I talked to Tsutako's father about many things and he greatly expanded my knowledge of science and technology. At that time, experiments were underway within the navy ministry into the production of nuclear bombs and there was excitement about the discovery of uranium. I bombarded him with questions and learned a fair amount about nuclear fission and fusion, the theory of relativity and quantum theories.

I was in Takamatsu on transport business on the morning of August 6th when I saw what looked like a thunder cloud rise silently in the blue sky to the west. Friends of mine said that a powder magazine had gone up, but before long reports came that it was a special bomb and because I knew, from what my father-in-law had told me, that there was a real possibility that America would develop an atomic bomb, I realised immediately what it had been. The image of that white cloud is, to this day, seared on my eyes. The shock of it was one of the things that later made me determined to harness nuclear power for peaceful uses.

Once it was settled that we should marry, the next question was who should act as go-between. My father and the others wanted to have Tokyo University Professor Rōyama Masamichi, a native of my hometown, or one of my superiors in the Ministry of Home Affairs, preferably the vice minister. I understood how they felt, but I had already decided on someone. This was Ochiai Tatsuji, the teacher who had patted me on the head on the first day at North Takasaki Primary School and had said, 'This boy will be like Saigo Takamori.' I told my father, 'I don't want someone chosen as my go-between because of their social status or prestige, I want someone who has really understood me, someone who has held me in affection.'

Mr Ochiai had retired from teaching and had taken a job at the Takasaki Commercial School. His wife taught needlework and they made a modest living at a time when material things were in short supply. I went to his house to ask him if he would do it but he refused point blank and, when I persevered, he told me that he did not have a morning suit to wear. I pressed him saying that there was a war on so why not have everybody wear national civilian uniform and, if that wouldn't do, that I would hire a morning suit, and with this he accepted. The ceremony took place at Takasaki Shrine and Mr Ochiai seemed happy. I think he saw it as providential that he should be asked to act as go-between for one of his own pupils.

My marriage with Kobayashi Tsutako at
Takasaki Shrine

Every year since I entered the Diet I have gone back to Takasaki North primary school on New Year's day to make a New Year's greeting. Every year I tell the same story of how I got big and strong by eating lots of rice cakes at New Year and doing callisthenics. I tell them that if they want to grow big, they must do the same. I tell the same story every year so by the time they graduate, they have heard it six times. After the second or third time, when I asked them to remind me of my story, they all chanted in chorus, 'Rice cakes, rice cakes.' The children who listened to this story grew up and voted for me. When the polar route to Europe was established I asked the children after the rice cake story, 'Can you guess where I went? I flew in a plane above somewhere where there are polar bears.' Lots of hands went up and they answered, 'A zoo, a zoo.' I had expected them to say 'the North Pole', but of course this was also a right answer.

Even now, each year, the graduating students come down to Tokyo in March and we have our photograph taken together in the Diet. They each bring me about two pages of something they have written. Primary school is the eternal home of the soul for us all. Whenever the school entry season comes round in April I find myself praying that every child who enters the gates so joyfully will be blessed with good teachers.

Younger brother Ryōsuke is killed in the war

Starting in February 1945 with the bombing of Tokyo, the whole country came under attack from air raids by the American task force. In March 1945 I was devastated to be told, in confidence, by a Sub-lieutenant Mizuno, in the Navy Ministry, of my younger brother's death. I was told it had happened on the southern coast of Honshu.

Ryōsuke had graduated from Otaru Higher Commercial School and it was his intention to become an officer in the paymaster's corps on a short-term commission as I had done, but because he was physically strong and had twenty-twenty vision, he went, as was the way at the time, as a reserve student in the fleet air arm for which there was an urgent large-scale call up. Around October 1944, he went to the base in Bihoro, Hokkaido, as an acting Sub-lieutenant on a medium-sized, naval attack vessel.

One night in December when a cold wintry wind was blowing, he arrived unexpectedly at my lodgings in Iikura in Tokyo with a bottle

47

of *sake*. He said he had come from the base in Kisarazu. We huddled round a brazier and drank the *sake* and ate dried squid and talked of our family back home and the way the war was going. At about 11 o'clock he said he was going back to Kisarazu and rose to leave. I was uneasy about what he could have come to Tokyo to talk about and as I walked him to the nearby station I warned him, 'Take care of yourself. The outlook for Japan is bleak. We are nearing ruin, but at all costs we must survive and work for the country.' I returned to my lodgings and wrote:

> *A winter's wind of war swept outside,*
> *As little brother and I shared two bottles of sake.*

No notification came of my brother's death. I knew how devastated my old father would be and decided to say nothing to him, or to my elder brother or sister, until the official notification came. My father kept writing asking me what was going on because the letters from Ryōsuke had just suddenly stopped arriving. I wrote back, 'Pilots are always on the move from one base to the next. He probably can't write because he doesn't have a proper address.'

For a time after we married, Tsutako and I lived with relations of mine in Kita Urawa. In the air raids of 10 March the downtown areas of Tokyo were reduced to stretches of burnt ruins and the Naval Ministry too was fire bombed. I felt that the time for investigations and plans was past. I didn't want to be doing office work in the Naval Ministry at a time such as this, I wanted to be making a visible difference, to increase the number of planes produced or the number of shells manufactured if only by one. I worried that Japan was being driven into a corner.

Working in the Naval Ministry left my evenings free except when I was on duty and I wanted to use this time do some manual labour that would contribute to the war effort. Faced with the death of my younger brother, it was a way, of atoning, for still being alive. There was an Oki Electric factory to the side of Warabi station. I made myself known to the boss of the factory and was put on the production line making machine gun bullets. All around me girl students in headbands were hard at work.

By this time, even within the Naval Ministry, estimations were being made of when the war would be lost. I struggled to do my best as a citizen and as a naval officer at a time when I was overwhelmed with anxiety about both the impending defeat of Japan and the death of my brother.

Coming in by train from Kita Urawa to Tokyo you could see, from the top of the iron bridge at Akabane, a temple with a bronze roof on the right bank of the Arakawa and it was there that I went one Sunday and told the chief priest about my brother. I told him that no official notification had yet been issued and asked him to say a quiet, private memorial service. The Buddhist priest consented readily. He lit candles and offered incense and chanted the sutras.

The official notification of Ryōsuke's death came after the war had ended. There were few details apart from the news that it had happened at sea off the southern coast of Japan. Even when I searched in 1970 when I was Director-General of the Self Defence Forces, I couldn't find out any more. In 1975, a classmate of my brother, Nemoto Masasuke, put an advert in the *Chūkōkai*, the magazine put out by former crewmen on mid-range naval fighters, asking for information on my brother. As a result of the advertisement, information came in that, according to the flight records preserved by one of the members, two planes had set off for Iwakuni at 06:30 hours and it was his recollection that, 'That day we ran into a blizzard at high altitude over Mt. Suzuka and I made an emergency landing at Toyohashi; the plane that had sortied with me went missing. I believe that was Nakasone's plane.'

I made inquiries through the governor of Mie Prefecture whether there might be further information in Mie police headquarters. What I learned was that, 'On the 25 or 26 of February 1945, a naval plane had crashed near the summit of Mt. Kyokugatake in Iinamigun and that local people searched but were unable to reach the site of the crash because of the fallen snow.' In February the following year, hunters came across the wreckage of a plane and the bleached bones of eleven dead and reported their find to the local police station when they got back down. The locals recovered all the remains and enshrined them in Kōfuku temple in Iinamimachi and buried them as deceased without relatives.

This was how we came to know that on 25 February, orders were received from Kisarazu Air Corps, 'Enemy task force approaching, strong probability of air raid. Scramble to safety.' and that fourteen planes took off toward China and Kyūshu but that owing to a blizzard in the Suzuka mountain range almost all made emergency landings in the Tōkai region. My brother's plane crashed near the summit of Mt. Kyokugatake and all on board died.

On 19 May 1979, I called together all the bereaved families and held a memorial service on the spot in Kyokugatake. At Kōfuku temple I apologised on behalf of the pilot. Later the remains of the eleven naval men were moved to the cemetery for war dead in Chidorigafuchi and enshrined together after which they were enshrined in Yasukuni Shrine. I felt at peace at last

> *Bush warblers have guarded*
> *the souls of fallen warriors*
> *For some thirty years.*

———————

CHAPTER THREE

THE ROAD TO POLITICS

Seize the chance

Another anniversary
Of the last War's ending:
Still cicadas sing
On all our islands.

It was in Takamatsu that, on 15 August, I listened to the Emperor's broadcast. Toward the end of my naval service I had been transferred to the newly-organised Takamatsu naval transport division as a part of the rearrangements for the last decisive battle on the mainland which would put even office workers on the front line. My job was to see to transport and communications for the special attack forces being developed in Kure and Tosa Bay. My office was set up in a classroom belonging to the Prefectural Girl's High School.

There was a lot of atmospheric interference during the Emperor's broadcast and it was difficult to make out a great deal of the content, but from about the 9th we had been hearing of moves within the palace to end the war. I was worried by the prevarication at a time when Soviet troops were advancing but of course I knew nothing of the debate about the pros and cons of accepting the Potsdam Declaration.

Consequently, I could only guess at the content of the broadcast from the few words I could understand, but I knew the war was over and I cried. My heart went out to the Emperor. Despite the poor transmission, grief echoed in his voice.

But there is no denying that, in one sense, it was a relief. I had survived, and from then on there would be no more blackouts. The only noise was the sound of the cicadas in the school yard.

A few days later orders arrived from the naval stores section in Kure, the gist of which was that I should get steam ships ready and

51

collect the heavy oil that was left in Kure naval port and distribute it where it would be most useful within Kagawa prefecture. I prepared five boats and set off from Takamatsu to Kure.

As the steam ships chugged along through the calm of the Inland Sea, I lay spread-eagled on the deck, looking up at the summer moon. I lay there in the centre of this huge power vacuum pondering, with no real hope of coming to any conclusion, what was to become of Japan. The era of militarism and the military man was giving way to the era of ideas and the civilian. I had thrown myself into winning the fight but this did not mean that my life had been in vain. My most important role was yet to come. I felt a shiver pass through me.

When I had filled the cargo space with drums in Kure I returned overnight to Takamatsu and immediately got on to the leaders of the fishing co-operative. I told them to take the oil because it was free and to use it to improve their catch of fish to supply the people of Kagawa prefecture. I gave strict orders against diverting so much as one can of the oil into illegal channels. At the time, a lack of heavy oil kept the fishing boats in dock, so the members of the fishing co-operative danced with joy at the decision. I was asked up to the second floor of the executive's house and they drank my health. My war was over.

My four years in the navy taught me many lessons. My first experience of society after I left school was of the military. It was there that I shared the joys and the sorrows of two thousand drafted men; there that I saw uncelebrated workers fight the good fight and there that I understood that the Japanese people are more emotional and more patriotic the closer to the bottom of society you get. When the war ended and I was demobbed I returned to the Ministry of Home Affairs but I felt that, with the country in ruins, the engine of regeneration could not be driven solely by the bureaucracy, that they had to join forces with the people, to become of one mind and to rise like a tidal wave across the country.

As expected, with the end of the war, communism spread and broadcast the seeds of violent revolution throughout the country. Some foreigners, acting out the role of victors in the war, ran amok in the towns. As a part of the bureaucracy during the early period when occupation policy was aimed at the dissolution of Japan, I could do nothing to oppose this drift. There was nothing for it but to rally forth in the name of the people. When, following the defeat, I decided to resign from the bureaucracy and return home, it was as a result of the deep impression that the ordinary people in the construction corps had made on me and of the ruination of post-war Japan. In my dealings as a politician I put to use the things I had learned in my time in the navy and under fire.

When I assumed office as prime minister,[1] I announced, 'the Nakasone cabinet will be an entrepreneurial cabinet. It will challenge taboos.' In so doing, I was following the naval motto, 'In times of storm, face into the wind, that is the secret of success for steering a warship.' 'Vigilance to both right and left,' 'Ship's position always accurate,' as the basis for action applies equally to Japan's diplomatic principles and to internal party activity.

I have been vilified as a 'weathervane', but knowing which way the wind is blowing is the first step in steering a ship of war. The body moves with the wind but the footing is steady. That is what a weathervane is. Who serves the national interest better, the rigid, obstinate politician and his politics caught up in ideology and moral justification, unable to shift with changing conditions, or the one who is suitably flexible?

There is a saying 'seize the chance' (*senki ni tōzeyo*) which means, wait patiently until the chance arrives, and when it does, grasp it without fear. This might sound like self-justification, but I am a disciple of Kōno Ichiro who survived as a minority current under the vast, so-called conservative mainstream politics that began with Yoshida and continued with Kishi and Sato,[2] and I am witness to that history of frustration.

Kōno and others in the minority faction were subjected to slanders, rumour mongering and name calling by the mainstream and by their increasingly powerful supporters in the press. I personally was attacked fiercely by the left-wing camp. This strengthened my belief that it is no good being impulsive and single-minded if you are committing yourself to a struggle for power. You need strategy and tactics to succeed. You only win the power struggle when you have understood the prevailing climate and the position of your opponent, and seized all the chances both big and little.

When I became prime minister and formed my first cabinet I chose men of note from the Tanaka faction: men such as secretary general Nikaidō and chief cabinet secretary Gotōda, and appointed them to central positions within the political structure. For this my cabinet was attacked as a 'Tanakasone cabinet' or a 'Lockheed shift'. But I had in mind the strategy of Admiral Togo when confronted by the Baltic Fleet. The formation of this first cabinet was likewise, the seizing of a chance.

At the time, relations with America were at their lowest point since the war and relations with China and Korea were at an impasse. At such times the only thing to do is to involve every available source of fighting power within the system and to lay down a structure which will fight the decisive battle to break the status quo. It makes no difference if something is right and reasonable: if it doesn't achieve results and get you what you wanted then it isn't politics. Politics isn't a university lecture or a church sermon. Politicians have to win political battles, not give in to silly opposition baiting.

I had witnessed the patriotism of the conscripts at first hand, and had seen my younger brother die and I found it hard to contain my anger at the people who had led Japan to war and to defeat. I felt the defeat as a humiliation in the history of the nation. At the time of the defeat I was not a national leader but, as an individual citizen, I thought an unforgivable stain had been left on the history of Japan. I became a politician in order to rebuild and rehabilitate Japan and, as someone who had come home, to repay the ones who had not. When I was attacked, I would remind myself why I got into politics in the first place and brace myself.

The country destroyed, there are mountains and rivers

I was demobilised in October 1945 and returned to the Ministry of Home Affairs, to the secretariat. It was my job to deal with special stores; the stores left behind by the armed forces. These had come under the jurisdiction of the Supreme Commander of Allied Powers, General Douglas MacArthur, [SCAP], and were released to the people and used to fill both government and public needs as a measure for maintaining stability and promoting industrial regeneration. I worked as an official contact with Lieutenant Colonel Eichelburg of the 8th Army which provided the occupying forces, and my direct contact was a Colonel Barado.

My first problem was English. I bought a set of conversation texts and crammed as if for an exam, but there were so many differences in pronunciation and in the sort of slang used in English and American, that I was getting nowhere. Fortunately, at that time, we had ten American military policemen guarding the thought control police records that were kept locked up in the basement of the ministry building and I wandered into their office and asked them to teach me American. They were very obliging and mostly it was the non-commissioned officers who taught me conversational English during the lunch break.

Colonel Barado was a gentle man, a former lawyer, who did not swagger and who did all he could to grant our requests. I wondered how a Japanese occupying force would have behaved in their position. I had great admiration for every action taken by Colonel Barado and the other officers and soldiers and I felt keenly that we had been bound to lose this war and that, had we won, Japan would have become puffed up with pride and would have been loathed throughout Asia.

I invited Colonel Barado to visit the Kobayashi family home of my wife. It was the first invitation he had had to visit a Japanese family since he had come to Japan and he accepted happily. We couldn't provide him with anything very good to eat of course, but we did what we could on the black market. I took him to Nikko and we stayed at Lake Chuzenji and played silly party games with geisha. While I was there, my eldest son, Hirofumi, was born. Even now, my wife still keeps on at me about how I left her in labour to go and mess with geisha and paint the town red with the occupying army. She tells me that no modern wife would put up with it; that I would end up divorced. I always tell her that I was on national work; that we might have been called the Ministry of Home Affairs, but we were actually more the office for geisha affairs.

It was round about this time that my old colleague, Hayakawa Takashi, resigned from the Ministry of Welfare, whence he had returned on being demobilised, and went back to his hometown of Wakayama Prefecture, to stand as a candidate in the forthcoming election. He wanted to publish a newspaper in Tanabe City as a way of starting his campaign but he couldn't get hold of either a printing press or paper. I went to see Machimura Kingo, deputy mayor of Tokyo (in current parlance deputy governor) and formerly in charge of personnel, and got stocks released from special stores.

It was a troubling time. Members of the communist party had been released and their leader, Tokuda Kyūichi had gone to the Supreme Commander of Allied Forces, General MacArthur, and shouted 'Banzai for the occupying forces.' Labour unions were being organised in every town, there were growing demands to know who was responsible for the war, and the occupation forces were giving them every encouragement in order to destroy the established order. Just as the purges from public office were beginning, former Prime Minister Konoe was designated a war criminal and committed suicide. There were even demands from abroad that the emperor be investigated for responsibility for the war.

In February 1946 I was transferred to become administrative chief of Kagawa Prefectural Police. It was my second time there since I had worked in the Takamatsu naval transport section toward the end of my service with the Navy Ministry.

At first I borrowed a room in a corner of Tamamo Castle which had escaped the fires in Takamatsu. Matsudaira Yoriaki, the head of the family, and grandson of the former *daimyō*, and his wife were resident in the castle. Yoriaki invited me to take part in a tea ceremony class with a master of the Mushakōji Senke school who came once a month from Kyoto. I learned how to walk on *tatami*,[3] how to open the sliding doors to the tea room and how to eat ceremonial food. We conducted ourselves formally, but I was not equal to learning the real procedures of the tea ceremony and studied only a simple, informal form of tea ceremony.

By and by I was offered the use of an empty house in the compound of Yajima Shrine, a house with one room of about twelve feet square and a kitchen that had been used by the Shinto priest as a place to change his clothes. It was like a hermit's cell; a place where the sighing of the pine trees in the pine forests of the mountains of Yajima echoed. I lived here with my wife and three month old son, Hirofumi, but so many centipedes fell from the ceiling that we were forced to hang mosquito nets when we put him down to sleep, even during the day.

I usually travelled by bicycle to the Prefectural office in the town, but occasionally I would take the electric tram. It was always full and I would hang on to the door. At Kawaramachi station where I got off there was a big open-air market where middle-aged men in demob suits and women in scarves sold things on the black market and young vagrants milled about. People's eyes sparkled with the joy of being alive and the smell of sweat and dust filled the air. It is said that, 'When a country is destroyed, the mountains and rivers remain' and I was keenly aware of being in a defeated country.

The main challenge for the police force was to stop thinking of itself as a coercive and political security body and to see itself as a police force which would serve the community. To that end, it was necessary to change the ideas of police leaders and those working in the front line alike; to guide them into putting the new ideas into practice, and also to publicise these changes. Sabres were changed for truncheons. Raids at hotels and other such opportunities for individual interrogation were banned. A woman's police force was set up relatively quickly. Lecturers were brought in from outside and classes, including tea ceremony, were used as a way of raising the levels of cultural education in the force. Masuhara Keikichi, the government appointed governor, was well aware of what the situation required and made sufficient funding available.

Another facet of police work was to monitor black market trading, particularly the pernicious trade between Hamamatsu and Osaka, whilst dealing leniently with ordinary individuals buying daily necessities for themselves. The MacArthur headquarters' counter-intelligence-corps (CIC) also cracked down on the black market but they were apt to be overzealous and it was sometimes hard to explain the circumstances and get them to exercise restraint.

It was about this time that Hayakawa's election campaigning began. There was no rule at that time against public servants taking part in election campaigns outside their own prefecture and so I sent out letters of recommendation saying 'Support Hayakawa, Hero of Wakayama. Kagawa Prefectural Police Section Chief, Nakasone Yasuhiro', and on my days off, I would go to Wakayama Prefecture and help with the speech-making from Tanabe city to as far as afield Shingū city. My letter of recommendation was distributed in the form of handbills. It was an odd period: we called ourselves a democratic police force, but we were allowed to campaign in our official capacity.

The birth of the *Seinen Konwakai*

In November 1945 my friends were demobilised one after another. The country was in confusion. Increasingly we wanted to discuss national policy, to do something to help rebuild Japan, and that is how the youth group, the *Seinen Konwakai*, was born. The founder members included several friends from the Bureau of Naval Affairs in the old Navy Ministry, myself, Hayakawa Takashi, Akazawa Akira, Nakagawa Kojiro plus people like Takahashi Mikio, Ozawa Tatsuo, Sawaki Masao, Seto Jūtaro, Minagawa Hiromune, Abe Takeshi and Gotō Susumu. Gotō was the only ex-army member. We held passionate discussions in the second floor tatami room of a *soba* noodle shop in Toranomon sitting in a circle around an electric heater still wearing our overcoats. We talked about how to maintain social order, the labour movement, food policy, industrial regeneration, and about reconstructing education and national ideology.

Hayakawa and Takahashi reported on public security and SCAP policies, Akazawa, who was deputy chairman of the Ministry of

57

Commerce and Industry's labour division, reported on the state of affairs in the labour movement and on conditions in the factories. Nakagawa gave us his opinions on the financial situation, Sawaki talked about trends in the Far Eastern Commission, Gotō and Minagawa told us how things were in company management, Seto talked about energy problems and Abe gave us his opinions on trends in medicine since the war. We lacked expertise on agricultural issues and later Higaki Tokutarō was included to give us someone who was knowledgeable in this area.

Gotō was the one who procured the food. At the time, he was Director of General Affairs for Tōkyū rolling stock manufacturers in Yokohama and he would buy cheap rice wine and bread and dried sardines from the black market in front of Sakuragicho Station and bring them in wrapped in a big paper bag. Everyone was very grateful that this son of Gotō Keita would habitually arrive bearing a large bottle. It was Gotō's way to listen, in silence, but at the end to put forward his own conclusions.

We met roughly once a month, but funding for the meetings was scarce. It was mainly Gotō, Akazawa and myself who went around the business community. Gotō Keita not only provided us with wonderful black market food but also gave us what was in those days the considerable sum of ¥30,000. It was through young Gotō's introduction that we met his father-in-law, Kuhara Fusanosuke. The Kuhara residence was what is now Happoen in Shiroganedai, Tokyo. When we all visited there on one occasion, we were overwhelmed by the scale of it.

I asked Kuhara if he would go back into political leadership when he was depurged. He replied, 'I've no interest in domestic politics. I wouldn't mind working to build a united Asia but even if we strain ourselves to get independence and peace, until America and the Soviet Union fight, its a waste of time and we should save our energy. I don't want to be a spoilsport. You can count me in if you are planning an excursion. An insubordinate, uncooperative united states of Asia is a historical inevitability, and Mikage in Hyōgo Prefecture will be its capital city, you mark my words'

In his memoirs, Gotō recorded the conversation he had with Kuhara when the latter called him back after this meeting and asked, 'Is Nakasone single?' When Gotō said no, I was already married, Kuhara asked Can't he be made to separate? I'd like him for my daughter. He has a good voice: the voice of a politician who will do well'.

It was after this that Gotō gave me a copies of records of Kuhara's support for the revolutionary movement of Sun Yat-sen, the father of China. Seeing the loan contracts for ¥1,000,000, for which Kuhara must have been the backer, and the loan contract for ¥700,000 and promissory notes for ¥100,000 from Sun to Kuhara made me realise what operators politicians were in the past. The date on them was the fifth year of the Republic of China, so it was from 1916. The loan was said to be for co-operation in the development of mining in China but when Sun Yat-sen ran into difficulties, the mining venture ended in failure. However, the funds seem to have been used to buy arms for the Strike North forces.

The *Seinen Konwakai* was restructured and expanded its member-ship in 1948. In 1954, when Gotō became chairman of Tōkyū, he was having difficulties with a group company, Tōkyū Kurogane Indus-tries, which was heavily in the red. Coincidentally, we were invited to dinner by old Mr Gotō. When we arrived at the restaurant in Shibuya, old man Keita, dressed formally in *haori hakama*, bowed deeply and said 'Please support my son Susumu.' I was taken aback that old man Keita, who could call on distinguished business people like Ishizaka Taizō, Kobayashi Ataru, Nagano Shigeo and Sakurada Takeshi for help, should pay underlings like us such consideration.

The *Seinen Konwakai* continued to operate. Eventually I became prime minister and Gotō became president of the Japan Chamber of Commerce, and the group members, now occupying strategic places, supported me strongly: it was particularly difficult for Gotō when, at the time of the consumption tax issue, he was caught between myself and the people in commerce and industry who were opposed to the tax. I'm afraid that it was this worry that made his illness worse. When he was better, it was Abe, a medical doctor and founding member of the *Seiwa Konwakai*, who became his confidant and it was Abe who told us it was cancer.

Gotō, Akazawa, Nakagawa and myself were playing golf at the Three Hundred Club when Gotō announced that he had decided to retire from the presidency of the Japan Chamber of Commerce and Industry and asked our advice about a successor. Gotō himself favoured Ishikawa Rokuro.

On 28 January, 1989, Gotō came hurrying in to open the regular meeting of the *Seinen Konwakai*. That day he had been officiating at the funeral of a famous old geisha madam by the name of Gorōmaru, and had been greeting mourners on the street in the freezing rain. He left before me, looking his usual kindly self, but that was the last time

I saw him well. After he retired from the front line, he made it his life's work to build a grove for the village shrine, to lead the fashion world and to address the problems of the Pacific Ocean. I would have liked to see him carry on working for another ten years at least.

I give up the bureaucracy without my father's knowledge

I wrote repeatedly from Takamatsu, where I was section chief in the Kagawa Prefectural Police, to Takasaki, to seek my father's blessing for my leaving the Ministry of Home Affairs. My argument was that, 'Young, educated people must defend the country against the radical left wing'. This is one letter dated April 30, 1946 and addressed to my father and brothers.

Greetings,

Many thanks for your letter which I have just received, and thank you also for all your trouble. We are managing all right here for money so please don't worry about us on that account.

The fact is, I want to ask your approval for something: something I proposed some time ago. I know that I have very little experience and will probably need to be patient but I am not saying this because I feel restless or because my friends have become Diet men, and I want to do the same. I am young, and I don't know much about the world, but I know at least that in the official world everything is changing and that the time to fight is now or never. Since I came to this district I've come to feel most keenly that there is a shortage of educated young leaders in the regions and that young people here are searching for such leadership. I have only been in Kagawa for three months but I have been approached by a number of outstanding young people since I came and have been asked to resign my post and lead their movement. I'm not saying this out of vanity. If I am to become a powerful leader in my home district, I must start early to win people's hearts and to build an organisation and a base. That is what is most important for Japan right now. Even if I come home now I won't run in the autumn prefectural elections. What I will do is rally the young intelligentsia in Gunma and they will volunteer to spread the word to the young people of the towns and so on and create a youth movement. If we do this, we will ensure that half the members elected in the autumn prefectural elections will be young people like us, in their thirties. But this in itself would not amount to much. Afterwards, I will spend the next year or two studying prefectural politics.

Only then will I stand for the Diet. I have already more or less learned what I can from inside the Prefectural office and from the police. One thing we have to realise is that the way the world is going it will not pay to have too much of a history as a bureaucrat. And to wait until everything is stable to come forward would be to miss the opportunity. Diet men now are nothing but brokers and servants. I don't want to be that sort of fickle, rootless representative. I want to win the hearts of the young people and then gradually to build an organisation and a support base, using our own resources. Then we can begin. The world might appear rational but it holds surprises. Please grant me this heartfelt desire. I decided to do this even before I was posted to Kagawa prefecture and what I have seen since has made me all the more determined. In fact, it was while I was in Tokyo that I made up my mind after going to talk, at his home, with a professor who taught me at Tokyo University, a famous professor of political science called Yabe Teiji. The reason that I have waited until now was that I thought I would take a look at how regional administration worked. I have looked for three months and I have seen enough.

Father, I know I'm asking the impossible and that it must appear to you to be crazy talk, but from where I'm standing, seeing the way things are going and the way history works, it seems to be absolutely logical. Please forgive me. You know one of the Satomi Nakasones was chased out by his father as a lunatic. He studied in Tokyo and was successful. Everything happened as he had hoped and forecast. This time too, this really is my life's work. Having worked hard for the higher civil-service exams and passed in the eighth rank, to leave behind a comfortable, powerful position now, by choice, I will need to be very determined. But because this is my life's work I have thought about it earnestly and I have made up my mind. Please understand how I feel and grant me your indulgence. I know that when I get home it will be difficult to make ends meet, but think to yourself that you are cultivating a great man and take care of us. I will do whatever I can to get an income. It is a thing of the past to train for two or three years, or to think of waiting until you make section chief or something. The world now cannot be judged by what was common-sense in the past. The time will soon be ripe.

Please give me your blessing because otherwise I will have to do it without.

It was a time when it was said that, 'Democracy is life through demonstrations', and I felt a violent impatience at the way Marxism and related ideas took advantage of the spiritual vacuum to spread like wild fire.

The new draft constitution was delivered from SCAP in February 1946 and put out as a Japanese government plan in March. This constitution brought massive structural changes in politics and speeded up social change. Japan was in the midst of an unprecedented frenzy.

As a result of the purges from public office, the politicians of the pre-war *Seiyūkai* and *Minseitō* parties had been driven out, but no strong, alternative conservative leaders had emerged to take their place. In Takasaki the conservatives had been overpowered and silenced. The Communists dominated a wide area in the person of Kyoto University professor of agriculture, Yamada Shōjirō. Leading lights of the Communist party like Kameda Tōgo were very active making speeches and building organisations and had joined up with the left wing of the socialist party under Muto Unjūrō.

I had made up my mind to become a politician but my father would not agree. It was not unreasonable. My timber merchant father had spent his savings launching his son on a career as a bureaucrat. Then, just as the terrible war was over and it was safe to breathe again, he was thrown once more into the maelstrom. I pressed him so hard in my letters to give his consent that he sent my older sister's husband, Nakasone Eiichi to Takamatsu to persuade me to drop the idea. I did not listen to him and in my last letter home before I left Takamatsu, I wrote these words.

> The best way that a soldier who came home can repay the spirits of those who died in the war is to stand in the front line of politics and tread the road of suffering and uncertainty that will rebuild Japan. I am confident. There is a time for fighting and now is that time. We were lucky, our house did not burn, we lost only a little land in the farm dissolutions, our factory and mountain forests survived intact. Please look on this as something lost in the war and give me the money for election funds.

I was transferred to Tokyo as a police supervisor with the Metropolitan Police Headquarters, 6th district which encompassed the downtown areas from Honjo and Arakawa to Adachi and Katsushika. My duties were to supervise and observe how police administration was working in practice, and in particular to guide the front line police chiefs. I paid particular attention to learning about the organisational theory of communism and to finding out about the activities of communist parties in other countries.

I read Mao Tse-tung's book *Guerrilla Warfare*.[4] This book on strategy and the principles of action opened my eyes. A number of things made a particularly deep impression on me: the hardships on the long march from Jueichin to Yenan; the training and discipline for the soldiers of the Eighth Route Army; the maintenance of military laws such as, 'If you borrow a needle from a farmer, return it' and 'Don't go into the farming villages. Sleep in the open'; the combination of political and military wisdom in such injunctions as, 'seize villages, encircle towns', 'take refuge when the enemy is strong, strike at the weak points'.

At the time, the Nationalist army was still strong and the communists not so secure. But, by following these principles, they gradually began to capture both towns and villages. While laying siege to cities by tactics of infiltration, they sent in activists to watch developments and I worried that they were becoming an invincible force

Another memory I have is of the *Tōenkai* [Peach Orchard Club]. The club, which revolved around three professors Yabe Teiji, Sassa Hirō and Abe Yoshishige, had very few members. When I arrived in Tokyo and met up with professor Yabe, he asked me if I would like to take part in an informal gathering to discuss the current situation. He said that a Mr Asami, would also be there and that he was donating food and drink. Mr Asami had been born at the foot of Mount Haruna, near my home.

The name 'Peach Orchard' was taken from the Peach Orchard oath of the three heroes of the History of the Three Nations Period of China, Ryūbi, Kanu and Chōi, who spoke with great reluctance but to great critical effect. It was a frank meeting in which people were very open: Professor Yabe sat and caroused, professor Sassa ate white rice with *sake* poured over it, professor Abe sang Meiji songs. All three believed in co-operative democracy so they were critical of both the doctrinaire left-wing which they thought flattered the workers and farmers and also of the lack of discretion and self-respect of the conservative camp. They preached a quiet social democracy after the manner of the English Fabians. And of course they espoused the idea of *Gemeinschaft* and therefore strongly emphasised the retention of the emperor system and the protection of Japanese traditions.

At the time they were castigated as the three turncoats, but in truth the turncoats were three other scholars, let us call them M, N, and Y, who made sharp turns, and changed their dress to suit the cut

63

of the times and caused professor Yabe and the others great indignation at their degree of opportunism.

Amidst all of this, my correspondence with my father continued. In the end, I handed in my resignation to Inspector General of Police, Suzuki, without my father's agreement. They were very reluctant to accept the resignation and bemoaned the crisis in manpower they saw coming. But it made no difference, I packed our belongings in willow baskets and returned with my family to Takasaki. My father and brother and younger sister were surprised, but at this point my father accepted the inevitable with these words. 'If you're going to be a member of the Diet be like Sakura Sōgorō.'[5]

Speech-making on a white bicycle

When I left the metropolitan police, my retirement pay came to ¥2,800. I used this money to buy a bicycle from the Fukuda Bicycle shop which was run by a playmate of mine from primary school. I painted the bicycle white: a white charger to fight the red flag. I used the bicycle to travel around the district meetings, speaking. A friend of my father, Sakurai Ihei, a former member of the House of Peers, became my backer. He recommended a purged prefectural technical school teacher, Satō Harushige as my secretary. Satō was a hot-blooded man of my own age and together we began to form a network and promote a youth movement. At that time, Takasaki was becoming a centre for the radical labour movement and members of unions affiliated with both the socialist and communist parties were mobilised in the lecture halls to boo and jeer and get people going, so that conservative speakers were at their wits end. I used to appear on the stage in a variety of dress, workman's clothes, navy uniform with insignia removed or a suit and I didn't give an inch.

> We must formulate the blueprint for a social revolution based on the preservation of the emperor system. We must be kind to those who are damaged, comfort those who are sad and protect the special characteristics and traditions of the people. Whilst we do these things we must keep our eyes firmly fixed on independence. The socialist party is agitating for guarantees of rice rations of three *go*[6] for the towns and for the suspension of deliveries of rice rations to farming villages. I say that there is nothing for it but to insist that deliveries be made to farmers as well, that minimum rations be made available to the people

Electioneering on a white bicycle

and that MacArthur be asked to give emergency aid to make up the shortfall.

I appealed to them frankly and honestly. New, twenty-eight years old, and full of conviction, I attracted support both from demobbed soldiers and from the old, conservative leaders who had been chased from their positions in local government. Rumours spread of, 'the emergence of a young hopeful in Jōshū'. I wrote a book, and contributed articles to newspapers in favour of, 'a revolution in education'. The book, *Seinen no Riso* (Young Ideals), was advertised as 'written by Nakasone Yasuhiro with a preface by former Tokyo University professor, Yabe Teiji' and immediately sold 43,000 copies.

In, 'Meditations on the Prefectural Character' for the Jōshū Newspaper, I wrote these words.

> The four characteristics of Gunma prefecture are volcanoes, thunder, dry winds and petticoat government. You can grow mulberries on volcanic ash, so silk worm culture became popular. Women are the workers in sericulture, so naturally we have petticoat government. Summer thunder and winter winds make for angular characters, not gentle folk with rich men's airs. Furthermore, because we are not so far from Edo, the Tokugawa Shogunate did not put in one of the large clans

to govern, but sought to divide and rule through direct Shogunate control in each area.

Gunma people are rich in public spirit, warm-hearted, emotional and easily moved to tears. As we stand at the turning point of defeat in war, we must think these things over and begin with a revolution in education.

Labour unions whose leaders were affiliated with the communist and socialist parties planned a general strike for February 1, 1947. I made speeches opposing the general strike and spoke by invitation all over the prefecture, not just in my constituency, but as far afield as Maebashi, Kiryū, Ōta and Tatebayashi.

In the end, the general strike was stopped on MacArthur's orders and, despite the spiritual vacuum, the people of the prefecture began to realise that, for Japan's sake, we had to think more constructively. This was in large part due to the efforts of intellectuals across the region within their own communities. I played a part in that as one of the demobilised soldiers.

As the date of the second post-war Lower House election, the first under new constitution, approached, the question arose of which party I should stand for. Because I was close to Hayakawa Takashi and to Yabe Teiji's school of thought, the small National Co-operativist Party [*Kokumin Kyōdōtō*][7] which was made up of a number of parties, was a likely choice and I spoke with the supporters. Among Sakurai *sensei's*[8] connections were a large number of people from the old *Seiyūkai* party. In the end, because Komine Ryūta was in the Japan Liberal Party [*Nihon Jiyūtō*][9] which was descended from this line, I became a candidate for the Democratic Party, [*Minshutō*][10] formed just before the election by Ashida Hitoshi and others.

Sakurai *sensei* advised me on tactics. He told me, 'Nakasone, you'd do well to keep the fact that you are married quiet. It isn't cheating and you'll get more votes if they think you're single.' So, my wife wore an apron over her pregnant belly, stoked the kitchen stove and made rice balls for the campaigners and didn't show herself in public any more than was necessary.

My first child, Hirofumi, was one year old and my second, a girl we named Michiko, had been born just two months earlier. For my wife, with two babies to attend to, it was a tough fight. As the wife of a bureaucrat she had dreamed of a quiet life, but with one turn of the wheel, she had been thrown into the midst of relations she barely knew and forced to bow her head to supporters. Whatever way you look at it, it was a real ordeal. But we were not discouraged because we considered we were fighting a continuation of the war under a different name to achieve the independence and regeneration of Japan.

My father rented us a house opposite the factory as a home and campaign office and it was there that the young people and I shared simple meals, stayed up until late at night talking, and even bathed together in the small tub. Meanwhile, my wife gallantly did everything from cooking their food to making their beds and washing their night-wear. Of course, we didn't have washing machines in those days, and everything was washed by hand.

When I was making speeches in the streets on my white bicycle I would be surrounded by large numbers of young people, themselves on bicycles, wearing headbands and waving megaphones. I have fond and moving memories of these nameless young people, late at night, in the towns and along the paths between the rice fields, their calls of, 'Vote for Nakasone', cutting the darkness. These young people subsequently became the nucleus of the Blue Cloud School.

On 25 April, 1947, I was elected for Gunma third district with the largest number of votes cast, an unforgettable 65,484. This was the fifth highest number of votes cast for one candidate anywhere in the country, despite the fact that Gunma third was not a constituency with a large electorate. At twenty-eight, I was also the youngest person elected to the Diet.

If only I cold offer
This bunch of irises
To my dead mother.

I took the election result to my mother's grave.

Some of the women who heard this *haiku* set up a women's support group called Ayamekai [Iris Club] that would stand in for my mother in supporting me. The Iris Club and the Blue Cloud School [*Ayamekai* and *Aogumo juku*] have remained my two biggest sources of support ever since.

Young Turks in the Prime Minister's official residence

The first general meeting of Democratic Party Diet members after the election was held in Ueno at a Western style restaurant called *Seiyōken.* When I arrived in Tokyo surrounded by young people, I found a big man waiting in the corridor outside the meeting place. He stood up when he saw me and offered me his hand saying, 'You must be Nakasone. I'm Kawasaki Hideji.' Kawasaki was a reform conservative who supported reform within the limits of the existing structure. I didn't join his group: instead I formed a group of young, first-time members with Sakurauchi Yoshio and Sonoda Sunao with the aim of shedding the less favourable aspects of conservatism.

The election of the Democratic Party president was imminent and the candidates for the post were Shidehara Kijurō, Saito Takao and Ashida Hitoshi. I favoured the Foreign Office diplomat, Ashida, who was younger in his ideas, over Shidehara who, I felt, would favour old Imperial Rule Assistance Association[11] men. Tanaka Kakuei supported Shidehara, and Hara Yasusaburō supported Saito.

I hurried with Sonoda, Sakurai and the others to the prime minister's residence where the old guard, Hitotsumatsu Sadayoshi and Nagao Tatsuo and the rest were holding discussions. We raced up the stairs to the second floor in our old army boots scattering the venerable red carpet with mud as we went, and called out Nagao from the meeting to press strongly for Ashida for president. The newspapers the next day referred to us as radical young officers or Young

At the time of the first election

Turks. In the confusion following the war, there was an atmosphere in which the power of juniors vis-à-vis their seniors grew, and with pre-war politicians under investigation, the natural order between young and old was confused, and we were quite wild. Ashida was chosen as president and our group of young Diet members joined the dominant stream of the Democratic Party.

The socialists came out of the election the biggest party and we advocated a national coalition cabinet with Katayama Tetsu, chairman of the Socialist Party, [Shakaitō] as prime minister. At first, Yoshida Shigeru's Liberal Party [Jiyūtō] agreed but subsequently they split off to try to cut off the left wing of the Socialist party. This caused great controversy within the Democratic Party over whether there should be a three party coalition of the Socialist Party, the Democratic Party and the National Co-operativist Party, or, alternatively of Liberal, Democratic and National Co-operativist Parties. In the midst of this, Miki Takeo, the National Co-operativst Party chairman vetoed an alliance with the Liberals and there was a political impasse.

Somewhat reluctantly we decided to form a coalition cabinet consisting of the Socialist Party, the Democratic Party and the National Co-operativist Party. This was done in the light of pressure from the outside world, which was distrustful of Japan, and with the aim of achieving domestic harmony following defeat in the war. Tanaka Kakuei, Hara Yasusaburō and Nemoto Ryūtaro were all violently opposed.

In June 1947, the Katayama coalition cabinet was formed by the three centre parties. In the first post-war Diet there was a pressing need to rebuild the devastated economy. The Economic Stabilisation Board was set up to deal with the major problem of economic regeneration and, on the advice of Arisawa Hiromi and Inaba Shūzo, a graduated production scheme was put into practice whereby capital and materials were diverted to increasing coal production which could then be used to increase volumes of steel and fertiliser and expand the whole basis of production.

A failure to put the coal industry under some sort of national administration and to concentrate what little there was of capital and raw materials in this way would have resulted in a loss of social capital. Nevertheless, the bill for the national administration of coal and steel faced problems and the Diet session was disorderly. Even within the Democratic Party there was opposition, and the group that was opposed, people like Nagao and Tanaka, withdrew from the party with Shidehara as their figurehead. The bill was rejected in committee and approved in the Diet. When it was finally passed, after extensive amendments, graduated production centered on coal began.

But the good-natured Katayama's nickname of Dr Shilly-shally was apt. His cabinet lacked decisiveness and leadership and was attacked increasingly by both left and right. Nishio Suehiro and Hirano Rikizō were at daggers drawn from the right wing, while people like Suzuki Mosaburō, attacked the establishment from the left. The cabinet crumbled and Ashida, who had constructed the coalition and had served as Foreign Minister, became the leader of the new administration.

The Finance Minister in the new cabinet was one of our circle, a man called Kitamura Tokutarō. Kitamura was a Christian, a highly cultivated man and very fastidious. He proposed a sales tax that was intended to address the lack of financial resources, but I had doubts about such a complicated procedure. Agreement was reached on a method of tax collecting through stamp duty, but in the end, serious opposition from commercial and industrial groups, combined with the coincidental breaking of the Showa Denko affair, resulted in the overwhelming defeat of the Ashida cabinet in the general election and Kitamura stepped down.

Ashida's successor as Democratic Party president was Inukai Takeru. Following a meeting with MacArthur, Inukai apparently, 'received divine inspiration on his way down in the elevator', and decided to form a coalition with the new Yoshida cabinet. The Democratic Party consequently split into an opposition faction and a coalition faction. My own group broke with Inukai, Hori Shigeru and Kosaka Tokutarō and, as part of the opposition faction led by Tomabechi Gizō, joined up with Miki and the National Co-operativist Party to form the People's Democratic Party [*Kokumin Minshutō*] in April 1950.

I comprehensively opposed Yoshida from the time of the Occupation to just after independence. I did so because the only effective way for an opposition party to show the occupying forces the views of the Japanese people was to attack the Yoshida cabinet which was pushing through Occupation policy in the Diet.

At heart I was more international in outlook than many of my colleagues in the opposition party and I respected Prime Minister Yoshida both for the way he excelled in the art of coaxing and for his sheer brazen-faced nerve. But in the political world, and particularly under the Occupation, every party and every politician had a role to play in deciding the ways and means of achieving goals, even those over which there was general agreement.

Above all, I felt that the opposition had an important role to play in encouraging the national spirit, in putting forward longer term national aims, and in rejecting the easy compromise. It was only natural that the government party should become an apologist for the occupying powers. The role of a healthy opposition party was therefore to monitor and attack the government and to represent the ideals of the people.

Comments by Tokutomi Sōhō

In the autumn of 1948, I went to visit Tokutomi Sōhō at his home at Izusan in Atami where he was living in comfortable retirement. I met him through my brother-in-law who was related to his grandson, Tokutomi Keitaro. Tokutomi was a great scholar, whose masterpiece, *A Modern History of the Japanese Nation*,[12] had shaped the intellectual history of Japan from Meiji, right through Taisho and Showa and I wanted to ask him his views on post-war Japan.

At the time, Tokutomi was suffering from facial neuralgia and I could only see him for a brief hour in the mornings. I would get up at six and jump on to the express train and then, after we had talked, I would dash back to Tokyo for the afternoon session of the Diet. I continued in this way until 1952.

Our conversations were conducted in a room, buried in books, which looked out on Sagami Bay. Like Tsukahara Bokuden,[13] Tokutomi would sit upright in a chair, his eyes half closed, dressed in formal Japanese style, with his long white hair tied at the back. I was surprised to find that he looked at everything, from newspapers to weekly magazines, and that he annotated them with a red line. I remember how he vented his anger, 'The newspapers are no good. I wrote a piece on the one hundredth anniversary of the birth of the Meiji Emperor and not one newspaper would accept it.'

One of the things that he argued was necessary in a politician was the ability to compromise.

> As Katsu Kaishū said, "We have to follow the momentum of the universe". Politicians aren't officers in the Salvation Army so there is no necessity for them to cling to established concepts and ideologies. The future will be a time of flux; provided that you don't lose the track of the

broader view, you should compromise to the limit. There was no one so fond of compromise as Saigo Takamori. He was like the New Year rice cakes that are lined up in rows to cook and stick to their neighbours so that they can't be separated. You must follow his example Nakasone.

China will never become a follower of Russia. Betrayal is all that Russia can expect. Mao has the potential to become more significant than Tito.

As for the path Japan needed to follow, Tokutomi laid especial stress on relations with China and America.

When you get involved on the continent, you have to do so with the utmost caution. Empress Jingu, Toyotomi Hideyoshi, the Great East Asian War, were all historical defeats and fingers are going to get burned again. So, for the time being, grasp America's hand and don't forget that, for now, America suffers from the weakness of being unable to cast Japan off, whatever unreasonable demands she might make. In the end, people cannot be happy under communism. But, America lacks wisdom, so there is much Japan must teach her.

Of the departure of Inukai Takeru and Kosaka Tokutaro to the Liberal Party, he said; 'Political parties are like crowded trains, without a seat, its hopeless. If you leave your seat, someone else will sit straight in it.'

Learning from Tokutomi Sōhō

72

I remember him saying too, 'You must be like Churchill and make the Diet your home. He was driven out of parliament but no one loved parliament like him. Now is not the time for the power of the individual, it is a period when we must work with the strength of the group, though the time when the power of the individual will again be prized may well return. If victory or defeat in the Diet are not more interesting than horse racing or cycle racing, democracy will be finished.'

One day when I went down to Izusan I asked him his opinion on the politicians of the day. This is what he said.

Ogata Taketora: a man who is criticised for having no faults. Has no pulling power but moves when pressed. In this he is more reliable than Nakano Seigō. He is straight as far as money is concerned and in terms of character is rather like Matsumura Kenzō. He is like a bass drum that gives a big sound when you strike it hard and a small sound when you strike it gently.

Shigemitsu Mamoru: lived for a long time in London, so when its misty he doesn't know if its clear or cloudy. The most suitable post for him is drafting diplomatic documents. He is a bureaucrat and therefore fainthearted so don't be too hard on him.

Yoshida Shigeru: a man who is very black and white in his judgements but who has recently become grey and unrecognisable. Getting old.

Hatoyama Ichiro: a liberal, just like his father. Raised in a political hot-house. Yoshida's skin is thicker. A good man at heart; gets taken in by people.

Miki Takeo: the sort of man Ōno Banboku would have been if he had become a lawyer. A gambler but of good character. Like Ōasa Tadao, he is engrossed in destroying his enemies and tripping up his opponents. You mustn't get involved in that; you must leave it to the experts.

Ōasa Tadao: A flatterer of the first order. Always the first to jump to attention. Just like an eel, he'll disappear you don't know where, and then suddenly pop out from a hole in the wall above your head. Good for settling quarrels and managing people. Close to money but clean so far as money is concerned, so can't keep it. He goes straight for young partners so he'll be coming after you.

Later, when the Progressive Party [*Kaishintō*] was formed and Ōasa recommended Kawasaki as Secretary General and myself as head of the Policy Research Committee, I remembered what Tokutomi had said.

The Blue Cloud School and the incident of the Japanese flag

Immediately after the first post-war election, some local friends and I set up the Blue Cloud School. The school had neither classrooms nor blackboards. We targeted the people who worked in neighbouring towns and villages and wanted to be centrally involved in the local party or to help the nation. The Blue Cloud School was intended to generate the energy for making things happen, and like-minded comrades all over were a 'thought militia'.

If you look at the Blue Cloud School 'Principles of Learning' and 'Our Statement', both of which I wrote, you can see that we aimed to build 'a country of brotherly love' by reform, within the system, and in harmony with Japanese traditions. Let me quote from the texts as I wrote them in 1947.

'Principles of learning of the Blue Cloud School'

1. Text book: all human life is our text book, all pleasure and pain, love and hate are teaching materials given by God.
2. Classroom: the classroom is in the hearts of those of like mind. If we travel with pure hearts we will all be educated together in the same classroom.
3. Foundation: If we create no sense of responsibility and no motive force, we cannot say we have learned. The cultivation of our minds begins when we gird our loins and overcome both internal and external resistance.
4. Procedure: The procedure for learning is personal morals, wise government of one's family, good government of the state and world peace.
5. Aims: the aim of learning is to leave the world having lived one's life like the best work of art.

'Our Statement'

The future awaits us. When we have overcome the hardships before the dawn, the sun will drive away the ominous clouds and a brilliant light will be shed on all creation. The life force of one hundred million people who achieved the Meiji Restoration and the Showa Reform, the life force of a race which has moved forward with great strides and with continuity, cannot be checked. Let us now reclaim the historical mainstream and pledge ourselves to fall fighting for Showa reform so that we may drive away the nightmare of national defeat and, bidding farewell to the old Japan, establish a new Japan for the sake of the Japanese and a proper, peaceful world order for the sake of all mankind.

Japan under the Meiji constitution was in its first period of constitutional government. Japan under the MacArthur constitution is in its second period of constitutional government. Japan under the Showa Reform which must now follow will be in its third period of constitutional government. We are standing at the dawn of this third period in the midst of the stormy blizzard. Let the storm come. We of the Blue Cloud will not be moved. We will calm the storm and greet the sun.

Comrades, let us now take up the great work of construction bequeathed to us by our patriotic ancestors since the Meiji restoration. Let us stand to the fore of the advance of the one hundred million to raise up the nation and carve the destiny of the world.

- With its nuclear bombs and hydrogen bombs, the world is in an historically unprecedented situation, poised on the edge of a dangerous precipice. We will appeal to man's intelligence and, with our creative and harmonious world view, we will eliminate opposition and conflict. We will get decisive action on fair international supervision of dangerous weapons and on arms limitation among the nations of the world, and insist on the realisation of a lasting world peace and an international democracy which is based on national self-determination and co-operation. In particular, we will humbly serve the regeneration of Asia based on our insight as Asians.
- In line with the period of creative enlightenment to come, we shall renew national politics with policies on labour and science as the mainstay and we shall build a national community. To this end, we shall establish a new Japanese national constitution and push forward the Showa Reform, which aims to strengthen an international co-operation that rests on an awareness of the unity of the world's destiny, to recover lost national territorial and other rights, to promote the complete withdrawal of foreign troops and to move forward from the Potsdam-San Francisco structure.

- We shall aim for social harmony under a spirit of joint friendship and build a society of brotherly love where native industry is awoken and communications opened and where those who suffered from their sacrifices in the war receive particular sympathy and those who are sad are comforted.
- By reforming the education of the young we will cultivate firm beliefs. By ourselves breaking with convention we will reform people's lives, and by means of sincerity and consistency we will become the backbone of our villages.

In the transition from the Tokugawa Bakufu to the Meiji period, lower class descendants of samurai and bright regional notables built a modern state. They carried out the revolutionary work of the Restoration and struggled for forty-odd years to revise the unequal treaties. As we stood at the brink of a second restoration we kept these great undertakings in mind whilst we tried to conduct a fair sort of politics where we planned national policy, revived the economy, developed the villages and brought succour to the war wounded and bereaved families.

We appealed for the international regulation of atomic and hydrogen bombs, for arms reduction, the establishment of a national self-defence force, the early withdrawal of occupation troops and the restoration of independence and we declared our humble determination to serve the regeneration of the Asian nations.

It was a time when the people were dispirited and mean, and in their inertia, were envious and testified against their brothers or took advantage of others. Some young people, pressured by a section of the occupation troops, even turned to the communist party. This being the case, we wanted to maintain Japan's identity (*shutaisei*) and at the same time to build a democratic community under a symbolic emperor.

I wrote passionately about how the fatherland I loved was now hungry, but how what it really lacked was not bread, but the food of the spirit. I believed that it was not arms which rebuilt a defeated Denmark, but the pioneering spirit of the farmers and how the source of Japan's rejuvenation lay in its education and its youth.

Membership of the Blue Cloud School grew to 40,000 and branches spread across the country. Films did the rounds and were shown on projectors bought by the branch members themselves. The profits were used to donate cleaning equipment to primary schools. In January every year, 4,000 delegates met for a New Year General

Meeting to discuss the plan of action for the coming year. I explained policies on constitutional issues, on textbooks and on nuclear power, and with their agreement took the issues up in Tokyo.

Over time, the members began to agitate for the building of a headquarters for the movement. My father, being in the timber trade, donated the materials, and a two-story assembly hall was built next to where I lived. When we asked for contributions, donations of 100 yen per person were made, totalling ¥1,750,000, more than two-hundred million yen at current values. I asked Tokutomi Sōhō to supply the calligraphy for the spot above the doorway in the entrance hall. We held Blue Cloud School lectures there and published texts.

The hall is in daily use even now as a public hall. At the time, such an active conservative group was unusual and attracted the attention of the Occupation forces. We used to raise the *Hinomaru* flag every day and one day U.S. military police arrived from Maebashi and warned us that it was forbidden under the occupation to fly the Japanese flag. They withdrew when I argued, 'In your own country, in the United States, the stars and stripes are flown in all the towns and villages. Why does the fact that we were defeated make it wrong for Japanese to fly their flag?'

The consistency of the Dodge line policy from 1949 brought a heavy increase of taxes in farming villages which resulted in plans by

Taking a break with my eldest son, Hirofumi and eldest daughter,
Michiko in a park in Maebashi

the communist party for a 'red flag demo' at the tax offices. Not to be outdone, we sent out a written appeal to our supporters across the prefecture and organised a '*Hinomaru*, Japanese flag demo'. Forestalling the 'red flag' demonstration, ranks from every area joined forces and headed for the Takasaki tax offices. One group, which came down the main road of Takasaki led by four ex servicemen in uniform sounding the march on bugles, carried a casket containing the mortuary tablets of the chief tax officer and the tax revision decisions. The communists carrying their red flags tried to join in with them but were rebuffed and forced to follow after. Meanwhile, I opened a second frontal attack, meeting with the Finance Minister, Ikeda Hayato, and the Chief of the Tax Administration Bureau in Tokyo and demanding a reversal of the various increases in income taxes. Before long our demands were satisfied. The more active we were, the more invigorated we became, and we revelled in the pleasure of flying the *Hinomaru* in the streets.

It was round about then that Tanaka Kiyoharu brought information that there was a violent revolt being planned, and that the power plant upstream at Tonegawa river was in danger. The information seemed plausible; there were many incidents involving unrest at the time and the Electricity Workers Union was the most combative of unions. The members of the Blue Cloud School firmly opposed what was going on and a number of them, including Tanaka Densaku, Takahashi Kogure and Kabasawa Eiichi visited the homes of the plant employees to persuade them not to side with such a movement if it should occur.

Overnight we stuck up posters in all the important places, warning of the danger of explosions and the union spent all night tearing them down and putting up their own. The scenario was repeated when we tore their posters down and put up our own again. Battles like this were played out over and over again but as we proclaimed our warnings in street-corner oratory, the Electricity Workers Union members gradually woke up to what was happening. A sympathetic faction, the Midori Club, was set up inside the union and unseated the chairman of the committee who was affiliated with the communist party. As a result, the Electricity Workers Union split and became a moderate union. The solidarity of the Blue Cloud School was noticeably strengthened.

Politics during the occupation was carried on with one eye on the complexion of the Supreme Commander of Allied Powers, General Douglas MacArthur. Prime Minister Yoshida was often able to force things through by wearing borrowed plumes and referring to, 'the intention of the authorities'. There were even rumours that there had been some trick using MacArthur in the purging and then subsequent release of some important people such as Hatoyama. Yoshida's close associates seemed to interfere in both cabinet and party personnel affairs using Yoshida's autocratic power.

Nevertheless, we should give Yoshida his due for what he did to show Japan's repentance and for earning the goodwill of the Occupation, and regenerating the economy of Japan. He undoubtedly made mistakes, for example in regarding the right of self defence as harmful, but he maintained the proper recognition of the emperor system as the backbone of the nation and supported the country during a critical time. Apart from a period at the end of his administration, he understood the broad picture and managed the handling of the occupation forces well. As far as history was concerned, he expected to be cursed as an agent for Occupation policies but, behind the smokescreen of his cigar, his feet were shod in traditional footwear. He was without a doubt, 'an old fox', inedible whichever way you cooked him.

After Ashida's resignation, Allied Forces General Headquarters [GHQ] Public Administration Department sent a suggestion that, 'the Secretary General of the Democratic Liberal Party [*Minjitō*], Yamazaki Takeshi, would be suitable as leader of the next cabinet.'[14] The opposition executive began a movement against this happening. Within the Occupation headquarters at the time, different groups were also at odds: there was Brigadier General Whitney and Colonel Kades of the Public Administration Department, who were relatively close to the opposition party, and the so-called G 3 group, which included Major General Willoughby et al, was closer to the Democratic Liberal Party. The opposition executive planned to use Yoshida's overthrow to split the Liberal Democratic Party. At first, Yamazaki let it be known in the Public Administration Department that he would accept if he were named by the Diet with the result that, for a time, Yoshida lost hope. However, eventually, after some persuasion by Masutani Shūji, Yamazaki resigned from the Diet and the idea went no further.

In the normal course of constitutional government, such an attempt to use the shelter of the authority of GHQ to recommend as prime minister a man who was not the leader of the majority party, was clearly wrong. Had it succeeded, it would have brought the Occupation and its constitution into disrepute, and would have attracted severe criticism.

At the time, although I worried about losing my seat, I would have been happy to see the plans for a second Yoshida administration fail and, consequently, I did not take proper stock of the situation and actively condemn the error. This was a big mistake. As a result of this strange incident, public support for the Yoshida administration was strengthened and Yoshida's Democratic Liberal Party took an absolute majority of 264 seats in the next, three party, election. The verdict of the people was absolutely clear.

CHAPTER FOUR

THE CHALLENGE OF NATIONAL RECONSTRUCTION

Petition to General MacArthur

Today .... we arrived, I believe, to a stage where, pressed by various conditions, Japan's affairs, whether in domestic politics or in national defence, should be dealt with [through the] responsibility and honor of the Japanese themselves .... Long occupation makes both the occupier and the occupied deteriorated. It is impossible for a general, however sagacious, to subjugate a modern nation craving for freedom of personality under occupation for more than five years solely by his personal character.[1]

These were the opening phrases of a 7,000 word petition composed in English and running to twenty-eight typed pages. As Dr Williams, head of GHQ domestic politics bureau read it, he blanched and his hands trembled. He told me, 'I can't accept a document of this nature', and I replied, 'You can accept it or not, as you prefer, but copies have already been sent to the Chairman of the Foreign Relations Committee, Senator Tom Connally, to Senator Robert Taft, Senator Margaret Chase Smith and others, and I would like you to show it to General MacArthur before the members of the U.S. legislature see it.'

When I told Dr Williams that the note had also been sent to influential members of the United States Congress, he turned as red as a turkey cock and retorted angrily, 'Under the Occupation no Japanese may send material critical of Occupation policy to U.S. politicians.'

I replied, 'I am a member of the Japanese National Diet, and it is my right and my responsibility to decide what to send and what not to send.'

'I'll have to take this up with the General.' Dr Williams' angry voice followed me from the room.

This was on 23 January 1951. I made my representation at this time because certain circumstances had led General MacArthur to speak in his New Year greeting of an early peace with Japan, and because a visit by special plenipotentiary John Foster Dulles to discuss peace with Japan was being planned for 25 January. It was an escalation of the Korean war at that time which had prompted this. The United Nations forces which, for a time, had been pushed back as far as Pusan, had, as a result of the success of the strategy of landing at Inchon, crossed the 38th parallel and had arrived at a spot 50 kilometres from the Yalu River. However, when the Chinese People's Liberation Army entered the war, the UN Forces were forced back again and on 4 January, it looked dangerously as if the re-occupation of Seoul was imminent.

Writing about what Japan would be like after independence, I said, 'Under collective security, Japan will have to be defended by the Japanese themselves, and for that, patriotism has to be revived. Unless there is warm backing of the bereaved and wounded and those who made sacrifices in the war, some people will wonder why they should defend the country again. It was a mistaken war, but it was not their fault.'

On the Peace Treaty, I pointed out that, 'What the Japanese people hope for the U.S. to do in regard to the peace issue is U.S. determination to push unhesitatingly ahead [in] what she believes in. A majority of the Japanese are implicitly praying that the U.S. without having a regard for the Soviet Union and other countries proceed with her faith in justice in a long reaching plan'. As for the formula for Japan's defence and politics I argued that, 'The matter is desired to be based on self-determination of the race, stipulating no restriction in the peace treaty and leaving the matter to the free will of the nation. The Japanese people are heartily desirous of participating in the United Nations Organization, and when our desire [is realised], we are not going to shirk our duty only asserting our rights ....'

On rearmament, I insisted on five points: 1. A prolonged period of spiritual re-education of the people. 2. Complete independence and equality internationally for Japan. The defence of Japan can only be achieved through an alliance of equal, freedom-loving peoples. 3. The relaxation of measures to remove excessive concentration of economic power. 4. The military to be under the control of the Diet and not to be used, as a rule, outside of the country 5. Financial aid for the Japanese economy by lend-lease, or other means.

Taken as a whole, for those days it was very frank and clashed directly with the way a lot of people thought. On reflection, I feel that when I wrote, for example, criticising Yoshida for declaring that the current cabinet would sign a peace treaty, or attacking the treaty proposals as something drawn up by aristocrats and bureaucrats far removed from the realities of ordinary lives, that I might have been somewhat carried away by youthful enthusiasm.

On 6 February, I received a letter from Senator Taft agreeing with much I had written about the problems of the peace treaty with Japan,[2] and on 16 February I had a reply from Connally [FRC] which said, 'America wants a speedy end to the occupation. I believe that the Japanese themselves should reassume all responsibility in order that the people might maintain their real character and their complete independence. This is an essential condition for peace in the Far East.'

More than thirty years later, on August 4, 1983, I received a visit from Dr Williams at the Prime Minister's residence. The exchange we had then is reproduced below.

Dr Williams: I'm very happy to have the opportunity to meet with you Mr. Prime Minister. I always thought you would be prime minister one day; I believe I even said something along those lines to you thirty years ago, so I can take particular pleasure. You know, before I came to Japan this time, I looked up the petition that you presented to General MacArthur during the Occupation, and the points you put forward in that document were really excellent. General MacArthur didn't take kindly to your opinions though, not least because some of your judgements on the policies of the Occupation were critical. On the very first page of the petition for example you wrote that the Occupation had lasted for too long.

Nakasone: How was my petition handled within GHQ? Did it go from Major General Willoughby to General MacArthur?

Dr Williams: No, it was not given to Willoughby. It went to Brigadier General Whitney and from Whitney to General MacArthur. As I said before, the petition was so critical of the Occupation in places that the general tried to rip it up, but at twenty-eight pages long it was too thick so he dropped it, as it was, into the bin. I heard about this and retrieved it and took it back to America. I believe it was an excellent document; I don't believe that the contents were unfriendly to America, I think that they appealed to Secretary of State Dulles and the Democratic members of the Senate.

Nakasone: I sent the document to General MacArthur, but immediately before that I had sent copies airmail to the Chairman of the Senate Foreign Affairs Committee, Connally, and to Senators Smith and Taft.

But there is something else I would like to ask you about. When, after the war, the Emperor made his first visit to meet with General MacArthur, it is said that the general was very impressed by his Majesty's personal character. Is that in fact true?

Dr Williams: There was no diary entry by General MacArthur for that day so there is no record, but I believe that to be the case.

Nakasone: It is also said that on that same occasion, the Emperor asked that his soldiers and officers be spared punishment and that all punishment instead should devolve on him and, furthermore, that he asked the general to extend his hand to help a hungry and devastated Japanese people ...

Dr Williams: I believe that is so.

Nakasone: When Secretary of State, Dulles pressed Japan to rearm, is it true, as it is so often said, that Prime Minister Yoshida resisted this proposal?

Dr Williams: I can't say. It was the opinion of Secretary of State, Dulles, that until he was confident that Japan could be defended comprehensively (that is to say from foreign invasion), a peace treaty was not necessary.

There is actually something I would like to ask the Prime Minister. I realise it is a very delicate issue, but I would like to ask if you believe that the constitution should be amended and if so, which provisions should be revised?

Nakasone: The issue is too delicate to be firm about anything. However, let me say that no matter how painful a problem might be, I believe in confronting that problem head-on, not evading it.

The petition I wrote was retrieved from the bin. The English original now titled '"What the Japanese are thinking", opinions presented to the Supreme Commander of Allied Powers by Nakasone Yasuhiro MP', is currently in the Asian Collection of the University of Maryland Library with a Japan Times article from the same time.[3]

Opinions on the defence of Japan

My first post-war visit abroad was in June 1950 as a member of the Japanese delegation to the World Peace Movement, Moral Rearmament [MRA] conference. We flew in a charter plane belonging to

Philippine Airlines and landed in Chur, Switzerland. The movement for moral rearmament was advanced by an American, Dr Bookman. MRA rejected both ideology and religious coloration and practised the moral precepts of 'absolute honesty', 'absolute integrity' and 'absolute unselfishness'. It was a human-friendship peace movement intended to join hands around the world.

The leader of the Japanese delegation was a man called Ishizaka Taizō. A woman called Sōma Yukika was the moving spirit behind the movement in Japan, but it appealed to people from all walks of life. From the financial world there were people like Hirose Gen, Yuasa Yūichi, and Ōhara Sōichiro who became involved, while from the political world there was Kitamura Tokutaro, Kawashima Kanetsugu and so on. Journalists such as Kuriyama Chōjiro also took part. During the Occupation it was impossible to leave Japan and since I had a long-cherished desire to travel abroad, I seized the opportunity when I was invited to participate.

At the conference I was deeply impressed with the faith of those who supported the MRA movement and by their all encompassing spirit of service to others. However, I have always had trouble with the word 'absolute'. As a politician, this is something that I really can't believe in and, had I said I could, I would have been deceiving people. I therefore felt I couldn't join the movement.

On 26 June I was in a barber's shop in Chur getting my hair cut when a German man sitting in the next chair told me that war had broken out in Korea. We went on to France, Germany, England and America, but wherever we went I listened avidly to the news. With the U.S. and South Korean armies being driven toward the area around Pusan, my journey was punctuated by worry about the security of Japan.

In America I stayed at the house of Robert Fairly, who was working on the Japan desk in the State Department. I received a very warm welcome, but I was greatly surprised to hear that Fairly and his wife took it in turns to prepare breakfast. Fairly had been secretary to Ambassador Grew in Japan before the war and again, after the war, and had accompanied Dulles to Tokyo as his secretary in January 1951. It was through a special arrangement with Fairly that I was able to deliver a memorandum on the Peace Treaty to Secretary Dulles. The memorandum to Secretary Dulles outlined what I had written to General MacArthur and asked for a U.S.-Japan alliance treaty within the collective security guarantee. In particular it demanded that, 'Under the terms of the Peace Treaty, research into the peaceful uses of atomic energy and the construction of civil aircraft should not be forbidden in Japan'. Later Secretary Dulles said, 'I read those two points with particular interest.'

When I was in Washington I was fortunate enough to be able to talk with Vice President Alben Barkley, the Chairman of the Senate Committee on Foreign Relations Connally, and Senator Taft and to exchange views on the question of a peace treaty.

When I arrived back in Japan a police reserve had been set up by order of General MacArthur; things were changing rapidly both at home and abroad. During my time abroad I came to feel that after independence Japan needed a suitable defence force; that we should form a U.S.-Japan Alliance and that we must, with co-operation from the United States, defend Japan ourselves.

In October 1950, I was invited by Ashida Hitoshi to make a campaign speech in his electoral district. I was surprised to find that a room by the entrance to the hotel had been prepared for Ashida, whilst a higher grade room toward the back had been prepared for me, and I asked Ashida to take my room. Ashida taught me much about the behaviour of politicians and on the road from Kyoto to Ayabe, I made a cautious appeal to him.

> My recent travels abroad and the seriousness of the situation have strengthened my conviction that defenceless neutrality is not an option for an independent country. Although General MacArthur referred to Japan as "the Switzerland of the Pacific", when the Korean troubles began, he very quickly had the police reserves set up.
>
> The individual citizen's will and pride are the basis for any country's defence. Don't you agree that whatever alliance may be made with U.S., Japan must rearm adequately, have the U.S. troops withdraw as far as possible and reduce the number of U.S. bases. Otherwise Japan will continue to be occupied by foreign troops indefinitely, and will remain in a subordinate position.

Ashida agreed with me utterly, 'You are absolutely right Nakasone. So, you feel the same? Well then, let's start a movement.' When he returned to Tokyo, Ashida became the first politician to make public his opinions on the defence of Japan.

On 23 January 1951, Ashida, Miki Takeo, Narahashi Wataru, Kawasaki Hideji and others spoke to a large meeting sponsored by the People's Democratic Party in the Yomiuri Hall. Ashida and I spoke about the necessity for rearmament for the defence of Japan. I believe that herein lay the roots of the later Progressive Party position on defence.

Yes to the Peace Treaty, no to the Security Treaty

On 31 March 1951, the United States government published the draft of a peace treaty with Japan. Then, on April 11, President Harry Truman relieved General MacArthur of his responsibilities as Supreme Commander for the Allied Powers. Over the course of the summer, influential politicians who had been purged were released and on 4 September, a conference on peace with Japan opened in San Francisco. The era had all the wildness of a raging torrent.

The question of whether or not the People's Democratic Party would take part in the plenipotentiary delegation to the Peace Conference became a major issue. The general feeling in the party was that we must observe what was happening, and maintain our function as an opposition party to the end. The gist of the reasoning was as follows. 'The failure to return Okinawa, Amami Ōshima and the four Northern Islands, to Japan is a problem. There is a rumour about the creation of a U.S.-Japan Security Treaty but although this is inseparable from the peace treaty, the content has not been made clear.'

I supported the Peace Treaty on the grounds that, although there were a number of problems with it, its contents were relatively generous and, given the extent of Japan's war-making, sacrifices of this level were unavoidable. However, I was opposed to the participation of Democratic Party representatives as plenipotentiary members on the grounds that if we took part in the plenipotentiary group, we would also have to agree on the spot, not just to the Peace Treaty, but also to a security treaty, the details of which were still unclear. I did not feel comfortable with giving *carte blanche* to our delegates without checking the details of this important issue.

This was the situation when Prime Minister Yoshida, unhappy with the idea of the Liberal Party having to participate alone, suddenly turned up at the home of the chief representative of the Democratic Party, Tomabechi Gizō, accompanied by Upper House member Hayashiya Kamejiro, to beg him to take part. As a result of the visit, Tomabechi, did a sudden about turn and sought the understanding of the party in favour of participation. To make a precipitous announcement on the sort of issue which would affect the fate of Japan was unacceptable, so, day after day, the Diet Members Committee and a general assembly of Diet Members sat and engaged in serious discussion. In the end it was agreed that it would be inappropriate to deny the request of the party leader point-blank, and that Tomabechi could attend the Peace Conference in San Francisco as a member of the plenipotentiary group and could give his agreement to the Peace Treaty, on condition that he refrain from the signing of the Security Treaty.

On 8 September, Prime Minister Yoshida, accompanied by Tomabechi, Finance Minister Ikeda, Hoshijima Niro, President of the Bank of Japan Ichimada, and Tokugawa Muneyoshi attended the Peace Conference and signed the Peace Treaty. That evening, in the headquarters of the U.S. Sixth Army, Yoshida met with Dean Acheson and John Foster Dulles, the U.S. delegates, alone and signed the Security Treaty. The Socialist Party split into left and right wings in the controversy over the pros and cons of the Peace Treaty.

An extraordinary session of the Diet was convened on 26 October and both the Peace Treaty and the Security Treaty were passed by the Lower House. I voted in favour of the Peace Treaty but absented myself from the vote on the Security Treaty because I was dissatisfied with the content of it. Most importantly, in the event of domestic upheaval, and at the request of the Japanese government, American troops could be mobilised. Second, there were problems with the judicial jurisdiction rights of U.S. troops and army civilians. Finally, there was the problem of the lack of a set period for the treaty. These problems were put right in 1960 in the amendments to the Security Treaty.

On February 8, 1952, the People's Democratic Party merged with the *Shinsei* Club which consisted of newly depurged politicians such as Shigemitsu Mamoru, Matsumura Kenzō, Ōasa Tadao, Nakajima Yadanji and Miyazawa Taneo and became the Progressive Party. The new party also included the Farmers Co-operative Party (*Nōminkyō-dōtō*), supporters from the Upper House *Daiichi* Club, and the *Isshin* Club at the core of which were ex-officials such as Horiki Kamazō. Kitamura Tokutaro and I also joined in the capacity of leaders of a group consisting of Kawasaki Hideji, Sakurauchi Yoshio, Sonoda Tadashi, Inaba Osamu and others. Although initially the posts were vacant, Shigemitsu was eventually recommended as president and Miki Takeo and Matsumura Kenzo were appointed as chief secretary and chairman of the central committee, respectively.

The purpose of founding the Progressive Party was to provide a progressive alternative to the Liberal Party which had held power for so long. Not surprisingly, we were driven by a strong desire to correct those policies which had been undertaken by the Yoshida,

Liberal Party Cabinet at the instigation of General MacArthur, and which did not fit with the climate of Japan's politics and society. We were driven too by the desire to create an independent system for a responsible nation which could become a member of international society. Working with my colleague Kawasaki Hideji on the committee to establish the party, I threw myself into drawing up both the general guiding principles, and the specific policies for the Progressive Party.

General principles of the Kaishintō

♦ The party supports the dignity of the individual and the public good. It will reform politics and establish democracy.
♦ The party will ensure the independent defence of the Japanese nation. It pledges itself to the regeneration of Asia and the realisation of world peace.
♦ The party is founded on the principle of co-operativism. It will enhance the welfare of the masses and address the problems of capitalism.
♦ The party will bring together the cultures of East and West. It pledges itself to the arousal of the people's spirit and the promotion of world culture.
♦ The party will be at the forefront of progressive, popular power. It will carry out responsible politics.

Specific policies

1. Establish independent diplomacy; become an equal with the countries of the free world; promote early entry into the United Nations; extol the fundamental ideals of the United Nations, contribute to the establishment of world peace.
2. Restore good neighbourly relations with the Asian nations; contribute to Asian development and the improvement of life-styles through political and economic co-operation and technical and cultural exchange.
3. Demand the swift return of Karafuto, the Kuriles, Okinawa, Amami peninsula and the Ogasawara Islands and promote the revision of the Peace and Security Treaties.
4. Set up a democratic self defence force answerable to civilian power and replace the Security Treaty as soon as possible with a mutual

defence agreement and participation in a collective security organisation.
5. Undertake comprehensive re-examination of all laws and ordinances enacted under the Occupation, including the constitution, and while pursuing a progressive outcome, reject any which do not accord with national conditions or national strength.
6. Promote the restoration of diplomatic relations with those countries with which we previously had friendly relations but with which we have not yet concluded a peace treaty.

The principle of, 'ensuring self defence' was translated into successful Progressive Party support for the establishment of the Self Defence Forces. The principle of 'co-operativism' was not so well absorbed. It took the form, on the one hand, of an agreement with the Farmers Co-operative Party [*Nominkyōdōtō*] and on the other, of an extension leftwards; an expression of reform conservatism intended to make the party attractive to salaried workers and labourers.

These aims were, for the most part, adopted in the general principles and policies of the new Liberal Democratic Party in 1955 at the time of the conservative alliance. Of course, at the time of the formation of the Progressive Party, seventeen, out of the twenty-seven members of the People's Democratic Party, did not join because of the reformist policies outlined above. Those seventeen split off to form the *Minshu* Club.

Questions and answers about the constitution: Kishi and Nixon

On 29 December 1953, I met Kishi Nobusuke in Yotsuya, Tokyo in the Benkeibashi district, at a restaurant called Shimizu. There had been an unofficial decision by the Public Office Qualification Appeals Board to depurge Kishi on 18 April 1952 but Prime Minister Yoshida had flown into a rage at this because of newspaper reports which presented Kishi as more strongly 'anti-Yoshida' than he in fact, was. As a result, the depurging of Kishi, Iwamura Michiyo, Tokutomi Sōhō, Hatta Yoshiaki, Terashima Ken and Ino Hiroya was revoked. They were not even released from the purge in the final round of depurging but only when the Peace Treaty came into effect on 28 April.

After he was depurged, Kishi started the Japan Reconstruction Federation with Miyoshi Hideyuki and Ayabe Kentarō, and, together with Shigemitsu Mamoru they began a political movement. Kishi stood in the 'sudden assault' election of August 1952 as a Japan Reconstruction Federation candidate but lost. In January 1953 he joined the Liberal Democratic Party [LDP], and in March won a seat in the '*bakayaro*'[4] dissolution and, at Yoshida's request, became Chairman of the Constitutional Investigation Committee. Kishi was a proponent of constitutional revision.

At our meeting in December 1953 Kishi said he believed that prime minister Yoshida would retire the following May or thereabouts and would go abroad for about a month. Kishi also told me something that he had heard, in confidence, from Prime Minister Yoshida himself when he became Chairman of the Constitutional Investigation Committee. Yoshida had told him,

> I met with General MacArthur in the last days of the occupation and told him, "I want to revise the constitution comprehensively, not just amend parts of it, before the occupation ends." When General MacArthur was dismissed by President Truman not long after, I said the same thing to his successor, General Ridgeway. Ridgeway replied 'I have barely taken up my post and I don't know how long I will be staying. Wouldn't it be better to revise the constitution freely, from a position of independence, after the Peace Treaty is concluded?
>
> A lot of people think that constitutional revision is just a means of Hatoyama making a comeback in the Liberal Party, but I am seriously considering it and I have asked the Cabinet Legislation Bureau to study the possibility. However, I am of the opinion that it would be best for the party to do it. You could discuss it with Hatoyama, but as he's a sick man and will make various demands. You must select the people.

At this time it was whispered that, with the Peace Treaty concluded, this would be Yoshida's swan song. Hatoyama, Shigemitsu and Kishi had all regained the political stage and there were stronger efforts to move toward a 'post-Yoshida' era. But there was considerable confusion among the leaders and violent political confrontation between Yoshida and Hatoyama which lasted for three years, up to the end of 1954. Yoshida's recognition of Kishi's entry into the party was a strategem in his struggle against Hatoyama, and it was in compliance with his wishes that Kishi was appointed as Chairman of the Constitutional Investigation Committee. It was for this reason that he needed to be responsive to Kishi's wishes and for this reason that he relaxed his guard and spoke frankly.

When Kishi asked me how I thought the political confusion could best be resolved, I responded,

> It is vital that Japan should maintain an independent structure; that the political management practices of drift which grew up under the occupation must be done away with, and inappropriate occupation policies corrected. To this end, political ideas must be clarified, and a unified, popular concept of the nation reshaped.
>
> Yoshida politics scored quite highly for the way it dealt with General MacArthur and with the Peace Treaty, but now it has degenerated into trickery, and the economy has become the be all and end all of everything. Cronyism has grown rife and now, when what Japan really needs is a spiritual revolution, this administration is doing more harm than good.
>
> We have to take up difficult problems which the public shies away from; problems like the constitution and defence. We have to rebuild the spiritual order of the nation. We have to revive the economy and build the sort of structure that will enable us to rejoin international society. If we form that sort of administration with everybody working together, the political confusion might be resolved.

When I asked his views, Kishi said he agreed completely. The old men, the former purgees who formed Kishi's circle, were not able, by themselves, to advance his political movement and he had his eye on our group of so-called, 'young officers'. One month before my December meeting with Kishi, Vice President Richard Nixon had visited Japan and had become the first American VIP to say publicly that they had been wrong to impose the constitution on Japan. The Japanese newspapers ran the story widely with headlines that read, 'First statement by senior U.S. government official: Japan peace constitution a mistake.'

The gist of the articles was as follows. 'Vice President Nixon, who is visiting Japan, said in a lunch-time speech to the Japan-American Society and the U.S. Chamber of Commerce in Japan on the 19th, 'The disarmament of Japan in 1946 was at the insistence of the United States, and not of Japan. Let me acknowledge here that America made a mistake.'

In fact, Nixon's remarks did not come as a complete surprise. On 27 September that year, when I visited America, I was able to meet with Nixon, as I had hoped, in his office in the Senate. At that time the Crown Prince (now the Emperor) was in the middle of a visit to America, and the first thing I did was to express my gratitude. 'As a Japanese, I am deeply moved by the warm welcome given to our

Crown Prince, first by the President of the United States, and by every sector of American society.' Nixon smiled and said, 'The Crown Prince is a fine person. I still mix with the young so I'm very happy that I could meet your young Crown Prince.'

I went on to talk about Japan's problems with defence, the economy and economic independence. My purpose in speaking to Nixon was, above all, to try to make sure he understood the popular psychology behind the setting up of Self Defence forces by the Japanese before he visited Japan so that he would not make any mistaken judgements. I explained forcefully, word for word, as follows:

> The formation of Self Defence Forces would require constitutional revision in accordance with democratic principles. Japanese public opinion is generally agreed on this but, because of the terrible memories of the past war, opinion is very negative toward maintaining arms again. The left is taking advantage of the feelings of women and the young and engaging in vehement propaganda. How to promote a movement in favour of constitutional revision to combat this is a difficult and pressing problem.
>
> Given the current international situation, and the nature of the relationship between the United States and Japan, I believe Japan must take a brave step forward. Politicians must explain this to the people. They must seek co-operation from various quarters and endeavour to solve the problem with the support of the people. It is a matter of great regret that, because Japan has a one-sided protectorate relationship with the United States, we have been deprived of a voice on the issues of war crimes and Okinawa.
>
> I would like Japan to move to a position where it can defend itself and co-operate with the United States as an equal and independent friendly nation. The current U.S.-Japan relationship is an unhealthy relationship between protector and protected and urgently needs repair. The first step back to health must be the decision by the Japanese people to defend themselves.

I put forward four principles:

1. We will establish Self Defence Forces to defend the territory of Japan.
2. The existing U.S.-Japan Security Treaty will be revised into an equal alliance or security treaty. That is, Japan's position will be elevated so that the relationship vis-à-vis America will resemble that of America and England.

3. With the strengthening of the Self Defence Forces, the United States troops in Japan will gradually withdraw. There will be a time limit to this withdrawal by US troops. Under a new treaty, specified naval and air bases would be run by a joint committee.
4. The money to set up and expand the Self Defence Force will come from the Japanese people but the U.S. should help in those areas which are beyond Japan's capabilities.

Nixon said that the four principles were reasonable and that, for his part, he agreed with them. He told me he would shortly be touring Asia and would be visiting Japan, and he asked me what message he should be giving to the Japanese. I said there were two things he should be aware of

> First, the constitution. It is not unreasonable that you should find it hard to understand why the Japanese are negative toward amending the constitution. General MacArthur forced that constitution on the Japanese with the argument that it was the finest in the world. Now, the U.S. seems keen to see it revised, but has made no attempt to say that it was mistaken in its judgement in the past. Consequently, the Japanese people see no need to change a constitution that is still, apparently, the best. Unless there is some indication that America has reconsidered, the Japanese will be unable to do anything. Second: people in Japan are afraid that, if we have armed forces, it will ultimately lead to war and to troops being sent abroad. The establishment of armed forces and their dispatch abroad are issues to be decided by the Japanese people and not something that foreigners should be involved in; you could tell them that.

Nixon thanked me for an instructive discussion and said he was working out the draft of his speech with the State Department, and that, though he couldn't promise anything, he would do his best.

Two fundamental questions for the nation: Constitution and Abdication

On 31 January 1952, I put questions to the Lower House Budget Committee of the Thirteenth Diet on what were then the two most basic issues for Japan; defence and the Emperor.

If we take the Occupation as being the first formative period of post-war Japan, then this period of waiting, between the signing of the Peace Treaty in September and its coming into effect the following

April, was the start of the second period. I raised questions about the contradictions in the Yoshida Cabinet's half-hearted, makeshift handling of defence as evidenced in the creation of the police reserve force. This had brought to light the splits within the Yoshida Cabinet and had caused the situation to become unsustainable.

The next year Yoshida's Liberal Party lost half its seats in the 'bakayaro' election and was forced to co-operate with the Progressive Party. Talks were arranged between Prime Minister Yoshida and Shigemitsu Mamoru, the President of the Progressive Party through the good offices of Ikeda Hayato and Ōasa Tadao. As a result of these talks between Yoshida and Shigemitsu, a new organisation was set up with formal responsibility for national defence, and the preservation of the peace and independence of Japan from foreign threat. It was also agreed that the Peace Preservation Forces and Peace Preservation Office into which the Police Reserve Force had been reorganised, would be abandoned. Ozawa Saeki and Nishimura Naoki from the Liberal Party, Nakamura Umekichi from the National Liberal Party (*Nihon Jiyūtō*) and Arita Kiichi and myself from the Progressive Party worked together on the details and the three parties acted together to get the bills establishing the new organisations through parliament. The result was the Self Defense Forces (*Jieitai*) and the Defense Agency (*Bōeichō*).

The young Turk challenging Prime Minister Yoshida

95

This process presented me with a dilemma. The question was whether a new organisation could be set up without constitutional reform. Although constitutional reform was the ultimate aim, it was not going to be possible in the near future. However, when Japan became independent, defensive power would be essential.

I was very impatient with Yoshida's attitude of just 'getting through the day' during this period. But the very armaments which, up till then, I had attacked incessantly as a violation of the constitution, had now become an obstacle.

Salvation came in the form of the so-called 'Kiyose theory', advocated by Kiyose Ichiro, an old member of the Progressive Party, which stated:

1. The right to national self defence is a necessary condition for the existence of the state.
2. Moreover, during the Diet's enactment of the constitution, Ashida Hitoshi inserted into Clause 2 of Article 9, the phrase, 'In order to achieve the aims of the preceding paragraph'.[5]
3. Thus, being armed to the minimum level necessary to exercise the right of defence effectively, but not in order to settle international disputes, is not a violation of the constitution.

Now we are into the third phase of the constitutional issue where the discussion is no longer about the rights and wrongs of using defence forces for the defence of the country, but about the propriety of using them for international co-operation, beginning with co-operation with the United Nations. My personal belief is that the government's continual, unilateral moves to interpret the constitution ever more widely is confusing, and that suitable revision of the constitution should be planned according to the wishes of the people.

My second question concerned the Emperor. I asked it because I felt it was necessary to clarify the government's thinking as we approached independence. The possibility that the Emperor might abdicate needed particular clarification. I put it to the Lower House budget committee that, 'The government should ensure the Emperor's freedom of choice as a human being.' I felt that the Emperor should be free to abdicate if he so wished. Among the general population, I was not alone in feeling this. The pattern of questions in the Lower House Budget Committee on that occasion (31 January 1952) was as follows.

Nakasone: I would like to ask PM Yoshida how long his government intends to maintain the [Police] Reserve Forces in the context of the plans for a gradual increase in defensive strength?

Yoshida: We plan to discontinue the Police Reserve Forces from October of this year.

Nakasone: When they are discontinued in October, how are you intending to guarantee the defence and security of Japan?

Yoshida: We shall want to think afresh about defence forces (*bōeitai*) in the light of the security situation in Japan and of international conditions. We are currently studying the matter.

Nakasone: I would like to ask the Prime Minister whether the new, so-called, defence forces will be a force with the same equipment as the Police Reserve Force?

Yoshida: I will ask Minister of State Ohashi to answer.

Ohashi: It will be based on the Police Reserve Force and be run in a corresponding manner.

Nakasone: That being the case, as far as the Prime Minister is concerned, will their equipment include things like anti-aircraft guns and tanks and big guns or destroyers on loan from the United States?

Ohashi: It is our intention to continue to receive assistance from America in the matter of equipment.

Nakasone: You say that, but the Police Reserve Forces already have anti-aircraft guns and possibly naval vessels of the destroyer class. The question of whether this constitutes war potential is a basic issue. Anti-aircraft guns are for shooting at aircraft. Aircraft come from outside. It is not conceivable that the Communist Party at the present time has jets in Japan. In short, anti-aircraft guns are to be used to fire on things invading from overseas. The act of firing on things invading from overseas cannot be done unless the Police Reserve Force is replaced.

I have inspected the Police Reserve Force and it has an anti-aircraft battery.

Yes, that's what I said, an anti-aircraft battery! What is more, the organisation of the Police Reserve Force is military in nature. Even its internal affairs are like the internal affairs of the military. You claim it is not a military, but the armour shows below the sleeves of the sacerdotal robes.

If you ask me, this budget is a *Taira no Kiyomori*[6] budget. That such a budget of trickery as this should be put forward here makes one

97

suspect a violation of the constitution. Establishing a defence force would be an infringement of the constitution and would destroy the foundations of democracy. If the government can be so vague about such a thing at the start of independence, just how can we become ready for democracy? If there is no basic reform, just where does that leave politics? I would like to have the Prime Minister's clear opinion on this point.

Yoshida: The Minister of Justice will give a clear explanation.

Ohashi: As has been said before many times, the equipment of the Police Reserve Forces is fixed on the basis of the needs of internal security. It is entirely different in character from military forces.

Nakasone: I wish to put a final question on the problem of the Emperor's abdication. This is a very important issue so I would like Prime Minister Yoshida to be kind enough to answer.

It is a fact that the world at large, and the people of Japan, recognise that the present Emperor has been a consistent advocate of peace and that he bears no formal responsibility for the war. However, it is possible that the Emperor, who now has been released from the sacred divinity of the third clause of the old constitution, 'The Emperor is sacred and inviolable', to become human, may, like the rest of us mortals feel human suffering about the past war. If the human suffering of the Emperor cannot be relieved because of outside restraints, then it must be said that undoing those restraints is right for the new Emperor system.

What outside restraints might there be? One is the moral responsibility to the allied nations to stay in place in order to stabilise Japan and carry out our international duty. Another is the responsibility to the people of Japan to stay on the throne to limit the tragedy and confusion that resulted from war and the post-war circumstances and to promote orderly regeneration and stability in the peoples' lives.

These two problems have already been resolved or are in the process of being resolved. If the Emperor were to want to abdicate of his own volition then there have been several suitable occasions: the first was the occasion of the enactment of the new constitution; the second was when the Peace Treaty was ratified. The third and final chance, and the most appropriate, is when the Peace Treaty comes into effect.

Ultimately this is something the Emperor must decide for himself, and not in any way something we should be debating. However I think it is perhaps necessary to say that, judging the matter on the basis of the international and domestic conditions that exist now, then should the Emperor so wish, his suffering will be removed.

There are those who say that now, when the Crown Prince has come of age and we can give warm national thanks to the bereaved families of the war dead, the abdication of the Emperor by his own volition would make a deep impression on the bereaved and those who suffered in the war; that it would establish the moral foundation of the Emperor system, rejuvenate it and maintain it firm and steadfast. What does the government think? Would the Prime Minister be good enough to answer?

Yoshida: I think you would probably agree with me that this issue is not something that should be the topic of careless debate. I will answer briefly, not at length. This is a time when we must rebuild a glorious Japan; we are at the start of that project. If the Emperor, who is the symbol of the people's patriotism, and beloved and respected by the nation, were to abdicate, the stability of the country would be damaged. People who want things like this are traitors. I hope that the Emperor will remain on the throne and will persist in his efforts to lead the people toward the building of a new Japan.

When Yoshida heard my questions on defence and the Emperor he became extremely excited. He was so agitated that even I was afraid that he might suffer a cerebral haemorrhage.

CHAPTER FIVE

A NEW AWARENESS OF INTERNATIONAL POLITICS

Observing the Communist Bloc

I wanted to visit the Communist Bloc and the Middle and Near East. I felt that, unless I saw with my own eyes what things were like on the ground, I couldn't decide on a diplomatic strategy for Japan. In any case, I had a thirst for knowledge, for 'seeing and then doing', that the young were full of in those days. In July of 1954, I got my chance. At the time, politicians like Tanaka Toshio from the Socialist party, Sudō Gorō of the Communist party and Kimura Kihachirō of the Labour-Farmer party (*Rōnōtō*) and intellectuals like Mr Hoashi Kei and Mrs Kōra Tomi were all touring the country, praising what they had seen on their travels in the Soviet Union and China, and criticising conservative party politics and Japan's co-operation with America. Some of us in the conservative camp, seeing this, thought it necessary to observe the communist camp in order to correct the biased representation of the two countries. So I talked to Sakurauchi Yoshio, Sonoda Tadashi and others and planned a visit to China and the Soviet Union with the venerable Matsuura Shutarō and Nishimura Naomi from the Liberal Party.

Because there was a danger that they wouldn't let us in if it were just people from the conservative camp, we organised a cross-party inspection team which included Matsumae Shigeyoshi from the Socialist party and Kuroda Hisao from the Labour-Farmer party, and solicited invitations to the Soviet Union and China. The response was quick: invitations arrived in the names of the respective Overseas Cultural Associations.

However, there was one problem. The McCarren Act, in force in the United States of America, denied politicians, financiers and others who travelled in the Communist Bloc a visa to enter the United States. I went to the American Embassy and met with Ambassador Allison and explained the purpose of this visit to the Communist Bloc and asked for special consideration so that the law would not be applied to us. Ambassador Allison discussed this with his home country and provided us with a document which, though somewhat general, was what we had asked for.

Next, I visited Progressive Party president Shigemitsu Mamoru in his office in the Marunouchi Hotel to seek his approval. I was not expecting any difficulties and thought he would be encouraging, but Shigemitsu sighed deeply and said, 'Nakasone, I think you should give it a miss for now. This is going off the rails in a big way. You are a man who is going to be needed to work for Japan in the future. This will damage you badly. I'm giving you this advice more in the capacity of a friend than as the President of your party. I want you to drop it.'

Shigemitsu was a man of most distinguished service in diplomacy after the war. When he heard, immediately after General MacArthur landed in Atsugi, that the U.S. army would be running a direct military administration and military scrip was to be issued, he went straight away to the U.S. Army Headquarters in Yokohama and engaged in vigorous negotiations with Chief Staff Officer Sutherland. As a result of Shigemitsu's visit GHQ changed their policy and decided to govern indirectly through the Emperor and the government of Japan.

But the Shigemitsu who stood before me now was dazzled by the cold war policies of Secretary of State Dulles and reacted as a Foreign Office bureaucrat. Politicians, unlike bureaucrats, must catch the wind shifts and respond with sensitivity to the changes in the pressure charts. They must move on their own responsibility and, having prepared their data, their job is to be prepared to make detours in order to realise their aims. I was surprised by Shigemitsu's response, and without mentioning that the American Embassy had already given its approval, I withdrew, promising to give the matter serious consideration. Then I went ahead as planned.

We travelled to Moscow via Sweden and Finland and I wondered whether we might get the chance to go dancing en route. Sakurauchi, Sonoda and myself were all country lads who had run around battlefields during the war, and then devoted ourselves to politics since our demobilisation, so we decided to take dance lessons. We went to a big dance hall in Shimbashi called 'Florida', and I drove with the two of them in the old Austin I had bought in Washington. We got a puncture on the way, and since we didn't know how to change a tyre, we lifted the car to the side of the road and went on to the

Florida on foot. Then together, we three stern-looking men with bandy legs tried our best to learn the fox-trot.

In the Soviet Union we were put up at a Soviet hotel, and I was surprised by the dim lights and the poverty of towels, toilet paper and soap. When you turned the electric light switches they came away in your hand. We were taken to see what they told us were outstanding factories, but sixty percent of the machinery was manufactured in Germany and their equipment did not, in any case, seem particularly outstanding. The reality was quite different from the propaganda.

Behind the hotel was a row of poor wooden tenement houses that were unchanged from the time of the Romanovs. The people who lived there came to get their water from a faucet in the middle of the street, and carried it back to their houses. When Sakurauchi, Sonoda and Matsuura took pictures of these old tenements, they were investigated by the police on suspicion of spying. I stood a short distance away, filming this on a cine-camera, and I too was caught. We were taken to what might have been a committee room in the factory behind and released three hours later. It was forbidden to take photographs of factories, bridges and airfields, but not of tenements. We guessed that we had been taken in as part of some plain clothes policeman's quota or point scoring system.

At that time it was the Malenkov administration which was in power and Andrei Vyshinsky was the Foreign Minister. We met with Vyshinsky and demanded the return of the Northern Territories, the return of people detained in Siberia and the early release of soldiers convicted of war crimes. The Labour Farmer Party man, Kuroda, insisted that we didn't have to raise the issue of the return of the four islands at this time. We disagreed. Matsumae and the rest of us wouldn't defer and raised the issue with Vyshinsky who replied, 'There are no detainees, only criminals. I will look into the question of soldiers convicted of war crimes. The four islands are Soviet territory.' Later we were taken by car on an eight hour journey to a detainment centre for war criminals and visited General Yamada Otozō and handed over a care parcel.

When we crossed into China, and saw the people's faces, the appearance of the towns, and the fruit and vegetables in the shops, I felt as if I had returned to human society. The sight of the fresh red and green of the water melons on display outside the shops there has stayed imprinted on my mind. But the Soviet Union was truly the 'Gulag Archipelago'; it was a gloomy place and the eyes of the secret police were everywhere. I felt as if I were in a big prison.

In Beijing we met with the literary figure, Guo Mo-ruo [1892–1978] and Mrs Li De-Quan. We had to be careful of Mr Guo, who was very critical of Japanese imperialism and strongly anti-Japanese. However the helpfulness of the hotel staff and the warm welcome we received from the interpreters made a deep impression on me. Throughout Guo's speech, hotel staff members were swatting flies in full view. This was the slogan, 'To see is to act' made flesh.

The hotel staff wouldn't accept tips and when we took our leave of the interpreter in Canton, he said, 'As you know, I am inexperienced so if there have been times when you have not been satisfied with my services, please forgive me.' The factories and the streets were littered with slogans saying 'Devote yourself heart and soul to the study of the Soviet Union'. At that time, China was completely devoted to the Soviet Union and Communist Party members and service staff were full of the spirit of 'regularity and impartiality', and 'serve the masses', a spirit that the soldiers of the Eighth Route Army had shown during the war against Japan.

Tokutomi Sōhō's words, 'Mao Tse-tung is certain to turn out like Tito in Yugoslavia', were still ringing in my ears, but thereafter, so far as China policy was concerned, I had my own opinions, and I was careful to take a long and broad view. This was the reason why I was later seen as one of those people who had laid the groundwork for Sino-Japanese friendship.

When we reached Hong Kong, the free air smelled infinitely sweet, and I experienced a feeling of release as if my lungs were expanding and I was growing in height. We sat in a dazzling Chinese restaurant toasting the joys of freedom and democracy. Sonoda said he was going to deal with the China problem in the future; Sakurauchi said the Soviet issue was his. I claimed America and we drank on it. A quarter of a century later, Sonoda, as Foreign Minister in the Fukuda cabinet signed a treaty of friendship with China; Sakurauchi became president of the Japan-Soviet Friendship Society and led many groups to the Soviet Union. And when I formed my own cabinets I worked to strengthen the U.S.-Japan relationship.

The speech that was erased from the records

The speech I made to the Plenary Session of the Lower House as a Liberal Democratic Party delegate on November 27 1956, was erased from the shorthand record. It was erased in its entirety, the first time this had happened since Saito Takao's criticism of the military authorities on February 2, 1940.

At the end of 1954, the Soviet Union had made the first earth shaking moves toward restoring relations between the Soviet Union and Japan. At the New Year, Domnitsky, who was head of the Soviet mission to the Allied Council for Japan, passed a letter from his government to Prime Minister Hatoyama saying preparations were being made for negotiations on the restoration of diplomatic relations. At first, Domnitsky had intended to go to Foreign Minister Shigemitsu, but the Japanese Foreign Office had rejected the approach on the grounds that they did not recognise the existence of a Soviet-Japanese mission, since the Soviet Union had refused to sign the San Francisco Peace Treaty. The result was that Domnitsky took the diplomatically exceptional step of delivering a letter directly to Prime Minister Hatoyama.

Later, after many twists and turns, Prime Minister Hatoyama went himself to Moscow, and on 19 October 1956, in the Kremlin, signed the Soviet-Japanese Joint Declaration which provided for diplomatic normalisation. Eleven years after the ending of the war, five years after the San Francisco Peace Treaty, relations were finally restored between the Soviet Union and Japan, though the problem of the Northern Territories, of course, remained.

In my speech to the Lower House Plenary Session which was to ratify this Joint Declaration, I began by protesting against the Soviet demands for harsh clauses limiting Japan's sovereignty at the San Francisco Peace Conference. I went on to explain why most Japanese had not supported the arguments for 'overall peace', and I emphasised that, 'the signing of the joint declaration occurred because of the decision to go for peace by instalments. It is undeniable that this success came about in spite of the advocates of an overall peace.' It was then that the Socialist and Communist Party seats fell into uproar. I went on,

At the end of the second world war, the momentous events and activities which redrew the face of the earth left smoking volcanoes to both east and west. Viewed historically, these rumblings of national self determination, liberation and freedom, have a rightness about them.

Japan is a part of this volcanic belt. It stands ready to correct the system little by little; to move forward from the Potsdam-San Francisco system. With Japan's entry into the United Nations as a consequence of this declaration, the Japanese people will stand on a new historical stage.

But there is a lot that is wrong with this declaration; Kunashiri and Etorofu and other islands have not been returned; many of our brothers languish in detention and we are left ignorant of whether they are alive or dead. We have chosen this path because we have no choice.

We, the Japanese people, are not approving this declaration because we are bowing to some rule of justice. We are approving this declaration because we are bowing to the realities of power, because of our love for our brothers and because we judge it best for the development of the nation. For these reasons, we have no choice.

Let us remember that this declaration was built on the spirits of the millions who were the human cost of the Second World War, and on the sacrifices of our fellow countrymen. When we give this declaration our approval let us do so with our heads bowed and a silent prayer in our hearts.

The Socialists and Communists rose to their feet booing and jeering and pushing to the platform to protest, so that at times the speech could not be heard. I put my face close to the microphone and shouted until the sweat was pouring from me and I had completed the speech. I spoke for fifty minutes. When I had finished, the Socialist and Communist parties brought the proceedings to a halt with their protestations. Both parties demanded that the speech be deleted on the grounds that it was critical of the Soviet Union and injurious to our Soviet partners; that it was damaging to the restoration of diplomatic relations and that it was immoderate in its criticism of overall peace and dismissive of the views of the other parties.

My comrades and I were strongly opposed, but the government party executive could not get on with its Diet business and was anxious that approval of the declaration might be delayed. It therefore came to an agreement with the opposition parties and accepted the deletion. I often attended meetings by other parties where speeches were being made on the constitution and on defence issues and clashed with the Socialist and Communist parties. This was a concerted counter-attack, a sustained offensive to hunt me down. Looking back on it now, I realise that though I meant what I said, the violence of my expression and my youthful over-enthusiasm embarrassed my colleagues. But at the time, I couldn't help being disappointed at the erasure of the speech.

However, for every God who forsakes us, there is another who saves. I went to the *Yomiuri* newspaper and saw the president of the company, Shōriki Matsutarō. I told him that there was something I wanted the people to know and asked him to publish the speech in his newspaper. Shōriki said, 'Show me the contents of the manuscript and I'll consider it', and in the end, he published the complete text of the deleted speech in the morning edition of the next day's paper.

My real feeling was that I supported the declaration but not unconditionally. I wanted it to be made clear, both to future generations and to other nations, that the Japanese people retained grave reservations about a number of issues, including that of the territories. Because these feelings were erased from the records of the Diet, they reached the wider public through the medium of the press. I was moved by, and deeply grateful for, the many telephone calls and letters that came from all over the country.

Unexpected budget for peaceful use of nuclear power

On 3 March 1954, the Liberal Party, the Progressive Party and the National Liberal Party put forward an unexpected joint amendment to the Lower House Budget Committee just as budget deliberations were drawing to a close. The amendment was for ¥235,000,000 to research peaceful uses of nuclear power, and ¥15,000,000 for uranium resources; a total of ¥250,000,000. It was the first 'nuclear expense' in Japan's annual governmental budget.

Because it was totally unexpected there was opposition from every side. Newspapers dubbed it a 'reckless driving budget' and there were attacks from academics and from officials, including bureaucrats in the Ministry of Education, who called it 'imprudent and out on a limb' and 'premature'. The Chairman of the Science Council of Japan, Kaya Seiji, expressed his opposition to us, and the Ministry of Education insisted that appropriations be made for increases in the construction budget of the Nuclear Research Centre and to make up the deficit for the Scientific Research Institute. In this climate, people like Shiikuma Saburo, who had initially supported the budget, asked for it to be withdrawn, but those of us who had made the proposal, myself, Saito Kenzō, Inaba Osamu, Kawasaki Hideji and so on, could not be moved from our original intention.

We had a reason for this. In January 1947, at a stroke, Japan had been forbidden by order of the Far Eastern Council to study nuclear power for the duration of the Occupation. Prior to that, in November of 1945, the Occupation forces had thrown the cyclotron from the Science Research Centre into Tokyo Bay off Shinagawa, and a GHQ

106

order had forbidden research into the separation of uranium 235 and related isotopes. In 1951, when Dulles came as a special envoy to Japan, I made a particular request that the peaceful use of nuclear power after independence should not be limited by the Peace Treaty. I was anxious that, if the peaceful use of 'the biggest discovery of the twentieth century' were to be banned by the Peace Treaty, Japan would have to resign itself to the permanent status of fourth rate power.

Even from within the Science Council, in October 1951, Osaka University professor Fushimi Yasuharu, proposed that the freedom to undertake research into peaceful uses of nuclear power should be restored after independence. In July 1952, Kaya also emphasised, 'Now the Peace Treaty has gone into effect, it is necessary to establish a committee on nuclear power to look into the handling of the whole nuclear power issue.' However, there was opposition from the scholars connected with the communist-led Democratic Association of Scientists[1]. As a result, and in the light of the decision taken by the general meeting in April 1950, which stated, 'We will not pursue scientific research for the purposes of war', the majority thought it would be better to wait for a while. No decision was possible until 1953 when U.S. President Dwight D Eisenhower, in a speech to the U.N. General Council, announced, 'Preparations are underway to deliver nuclear fission material to new organs under the auspices of the United Nations to encourage developments in the peaceful use of nuclear power'.

In the summer of 1953, I made a detailed inspection of developments at American Nuclear Research facilities. I discovered that under the banner, 'Atoms for Peace', nuclear research, which had hitherto been the monopolised by the military, was to be opened up to the private sector. As a result, the Nuclear Power Industry Council set up by the financial sector became increasingly active. I remember how keenly I felt that Japan should not be left behind the rest of the world.

On the way back to Japan I went to see Dr Sagane Ryōkichi at the Institute of Physical and Chemical research at the Lawrence Laboratory in Berkeley, and I asked him how best to promote the study of the peaceful use of nuclear power in Japan. His answer was: establish long-term national policy; clarify national intentions through laws and budgets; guarantee stable research, and thereby ensure the supply of top class scholars you need.

I felt very strongly that the peaceful use of nuclear power was a national undertaking and that it was politicians who should be taking the decisions about it. Leaving responsibility with the Science

Council, which was under the thumb of left wing scholars, had led to endless debate and the waste of two or three years. I was convinced that the time had come to take political responsibility for development through legislation and the national budget.

However, the Progressive Party of which I was a member was at that time a minority ruling party and lacked the power to pass legislation or budgets alone. We were making slow progress when the Liberal Party lost more than half its seats in the '*bakayaro*' dissolution, and suddenly needed our co-operation to pass the budget and enact legislation. I saw this as a heaven-sent opportunity and talked to other like-minded politicians about the possibility of passing a budget amendment opening up research into the peaceful use of nuclear energy. Everyone was in favour, but because we anticipated fatal opposition from the press and academic world should there be leaks before the fact, it was kept secret and presented as a unexpected budget amendment.

For us it was a 'crime of conviction' so we were not about to give in, whatever the pressure. Inaba, in particular, was a man of strong beliefs. A doctor of jurisprudence and a professor of constitutional law at Chūō University, he was the most suitable man to challenge the Science Council. It was said at the time that I told scholars who came to object, 'Scholars are idling their time away dozing so we are waking them up by tapping them on the cheek with a bundle of money.' But in fact, this was Inaba's expression.

In response to a question asking why the grant was such a precise amount (¥235,000,000), the reply, 'Because enriched uranium is uranium 235 of course', caused a burst of laughter and the budget went through the Lower House. In the Upper House, there were various questions from the Socialist and Communist party members but a budget sent by the Lower House to the Upper House passes by default after thirty days. In the end, there were some constructive questions requesting, for example, that the government should indicate the basic direction of its nuclear energy policy and follow a sound budget, and the nuclear energy budget went through by default. The Science Council expressed their feeling that, 'It is regrettable that this budget was put forward without any contact with ourselves', but they also set out their demands that, 'The government should consult with the Science Council on the nuclear energy budget and on important matters relating to the issue of nuclear energy in the future.' The focus had changed, so to speak, to the question of how nuclear energy was to be used. A thick wall had been broken down and the hopes and ideas of a variety of fields had been brought together. Japan's research into the peaceful uses of nuclear energy had begun.

In response to a request from the Science Council, a Nuclear Power Usage Preparatory Investigatory Committee, including representatives from the academic and financial communities, was set up to study basic policy directions. Provision was made in the nuclear budget for large scale visits to Europe and the United States by investigating committees, and for participation in the conference of nuclear scientists in the U.S. in March 1955. Nuclear power sections were set up in the Economic Planning Agency [EPA] and the Ministry of International Trade and Industry [MITI]; administrative systems were established, and negotiations went without a hitch for delivery of enriched uranium from the United States in May of that year.

Establishing a legal system for nuclear power

In August 1955 four politicians, myself from the Democratic Party, Maeda Masao from the Liberal Party, Shimura Shigeharu from the Left Socialist Party and Matsumae Shigeyoshi from the Right Socialist Party, attended the United Nations International Conference for the Peaceful Use of Nuclear Power held in Geneva, as advisors to the Japanese delegation. If we had not pushed the amended budget through so quickly, this delegation would probably never have been dispatched. I firmly believe that politics is about taking responsibility and doing what has to be done when it has to be done.

This group of Diet representatives went to the United Kingdom, France, the United States and Canada, to make detailed investigations of their administrative systems for nuclear energy research development, and their research centres, and to study basic principles. Wherever we were, our research finished for the day, we would gather in one of the hotel rooms in our long drawers and T-shirts and engage in heated discussions. There, sitting on the edge of the beds, we canvassed opinions on the plans for Japan's science program, including nuclear energy research development, and the setting up of a government office for science and technology. All the Japanese Embassies expressed their respect for the group, saying they had never come across such a serious group of Diet representatives.

After our return to Haneda in September, the four of us put out a non-partisan declaration arguing the pressing need to prepare a system to develop Japan's nuclear energy research. This message reverberated around the country and, coupled with the international conference in Geneva, quickly fanned the flames of enthusiasm. After this, with the agreement of the four parties, a Joint Committee on Nuclear Energy was set up as a dual house, non-partisan consultative body, and a nuclear energy legal system was devised.

Without involving the government in any way, we made use of Sugata Seijiro and others in the Lower House expert committees, and of the Cabinet Legislation Bureau which was headed up by Nishizawa Tetsujiro, to draft an unadulterated piece of Diet legislation. Among the committee members drawn from each party were Narita Tomomi and Katsumata Seiichi from the Socialist Party. The committee members carried back the results of the committee discussions to the parties and with their approval, we prepared a bill. This was when the main provisions in the current nuclear energy laws were drafted: the Atomic Energy Act, the Atomic Energy Commission Law, the Nuclear Fuels Development Promotion Law, the Atomic Energy Research Institute Law, the Atomic Fuels Public Corporation Law, the Radiation Sickness Prevention Law and so on. Within six months we had drafted the eight main laws which regulate nuclear power and the law establishing the Science and Technology Agency.

At first, we had intended to make the Atomic Energy Commission an independent administrative/executive committee based on clause three of the National Government Organisation Act. But, believing that, during its formative period, the body we established would need to co-operate and co-ordinate with a government department, we in fact set up an advisory organ based on clause eight. However in order to distinguish it from other advisory organs, it was given a semi-independent character so that it drew up its own plans and took decisions without advising the government. Moreover, the cabinet was required to pay serious attention to these decisions.

The Atomic Energy Act owed a lot to the opinions of Matsumae Shigeyoshi and, because of the necessity to strengthen its cross-party nature, the demands of the Science Council were also taken into account. Consequently, the uses of atomic energy research came to have the following formulation: first, they were to be restricted to peaceful purposes; second, they were to observe the three principles of democracy, independence and openness, third they implied unrestricted international co-operation.

As the proposer of the Atomic Energy Act, I responded to the questions in the Diet about the meaning of 'peaceful purposes'. My answer was, 'The direct use of atomic fuel in weapons intended to kill and injure people is of course forbidden, but if, for example, a new steel could be created using an isotope, we do not intend to go as far as prohibiting the use of that steel in machine guns. When we reach the stage that nuclear powered ships are in general use and nuclear power it is used even in transport ships, we will approve the use of nuclear propulsion for submarines.

These 'principles of popularisation' were later also used for space development. Japan's space development was restricted to peaceful purposes. Nowadays, when communications satellites have become commonplace, the use of space development in Self Defence Force satellite communications is allowed.

One other arrangement is worthy of comment. The atomic energy budget for the various ministries and agencies was allocated in a lump to the Science and Technology Agency Atomic Energy Bureau. Budgets were then compiled to divide this sum across the ministries and agencies. This was an important exception in terms of execution and also because we were thereby able to gather together talented people by paying the research staff at the Atomic Energy Research Institute at advantageous rates of ten percent over the norm.

In a letter to Hatoyama from the conference in Geneva, 21 August, I wrote:

Greetings. I hope you are keeping well in the hot weather.

The Atomic Energy Conference ended without a hitch. The delegates from all the parties are agreed that Japan's participation in this conference was of the utmost importance for the county's future. The main points are as follows:

1. The conference has brought home to me the fact that the pivot of international relations has shifted to competitive cultural coexistence, and that the possession or otherwise of an atomic reactor, that is the extent of nuclear power development, has become the symbol of international status.

2. The position of Japan is comparable to that of Mexico or Turkey, while India, which has neither technology nor industry, enjoys first class power status through its skilful balancing act.

3. The Japanese government's recognition of this conference has been very poor and significant reform is necessary. The United States, United Kingdom, Soviet Union and France, each sent hundreds of delegates, but Japan sent its Consul General in Geneva to the

conference. We had so few people with technical knowledge that it was impossible to follow all the sectional meetings

4. The quickest route to restoring Japan's international position without irritating other countries is to join in this neutral scientific development program. Of the Asian nations only Japan can do it. If, in the future, Japan could become a member of the Council of International Organs for Atomic Energy, this would be an important step toward restoring our international position. To this end, our efforts to break into this programme must be made steadily, step by step. An important opportunity was lost at this conference because of the lack of a fundamental national policy.

5. I would like to see the Hatoyama cabinet open the door to a broad development of nuclear power as a legacy to future generations. The reasons are simple: this would be an historic policy which would resolve the problems of employment and population; it would be the best way to please the people and it would be easy to get all party support.

6. We, the delegates of all four parties, are in agreement with the points below, and each of us has pledged his party to their realisation. (There shouldn't be a problem with putting this into practise because all are influential experts in their respective parties.)

   a) The development of nuclear power should be kept free of politics, should be supra-party and pursued decisively.

   b) Concrete proposals:

   - To buy two experimental reactors from the U.S.
   - To complete a natural uranium heavy water reactor of 10,000 watts within three years. (The next international conference is two to three years away.)
   - To begin large-scale prospecting for uranium. (France spent about ¥25,000,000 finding a large vein of ore; there must be a big vein in Japan too.)
   - To bring American technology and Indian thorium together in Japan and to promote a co-operative Asian nuclear power body.
   - For as long as necessary, there should be strong national management, then when practicable, it should be opened to the private sector.
   - The above will take about three years and cost about ¥200,000,000.
   - A fundamental law on atomic energy must be passed.

This line has been agreed after discussions between the delegates of all the parties and Professors Komagata and Fujioka.

If the conservative government wants to come up with fresh policies, the only possibilities are social welfare and the promotion of atomic energy. With social welfare there will be opposition from the financial world, whereas there will be no such problem with atomic energy. After the Geneva Conference, the atmosphere at home should be ripe.

Consequently I would entreat the Prime Minister to make haste (if possible to take it up from where he is staying, in Karuizawa) to persuade the cabinet to take the matter up positively. The mood regarding the issue of nuclear power is so different in the domestic and international arenas that I am filled with trepidation.

Best wishes

Nakasone

p.s. I will visit reactors in France and Italy and investigate reactors and running costs in the UK, Canada and the US before returning to Japan on 10 September.

I can still remember my passionate desire to do something about this problem.

Thinking about it, it was a long journey. From the time that I saw what was evidently the atomic cloud over Hiroshima from Takamatsu in August 1945, I was convinced of the importance of science and technology and expected that the development of atomic energy research would become a litmus test for the level of development of industrial society and scientific research and for the strength of the nation. As a politician under the Occupation and again after independence, I strenuously applied myself to this problem and in the end, my efforts bore fruit. Now, roughly twenty-six percent of Japan's electricity generation relies on nuclear energy. When we consider environmental protection and global warning, the importance of atomic energy development grows ever larger. The more atomic energy is utilised, the more seriously we need to control safety procedures. I feel an enormous responsibility for the sound development of nuclear power.

When I tell my juniors, 'Diet legislation is the mission of the Diet member. Since 1955, the two major pieces of Diet legislation have been Tanaka Kakuei's construction of a national network of highways and the atomic energy legislation that we introduced.' my heart swells a little with pride.

The dawning of an Arab policy

In May 1957, I accompanied Prime Minister Kishi on a formal round of visits to Southeast Asian and Southwest Asian nations. In New Delhi, I split off from Prime Minister Kishi, and joined up with Nakatani Takeyo, a former Diet member, and Shimonaka Yasaburō, the President of the publishing company Heibonsha. The two of them were waiting for me there to go to inspect the Communist Bloc countries and the Middle East which was somewhere I had always wanted to visit. Shimonaka was eighty years old at the time; Nakatani was sixty. I was forty. Shimonaka had gone beyond being just a journalist. A distinctive character, and a patriot who supported anti-colonialist and independence movements, he called himself 'Potter Yasaburō'. Nakatani was a scholar of nationalism who left academic life for politics and later founded the Japan Arab Society.

Our first stop was Iran, where we were briefed on the details of the situation in the Near and Middle East from our Ambassador, Yamada Hisanari. The three of us agreed, in the event that we should meet with Egyptian President Gamal Abdel Nasser, to suggest to him that we should resolve the problems and bring the Aswan dam to a successful conclusion through Afro-Asian efforts and that Japan too would do her bit in a co-operative effort.

With Prime Minister Kishi and Prime Minister Jawaharlal Nehru of India

In fact, before we left Tokyo, I put it to certain circles in the U.S. that, 'Secretary of State, Dulles seems to be developing an anti-Nasser policy, but this requires caution. Egypt is the centre of the crossroads which connect Europe, Asia and Africa. It is the most important region in world strategic terms. It is a mistake to drive this region toward the Soviet Union. It might be difficult for America to come forward immediately, but Japan must cooperate in the construction of the Aswân High Dam so that Egypt is not driven into the Soviet camp. I am going to talk to President Nasser with that intention in mind. What about it?'

The reply came, 'Please wait a few days and we will get back to you.' Then, not long after, 'America will not raise any objections if you do this. We will wait to see what happens.'

President Nasser overturned a corrupt monarchical government, carried out the nationalisation of the Suez Canal, held out in a war against Britain and France and caused the Eden Cabinet to fall. Across the Arab world, pictures of Nasser were displayed, portraying him as an Arab hero. In response to these developments, President Eisenhower launched the 'Eisenhower Doctrine'. He sent special envoys promising large amounts of economic and military assistance to Arabs in the anti-Nasser camp and plotted to isolate President Nasser within the Arab world. For a time many of the pictures of President Nasser, which had been posted across the Arab countries, were torn down and only those in Syria and Egypt remained.

I visited Nasser at his home on the evening of 6 June. In Japanese terms the house he lived in was the sort that might have belonged to a company section head. I could hear the sound of children's voices clamouring in the next room. Speaking in English, I went straight to the point. First, I thanked him for supporting Japan's admission to the United Nations and told him that the Japanese people supported the nationalisation of the Suez Canal. I explained that Japanese diplomacy was in favour of national self-determination, anti-colonialism and the spread of international democracy, and I told him my thoughts on the construction of the Aswân High Dam. President Nasser thanked me and expressed his opinion with great feeling.

The Great Powers of Europe and America are putting out propaganda that I am trying to be an Arab Hitler and build a great power. But in my wildest dreams I have no thought, either of trying to become a great power, or of interfering in other countries. I desire only to prevent other countries from interfering in the Arab states and to achieve racial independence. The Arab peoples are uniting for this purpose. America is trying to separate all other governments and monarchs from Egypt, but this means isolating the governments and monarchs from the masses. They say I am a communist sympathiser, but the Communist Party has been legalised in Britain, France and Italy, whereas in Egypt it is banned, so what price that?

When Nasser asked, apropos the Aswân High Dam, whether Japan had the necessary construction techniques and power generators and so on, I told him about Japan's track record in the construction of the Suihō dam on the borders of Korea and China, and the dam then under construction in Burma (now Myanmar). His eyes lit up and he said, 'It's a good idea. I would like to have Japan's technical help and co-operation.' I formed the impression, as we talked, of an artless, honest man and an amiable leader. He was immensely attractive; his almond eyes were full of deep sadness and love. We were the same age, but he was already quite grey; perhaps it was the rigours of the revolution.

I telephoned the results of this conversation to the Director of the EPA, Takasaki Tatsunosuke, and asked him to consider the appointment of Kubota Yutaka of Nihon Kōei who had built the Suihō Dam.

When I got back to Japan I immediately persuaded the financial world to form a Japan-Egypt Economic Co-operation Council. On 13 September 1958, the first deferred capital payment of $30,000,000 was signed with the Arab League (Egypt and Syria) and, on the basis of President Nasser's promise, arrangements were made to accept Nihon Kōei in a central position. We invited the man responsible for the technical aspects of construction of the Aswân High Dam, Dr Aziz Sidki from Egypt and inspected other similar dams, such as Miboro Dam. Meanwhile, Nakatani set up the Japan-Arab Society. These events were the first steps in establishing an Arab policy for Japan.

Despite our efforts, the Soviet Union offered a long term loan with ultra low interest rates and got the order for the construction of the Aswân High Dam. Subsequently, Nasser's Egypt swung gradually to the left like Castro's Cuba, but then moved back to the right again under the influence of Anwar Sadat, Vice President under this administration. With President Carter's mediation, Egypt made peace with its long-term, mortal enemy, Israel and then distinguished itself as the leading moderate Arab state.

The Arab desert lives on and on, endlessly coming together and splitting apart; swallowing the sorrows.

Power struggle of the century

There was an unusual snowfall in Tokyo in the New Year of 1954; heavy and sustained. This was the prelude to a dramatic power struggle which unfolded over the next two years. It was a struggle of heroic and magnificent proportions, deserving of special mention in Japanese political history. One after another, there was the dissolution of the Lower House, votes of no confidence in cabinet ministers and the cabinet, the formation of the Democratic Party of Japan [*Nihon Minshutō*], the fall of the Yoshida Cabinet, the overwhelming electoral success of the Hatoyama Cabinet, the union of the conservative parties, the sudden death of Ōgata Taketora, the emergence of the Ishibashi Cabinet (an alliance of the parties in second and third position), Ishibashi's sudden illness, the formation of the Kishi Cabinet ... . In just over two years, the sort of drama that happens in the political world once in a lifetime, happened again and again, flicking past like pictures on a revolving lantern. The historical setting for the structure of Japan as an independent nation kept changing.

Even the Yoshida Administration, which could boast of seven years in power was gradually slipping and showing the symptoms of approaching demise. These symptoms of cabinet collapse were not only the result of 'the power of history' and 'the march of time'. It was 'the power of politics'; of ambition and skilful behind-the-scenes opposition which finally upset the foundations of Yoshida's administration. The 'pre-war politicians faction', purged, and then released and brought back to political life again, were the active players, the ones who contrived to weaken the Yoshida cabinet and create and direct the scenario for a change of administration. For a time, the so-called 'post-war politicians' faction' took a back seat to the veterans.

The cabinet started on the downward slope in July 1952 with the 'Fukunaga issue' in which Secretary General Fukunaga, appointed by Yoshida on the advice of people close to him, was crushed by the party faction within the Liberal Party. There had been a change in party dynamics. Then there was the failure of the 'sudden assault dissolution'. Yoshida had discussed this with only a few people close to him; not even with the new Chairman of the Lower House, Ōno Banboku. Ōno, who had been Chairman for three days, was exceedingly angry. The Liberal Party lost a half of its seats in the election. What was more, the day before the election, again at the suggestion of his close associates, Kōno Ichiro and Ishibashi Tanzan were dismissed from the party. This was the beginning of a subsequent rift.

117

In November 1952, MITI Minister Ikeda Hayato was forced to resign by a vote of no confidence after remarks that 'a few firms might have to go under'. Then, in February 1953, Yoshida made his '*bakayarō*', 'You fool', remark and a motion to discipline the Prime Minister was passed. A vote of no-confidence was also passed, and the so-called '*bakayarō* dissolution' took place. The Liberal Party was reduced from 240 to 199 seats. By early 1954, the ship building bribery scandal had also occurred, Justice Minister Inukai's move to invoke special powers attracted hissing and booing in the House, and Yoshida's resignation became inevitable.

There is a saying, 'A single man is powerless to save the country on the brink of ruin.' The 'single man' who tried to play such a role in this instance was Ōgata Taketora. with his appeal for the conservative forces to rally, and his statement to the effect that, 'The state of affairs is of such concern that the most pressing need at the present time is the need for stability in the political situation'. The Yoshida camp had decided that it would have nothing to do with anti-Liberal conservative influences, but this was, in effect, the first movement toward an integrated Conservative Party.

Amidst all this, my aim was to bring down the Yoshida Cabinet. Therefore, in January 1954, I asked an explosive question in the Lower House Budget Committee about the two Liberal Party members caught up in the ship building bribery case, and demanded a clean-up of the political world. There was a violent response from both government and opposition parties. The Liberal Party tried to pass a motion disciplining me but, having recognised that they stood to lose if the truth were exposed, they subsequently dropped it. Matsumura Kenzo cautioned me that, 'A politician of the orthodox school such as yourself doesn't turn to questions like that.' But Kiyose Ichiro told me I was right and that I should act with confidence. With hindsight, there were many occasions when I was borne along by youthful enthusiasm, but this certainly was a body blow to the Yoshida Cabinet.

I was also busily engaged in putting together a new party for the post-Yoshida era by aligning the Progressive Party with the forces affiliated with Hatoyama Ichiro, Miki Takeo and Kōno Ichiro, and Kishi. On 24 November, we launched the Democratic Party of Japan, (*Nihon minshutō*) at the Hibiya Hall. This forced the Yoshida Cabinet into a tight corner, and there were calls from party faction politicians within the Liberal Party, men such as Ōgata, Ōno, Masutani Hidetsugu, Matsuno Tsuruhei, for Yoshida's resignation. Those protecting Yoshida shrank down to just his close associates, Ikeda Hayato and

Sato Eisaku, but even then, Yoshida did not lose his nerve and determined on a dissolution. He only changed his mind and decided to resign as a result of strong opposition from Ōgata and Ōno. Both wings of the Socialist party supported Hatoyama for Prime Minister on the promise of a quick dissolution, and the Hatoyama cabinet was formed.

It took an immense amount of time and a complex process to bring down this administration. Politicians, especially the party faction politicians were resourceful, brave and selfless; they undertook this joint action, tying their fates together, out of a respect for ideas and beliefs. Of the so-called 'eight samurai' bound together by Miki and Kōno, two, Yamamura Shinjiro and Matsuda Takechiyo were refused re-admission to the Liberal Party and so the other six, including Miki and Kōno, 'died' a political death for the sake of these two and remained an opposition force.

The establishment of the Democratic Party of Japan and the formation of the Hatoyama cabinet were both popular events. The election in February 1955 saw a Hatoyama boom across the country, and the 120 seats grew to 185. Prime Minister Hatoyama's election commitments were to constitutional reform and the opening of negotiations with the Soviet Union. It was impossible not to feel keenly that there had been a change in the times when one saw such an overwhelming victory being achieved by someone who was openly advocating constitutional revision.

A meeting with Dr Kissinger

In July 1953, I took part in a seminar on international issues at Harvard University. I was told about the seminar by a man called Colton who was assigned to the Counter Intelligence Corps (CIC) and who often visited the Diet to gather information. Colton was a clean-cut, Harvard man with a strong sense of justice; he had no love for Prime Minster Yoshida, or for the Liberal Party, and it was this that brought us together.

To participate, I had to pass the Japan Harvard Committee English exam, and since my English was limited, I studied hard. All through the ordinary session of the Diet which began in January, I memorised words morning and evening every day just like a student studying for university entrance. Even in the corner of the Diet member's room, I sneaked a look at my word cards and opened up my English grammar study aid book. The exam was in English and there were questions on current affairs which you had to answer giving your views in English. I had taken a guess that three questions were likely to come up. The first question I prepared was on the new Far Eastern policy of the Eisenhower administration; the second was on the world economy in the aftermath of the cease-fire in the Korean war and the third was a comparative question about the American presidential system and the British parliamentary cabinet system, and the fundamentals of democracy. My linguistic skills were lacking, so I thought I would go for content.

The exam was held in the middle of February in the presence of equal numbers of American and Japanese members of the Japan Harvard Committee led by Komatsu Takashi. The question which came up was about the American presidential system. We had forty minutes to answer, and I think we were expected to write between three and five pages, but I scribbled down seven and a half pages, and gave it in without even the chance to check it over. The guess turned out well and, luckily, I passed. Among the others who were successful that time were Fujise Gorō, an NHK commentator Kaizu Yoshirō, an international lawyer, Fujimaki Shinpei, a member of the Policy Committee of the Right Socialist Party and a woman called Nakano Tsuya who was the chief clerk responsible for complaints in the Tokyo Metropolitan Government.

The seminar was attended by forty-five delegates from twenty-two countries. We were divided into three committees; in the morning we debated and in the afternoon we attended lectures by Harvard University professors and other learned Americans. Then representatives from each country made a speech. I was on the politics committee where we discussed international issues, regional problems, the principles of democracy, ethnic minorities, labour groups, pressure groups and the problems of religion.

The person assigned to look after us was an assistant professor in the politics department under the department head Dr William Greenleaf Elliot. His name was Dr Henry Kissinger. This was the start of a relationship which has lasted for more than forty years. A few years ago, at a discussion in Hawaii with Dr Kissinger on the theme of, 'A violent world', I confessed to him that I had only understood about thirty percent of what he had said at the time of the Harvard seminar and he grinned and replied, 'I had a very strong German accent then, and on top of that there were complaints that I mumbled so that I was unintelligible.' Before this seminar I was asked to 'give a public speech as representative of the Asian region'. I wrote a draft in which

Talks with Secretary of State Kissinger during the oil crisis

I spoke about conditions in Japan after the war and expressed the need for stability in the execution of politics so that Japan would avoid the path that Germany had taken under the Weimar Constitution, and I proposed the election of the Prime Minister by popular vote. This manuscript was translated into English and I practised the delivery with an American woman at Rikkyo University. The text follows below.

Present day Japan is under the Potsdam and San Francisco systems. That is to say, present day Japan is still the Japan that surrendered under the Potsdam Declaration and it is still operating under the Security Treaty System and the Peace Treaty of 1951. At the time that they were set up, these systems were constructed to fill contemporary needs. But now, when America has been betrayed so often by communism, conditions have changed and the time is ripe for the birth of a new, sovereign Japan. It is time for Japan to begin to move on from the Potsdam and San Franciso systems and head for a new horizon.

The present constitution, given to Japan by General MacArthur, has many strong points, and we must maintain the balance between pacifism, democracy, internationalism and nationalism, and the respect for human rights. But the content is not the only issue. One important strand of democracy is the way in which it is established.

This constitution was written in English by an occupying army and accepted by the people in their eagerness to regain their independence as soon as possible from that occupying army. If Lincoln's words 'Government of the people, by the people, for the people', are truths, then the Japanese constitution must be made according to the wishes of the Japanese people. If this kind of constitution can be achieved, America should rejoice with satisfaction at the birth of true democracy in Japan.

What is wanted nowadays in countries all around the world is political stability, and where a country suffers from such serious difficulties as Japan does at present, political stability cannot be assured under a parliamentary cabinet system where the assembly chooses the prime minister. Further, the functions of government in Japan have grown remarkably recently. Government has to take care of everything from day nurseries to the spraying of DDT. In particular it has to bring relief to the poor in society.

In Japan today, general elections are a frequent occurrence and parties are taken up with party politics. As a result, traditional bureaucratism is rampant and politics is in their power. In order to repair these inadequacies, I propose that we elect the prime minister by popular vote. Then we must make the separation of powers clear. The result will be a two party system, national stability and a strengthening of democracy. If the prime minister is chosen by popular vote the small parties will integrate gradually with the two big parties.

Japan needs the popular election of the prime minister in order to avoid the mistakes of Germany's Weimar Republic which gave birth to Hitler; that is to say, political confusion and instability. When we consider Japan's long feudal tradition, the severity of her excess of population and struggle for existence, and the limited nature of her territory, we cannot vouchsafe that there is not the soil for dictatorship if national irritation grows too much. Hitler under the Weimar constitution took advantage of the divisions into small parties and the political instability to abuse parliamentary politics. Japan can avoid this if she elects her prime minister by popular vote.

The audience was sizeable. I spoke slowly and clearly. They seemed to understand me and the speech received a favourable evaluation in terms of analysis and scope. Delegates from America, Germany, India and Pakistan came up to the podium and shook my hand.

The head of the faculty, professor Elliot, made copies of my speech and sent them to the State Department and to other professors at the University. Dr Elliot was a powerful figure in the American political world. He was an advisor to the State Department and a senior member of the National Security Council. Many of his pupils occupied important positions in the State Department and Defense. Under Secretary of State Robertson, who was Finance Minister Ikeda's partner in looking at Japan's defence problems, was one of them for example, and through Elliot's introduction, I met with Robertson and others.

My speech was broadcast on radio. When a party of us travelled to New York, we visited the mansion of an older woman who was one of the sponsors of the seminar. When I greeted her, the woman said, 'I've heard your voice somewhere before.' When I told her that I had made a public speech at Harvard, she nodded her approval and with a smile said, 'That's right. It was a voice with sex appeal.' It was then I learned the words 'sex appeal'.

CHAPTER SIX

HUMAN PATTERNS ON THE POLITICAL STAGE

Bandō Musha: man of spirit

Kōno Ichiro, a brilliantly sharp-witted politician, undoubtedly had intimations of the tragedies that would mark his life. He used to say he wouldn't be allowed to 'die a natural death' and that 'judgement on a politician was only decided when the lid was closed on his coffin'. The political stage is ablaze with energy and bright activity, but there is also, the darkness of the wings. I can't help but see his life as being filled with such light and shade.

Bandō Musha was a wild samurai, very simple in comparison with a court noble. Kōno had that samurai-like, unyielding attitude of mind, and I can be the same. He could be impulsive, lacking in patience, and though he was strong in battle, his failing was that he lost the wars. Let me give a few examples.

The first war was lost in June 1959. This was the time that the Kishi cabinet was restructured, when the Prime Minister pressed Kōno to accept a post. The Kishi cabinet was in trouble as a result of the departure of Ikeda Hayato, Miki Takeo and Nadao Hirokichi over the failure of the Police Duties Law. Ikeda had announced that he could not breathe the same air as Kishi, and so it seemed out of the question that he would join the new cabinet. If Kōno wouldn't accept a post, it seemed that the administration would probably fall. Kōno conferred with his senior factional supporters in the *Shunjūkai*. The leaders of the faction, especially Matsuda Takechiyo, strongly opposed Kōno's entry into the Kishi cabinet when it was teetering on the brink, so Kōno summarily declined and left for Osaka. But the dice did not roll as expected: by the time the night was out, Ikeda had joined the cabinet. Insofar as I failed to forecast such shameless behaviour on Ikeda's part, I too bore some responsibility for what happened. Perhaps it is the difference between Kanto and Kansai, or maybe it is the difference between being a military family and being in the service of the court.

With my mentor Kōno Ichiro

The second defeat was in July 1960 when the Ikeda cabinet was inaugurated and Kōno *sensei* decided to form a new party. He phoned and asked me to meet him urgently at his house. When I arrived he told me he was setting up a new party and asked me to become secretary general and help him in this venture. Though I was somewhat surprised at the suddenness of it, I said I would try to persuade the others, and I set about this in secrecy. However, with the exception of Shigemasa Seishi and Mori Kiyoshi, everyone was opposed. Afraid of the political damage that would be caused to Kōno, and convinced that we had to back off, I reconsidered my position.

Before very long I was called to the Imperial Hotel, to the room of the president of Daiei, Nagata Masakazu. Kōno *sensei*, Hagiwara Kichitarō, the president of Hokkaido Coal and Shipping Company, Kodama Yoshio, Shigemasa and Mori were there. When Kōno told them of his decision to set up a new party, Nagata was in favour, but Hagiwara and Kodama were negative about the idea. Kōno was emphatic that twenty-five people would act with him. Nagata asked my opinion. I replied honestly that about ten would join us, and of those there was a fair number who would follow only because they felt they had no option. Kōno *sensei* made a wry face.

By chance, a study session of the *Shunjūkai* was taking place at Karuizawa and the decision was taken to ask the opinion of all the members. Shigemasa, Mori and I took up position in a room in the Mikasa hotel and one by one, we questioned the members. The

125

majority were against. Everyone thought that patience was called for. When this was relayed to Kōno *sensei*, he gave us a verbal agreement not to go ahead, but publicly, he got about thirty signatures and went back to Tokyo in good spirits saying he had not given up on establishing a new party.

In the end, for form's sake, a messenger was sent to vice-president Ōno Banboku in Hakone where he was staying. Ōno, urging caution, handed over a card bearing the poem, 'Nothing is won without patience', and the new party movement was called off. Kōno *sensei* was fond of saying, 'a political party is a group enterprise and you are therefore doing well if you get ten percent of your own views adopted'. But he could be impulsive, and what he professed and what he practised were not necessarily the same.

The third lost war was in October 1964 when, on the day that the Tokyo Olympics ended, Ikeda announced that he was resigning because of ill health and asked Vice President Kawashima Shojiro[1] and Secretary General Miki Takeo to recommend a successor. Relations between Ikeda and Kōno had become extremely good by this time, and Ikeda had come to trust Kōno because of his support for the cabinet during the urgent business of organising the Olympics. On the other hand, the relationship between Ikeda and Satō Eisaku was cool.

Kōno thought that he would be named prime minister and he therefore told the members of the *Shunjūkai* that he wanted them simply to watch what was happening and to make no move. But in fact Satō, old high school friend of Ikeda and fellow disciple of Yoshida, was appointed. We were disappointed, but Kōno couldn't understand it and was devastated. In fact, although we were not aware of it, Ikeda had been coming under growing pressure starting within the financial sector but spreading to other groups, and an unofficial decision had been made on Satō two days previously. It could be said that Kōno was over-confident, but he was a fundamentally good man, and not given to doubting those he trusted.

Sixteen bouts in Japan-Soviet negotiations

'You know, Nakasone, that's it. Now there will be no more wars; there'll never be another world war.' Those were Kōno *sensei*'s first words to me when he got back from signing the joint declaration re-establishing diplomatic relations between Japan and the Soviet Union in October 1956. At the time we felt that he was inclined to make rash, dogmatic statements, but gradually his prophesies came true. It wasn't a question either of learning, or of guesswork: it was just animal intuition. It was a bit like the intuition that lets migrating birds find their nests from many hundreds of kilometres away. It was a natural talent and, in the dying days of the Yoshida administration, it enabled him to elaborate a number of scenarios with Miki Bukichi and finally to get Hatoyama appointed prime minister.

But with the exception of these times, the muse appeared to him only sporadically; he was not good at long-term planning and he lacked staying power. His was not a patient, intuitive power and he was therefore no match for Prime Minister Satō who, though muted in style, had both a keen bureaucratic insight and the systematic ability to get things done. He was routed too by Prime Minister Ikeda who, under the protection of Prime Minister Yoshida, had succeeded in putting down deep roots and building a strong political base in the financial world during his time as Finance Minister and as Minister for International Trade and Industry.

And yet, Kōno *sensei* was inimitable; a party man who derived his power from the party. He showed admirable coolness and decisiveness in his manoeuvring to get Hatoyama to go to Moscow to ensure the success of the Japan-Soviet negotiations. And during the struggle for leadership of the *Seiyūkai* immediately before the war he acted with dare-devil courage, occupying the *Seiyūkai* headquarters with labourers from the port of Yokohama in support of the Hatoyama-Kuhara alliance. The *Seiyūkai* matter was just a domestic disturbance in the party but Kōno's efforts in the matter of the Japan-Soviet negotiations were made in the national interest and out of friendship for Hatoyama.

In the final stages of the Japan-Soviet Fishery talks which had begun on April 29, 1956 as a part of the Japan-Soviet negotiations, Kōno *sensei* took part in talks with President Nikolai Bulganin. At this meeting, Kōno took an unexpected step which was later to invite suspicion and to be attacked as, 'Kōno selling territory for fish'. He left his advisor from the Foreign Office, councillor Niizeki Kinya, at the door of the Kremlin, and met for talks with President Bulganin without an interpreter from the Japanese side. The Soviet interpreter at this meeting attested:

> As the talks were drawing to a close, Mr Kōno suddenly put forward a suggestion. He requested that the Soviets should propose that, "If negotiations for restoration of diplomatic relations are not entered into

in the future, the fisheries agreement will also be void." Everyone was surprised. Even President Bulganin did not understand Kōno's reasons for making this request.

In the NHK feature, 'Japan-Soviet Negotiations', shown in the summer of 1991, both the interpreter, and the Ambassador to Japan, Troyanousky, gave the same evidence.

But this was very much a last resort for Kōno. It was a drama that came about as a result of Prime Minister Hatoyama's insistence that he himself should risk both his political life, and his physical safety, to go to the Soviet Union and see negotiations concluded satisfactorily. In the light of the situation in Tokyo, where both Foreign Minister Shigemitsu and the majority of the Diet members from the old Liberal Party were opposed, Kōno believed that unless the Soviet side engaged in this subterfuge, it would be impossible to reopen the negotiations to restore diplomatic relations and to send Hatoyama to Moscow.

It was a somewhat surprised President Bulganin who, when he understood this reasoning, complied. The Japan-Soviet Fishery Agreement signed on 14 May, five days after the talks ended, stated, 'The Agreement will go into effect either when diplomatic relations are restored between Japan and the Soviet Union, or, when a Peace Treaty is concluded.'

Negotiations to restore diplomatic relations shifted from London to Moscow and were reopened on 31 July with Foreign Minister Shigemitsu having full plenipotentiary powers to negotiate for Japan. The Soviets were unbending and there was no progress until finally, Shigemitsu asked for directions from Tokyo on his proposal to reach an agreement on the basis of restoration of just the two islands of Habomai and Shikotan. However no one in Tokyo would agree to this and instructions were sent to Moscow to refrain from entering into such an agreement.

Thus, Hatoyama sent a five-clause letter to President Bulganin saying they should leave the territorial issue for further consideration and announce the restoration of diplomatic relations. President Bulganin's reply agreeing to the reopening of negotiations was delivered on 12 September, and mutual consent to a joint declaration was reached during Prime Minister Hatoyama's visit to the Soviet Union on 12 October. Kōno, who had accompanied Hatoyama, met three times with First Secretary Nikita Khrushev for behind-the-scenes negotiations leading to this joint declaration.

The restoration of diplomatic relations secured the return to Japan of detainees and war criminals and facilitated Japan's entry into the United Nations. This broadened Japan's international sphere of action and became one of the foundation stones of Japan's subsequent development. It bore fruit in terms of results, and that is what counts in politics. However, there was strong criticism from financiers and journalists, most of whom owed their positions to the influence of the Yoshida mainstream, and Kōno's distinguished service was not always fairly evaluated at the time. However, his abilities were fearsome.

Certainly, it was not normal diplomatic practice to march into the Kremlin alone, without an interpreter, and to enter into talks with only an interpreter from the opposite side, and he was properly criticised for it. Nevertheless, he put his political life on the line, assumed responsibility and acted decisively. Had he failed, he would have been damned as a politician, but as he more than achieved his objective, ought not his political decisiveness and his success be given proper recognition? It is the fate of politicians to stake everything on a game of chance.

Another of his characteristics was his ability to carry out policies on behalf of the masses. Kōno, party politician and man of the world, had a talent for picking up on the demands of the masses and touching people's hearts.

When the Hatoyama Cabinet was formed, Kōno set out policies that were diametrically opposed to the policies of Prime Minister Yoshida with his aristocratic interests and bureaucratic self-righteousness. He began with things that were very visible such as dispensing with official ministerial residences, reducing police escorts and abolishing taxes on carts and bicycles. These policies aroused admiration for Hatoyama as a politician of the people and were the source of the Hatoyama boom.

During the Ikeda Cabinet too, Kōno acted in the interest of the masses. When it snowed heavily in Hokuriku he would pull on boots and head for Niigata and would mobilise the Self Defence Forces to shovel snow. When there were water shortages in Tokyo, he immediately pulled water from the Tonegawa in Saitama and loosened the limits on water usage in the capital. When a request was made for an international conference centre to fight land subsidence in Kyoto, it was built immediately. As the Olympics approached, by having construction workers toiling day and night, he made sure that all the necessary facilities were ready in time.

The people, who were tired of bureaucratic politics, were refreshed by Kōno's amazing ability to get things done. He commonly came top in opinion polls for 'favourite politician' and 'next candidate for prime minister'. People could see very clearly the difference between party politicians and politicians of bureaucratic extraction. There is no doubt that Kōno meant to follow in the footsteps of Prime Minister Hara Kei who was venerated as a politician of the people and the foremost political strong man since the Meiji period. Prime Minister Hara was brought down by terrorism, and forebodings of that sort may at times have crossed Kōno's mind too.

Kōno's achievements were of historic significance, but there was one thing he didn't achieve which he had secretly set his heart on: the normalisation of relations with China. There were senior people around Kōno, people such as Matsumura Kenzo and Takasaki Tatsunosuke, who were in the vanguard in the normalisation of Sino-Japanese relations. I believe that watching them, Kōno, decided in his heart, that he would one day sort out this problem himself. At the time, therefore, Kōno said not a word about either the China problem or the Taiwan problem, and this was almost certainly to keep his hands free to do something in the future.

Yoshida Shigeru and Kōno Ichiro

I think often about Kōno Ichiro the man. Why did a man with such insight, experience and ability to achieve things fail, and ultimately become neither prime minister nor party president? If one looks at his life history, there are very many scenes where he is running for all he is worth, not looking back, expending great effort, but to little effect.

His relationships with Prime Minister Yoshida and Prime Minister Kishi, for example, were like that. Both men assumed the office of Prime Minister as a result of Kōno's influential backing. In Yoshida's case, when Hatoyama was purged as president of the Liberal Party, it was Kōno, Hatoyama's advisor and secretary general of the party, acting under the guidance of Matsuno Tsuruhei, who wooed Yoshida, and Yoshida took office as the next president. In 1951, directly after he was depurged, Kōno met with Yoshida to present his compliments and they were very warm toward one another, but before very long he became resentful of Yoshida's complacency and cronyism, and made desperate efforts to bring Yoshida down.

Kishi, too, won political power as a result of strong support from Kōno. In that election for president I, as an ex-soldier, had certain things to consider, and I refused Kōno's request to support Kishi and voted instead for Ishibashi Tanzan. This insubordination actually required considerable determination since Kōno was very serious about recommending Kishi, and the entire membership of the Kōno faction was going around backing him. However when Kōno became dissatisfied with the policies of the Kishi cabinet, the relationship quickly deteriorated, and as a result, Ikeda Hayato replaced him as Kishi's successor.

It has a certain drama that the king-maker was never made king; it also has an element of tragedy. Kōno was described variously as able, perceptive, over-confident, a charlatan, simple, open, bashful, quarrelsome, arrogant and easily moved to tears. But the only way to appreciate the true worth of the man Kōno, was to meet him in the flesh and become acquainted with his idiosyncrasies. He defended his friends to the hilt and treated them with affection; toward his enemies he was implacable. Among powerful provincial families there was, traditionally, a particular creed of clannishness, and it could easily happen that, once you got caught up in this, individuals vanished, their reality obscured by solidarity and fellowship; friends could do no wrong and enemies no right.

I was always most careful about this because of the danger that the group would be prone to lose its intellectual rigour, and that policy and theory would be neglected for the sake of love and duty. In short, I chose not to be sucked in by Kōno's 'skinship'. For example when I visited the Kōno house in the morning, I would habitually be invited to eat with the family. But I always replied, 'I will wait in the reception room', and intentionally established a certain distance. Kōno himself, I am sure, thought me a stickler for rules and unable to blend in.

Kōno Ichiro, the man, was a supremely attractive being, full of warmth and human kindness. He was blessed in abundance with those things in which I, as a politician, was lacking and partly because I wanted to learn these things, I became a part of the Kōno faction. He walked round-shouldered, with a slouch, and when he came close, he would suddenly fix his eyes on your face. When you met him in the corridors of the Diet, you were conscious of a pressure in the air, but when he was in Japanese dress, at home with his family, or travelling, he was a gentleman and bashful. The fact that he was punctilious and a bit of a dandy, is surprisingly little known.

When he visited a barber he would always have his nails manicured. The reason he gave was that he was embarrassed by the state of his hands when shaking hands with VIPs abroad. It would seem that on one particular occasion when he was in Hollywood and took the soft, clean hand of the actress Deborah Kerr in his, his heart froze. From then on, apparently, it had become a matter of principle with him that politicians must keep their fingers clean.

Something called the 'Tuxedo club' was formed, sponsored by Nagata and Hagiwara. When one travelled abroad, a tuxedo was necessary. Large sums were laid out to have them made, and then, at that time, there was no chance to wear them in Japan when you had them. This was a waste so, once a month, we met as couples for dinner in the Imperial Hotel wearing black tie. About fifteen couples including Higashikuni Moriatsu and Funabashi Seiichi used to meet, but it was Kōno *sensei* who wore the finest clothes and whose hair was just so.

He was bold and obstinate. The obverse of this was the attention to detail that came from a keen insight into human nature. His long-time secretary, Ishikawa Tatsuo told of the following episode. Every month, Ishikawa would collect cash of ¥300,000 or ¥400,000 for expenses and keep exact accounts right down to details of newspapers bought whilst travelling and coffee and ice cream purchased on trains. On one occasion, Kōno told him, 'Make a disbursement of 10,000 yen and use it for expenses', since, 'When you keep exact records, there will inevitably be things that you will have to pay for yourself out of your own pocket, and it isn't right that you should be liable for that portion. Therefore, you must keep 10,000 yen extra on one side.'

When he handed over political funds to Diet men he always added: 'It is a shame that politicians' wives are kept working so hard. Use this to buy some shoes or a kimono neckband for your wife.' You have to hand it to the old politicians: he was probably imitating what Hara Kei used to do.

They say that godsends don't come in twos, and that really is true: when you get several at once their peculiar characteristics cancel one another out and you end up with an ordinary, average person. Kōno was able to overcome this. But, given his character, if he ever had become prime minister, though he could probably have done the job, there would have been clashes everywhere, and he wouldn't have lasted long. Kōno didn't engage in public office, so much as he represented public opinion in an oppositional capacity. He is better remembered as a party politician who resisted power.

In this sense Yoshida Shigeru, the ex-bureaucrat, and Kōno Ichiro, the party man, were both unparalleled prototypes of the post-war politician. Miki Bukichi was pre-eminent as a party politician who generated storms, but in terms of political richness over a whole lifetime Kōno was undoubtedly number one.

At the congratulatory party given when Kōno received the continuous long-service commendation, Prime Minister Ikeda made this address. 'When Kōno first stood as a candidate in 1932, he did not have official recognition. When he ran for a second time in 1936, he did so from the police station, where he was being held for electoral violations. In 1937, he ran, again without official sanction. During the war he was without the recommendation of the Imperial Rule Assistance Association. During the Occupation he was imprisoned for contravention of the public office purge directive. In 1952, when the purge was lifted, Mr Yoshida and I expelled him, and in 1954, he was expelled again.' Truly his was an heroic political career.

Then finally, on his return from a national speaking tour for the Upper House election, he suffered a ruptured aneurysm of the abdominal artery and died just two days later. It was the kind of tough political career that makes you want to bury your head in your hands. Two days before his death Kōno said three things to the executive of the Kōno faction. Though he didn't know it, it was to become his testament.

The first thing he said was: 'Don't be carried away by the party. A political party is a gathering of many people: it will do wrong and misguided things. Consequently you must not give blind obedience to party decisions. We have a responsibility as politicians to the nation. When we think the party is in error, we must put the party right.'

The second was: 'Politicians mustn't operate on the basis of profit and loss. We receive an annual allowance from taxes. Merchants work for profit and that is natural, but we live on our annual allowance. We mustn't operate for gain.'

The third thing he said was: 'Let us work from a national perspective. Let politicians always take the broad view and consider Japan as a whole when they act. Do not be swayed by the perverse demands of local pressure groups.'

This was 6 July 1965. Ordinarily he told the newly admitted Diet members when they came to pay their respects: 'A politician must not be afraid to make enemies', 'For a politician, there is no title more honourable than Member of the Lower House' and, 'A politician must always be able to feel at ease without a master'. Ten thousand people crowded Kōno's funeral service. Truly, with the closing of the coffin judgement was finally passed and he may rest in peace.

Sarcasm and the venerable
Miki Bukichi

When we look back over the period from the founding of the Democratic Party of Japan to Japan's entry into the United Nations, we can see what we owe to Hatoyama Ichiro's disposition, to Miki Bukichi's self-sacrifice and powers of persuasion, to Ōno Banboku's tolerance, to Kōno Ichiro's intensity, to Ōgata Taketora's breadth of vision, and to Kishi Nobusuke's ability to plan. Above all, Miki Bukichi's goals, his clever fighting strategy, his final, unselfish effort gave us an unforgettable lesson and left a deep and lasting impression.

Even political reform, a topic of such interest now, would not have come to this pass if Miki had been here. He had an amazing ability to cause waves in order to achieve his ultimate goals. He set his sights on particular people in the party, sometimes he would flatter and sometimes he would threaten, and he would mobilise anyone who could play a part. In comparison, today's politicians are hide-bound by rules and bureaucracy. They lack the capacity to mobilise people or to whip up a storm.

Miki wore traditional Japanese dress of *hakama* with *zoori* and hobbled along the red carpet of the Diet with a stick. If you crossed Yoshida or Kōno Ichiro in the corridors of the Diet, you felt a surge of wind pressure as if an express train were passing through. As for this tottery old man, there was something weird about his eyes. When he chanced upon someone, they would open suddenly and he would pierce them with his penetrating gaze. There was no sense of pressure but, momentarily, it was as if there had been a surge of electricity.

In September 1954, we were busy bringing down the Yoshida cabinet. In order to deal with the Liberal Party's loss of more than half its seats in the election, talks were being held between Prime Minister Yoshida and Progressive Party president Shigemitsu. Suddenly, this 'general of the eight samurai' burst into the Progressive Party ante-room where we young Diet men were waiting, and brandished his stick.

He turned his usual glare on us, fired off this one shot and wandered out. 'What a sloppy bunch you lot are in the Progressive Party. You have this splendid opportunity to beat Yoshida in the election and get him out. Why don't you put your backs into it? What do you young Turks think you are doing?' I was conscious of what a patriot he was.

Miki Bukichi

It was Miki who was the most encouraging and supportive when I was pushing for a nuclear power policy both in the Progressive Party and subsequently the Democratic Party. He said with a grin, 'What you are doing will have an unimaginable impact on the future of Japan. I have had dealings in mining and been called a miner, and I have an eye for these things. I used to joke that 'Miki' would join 'Mitsui', 'Mitsubishi' as the *zaibatsu* in Japan and that hasn't happened yet.'

Whilst he was pushing for the merger of the conservative parties, he made a point of showing up at any sinister-looking gathering of the party's Diet members and inviting the unruly groups out to a restaurant to work on them. I was truly amazed at just how whole-heartedly he strove to achieve his aims, and how close he worked himself to his physical limit.

I, too, was against the merger of the conservatives in the beginning. I felt it would lead to upheaval and that the political confusion would be prolonged. If the conservatives formed themselves into one party and the government lost power to the opposition in an election, there would be a socialist administration. The Socialist party then was a Marxist, labour-farmer Socialist party dominated by the left-wing, and I felt the necessity for the sort of neutral zone that would result from multiple parties. It was against this sort of atmosphere that Miki worked so hard to persuade us. Miki called me, along with Ishida Hakuei, Kawasaki Hideji, Kuraishi Tadao, Sakurauchi Yoshio and others to Akasaka, and spoke with spittle

135

flying. He knew that he was ill, and it even occurred to me from his impatience for the conservative merger, that he was, deep down, confusing the political life of the country with his own physiological life span. Even so, I was moved by his almost unearthly powers of persuasion.

The next objective was to achieve membership of the United Nations. For this, the stable political situation that would result from a conservative merger, was indispensable, and I came to believe that there was nothing for it but to fall in with Miki. The inaugural meeting of the new party was just like a piece of marquetry work. There was a feeling among the young party members that they had been pulled around in a high-handed way by Miki and led into it willy-nilly. There was also nostalgia for the old home. However, once the new party was formed, right then and there, everyone jumped into action. But I guess that's youth for you.

The Japan-Soviet negotiations of the Hatoyama Cabinet were conducted with great care in order to avoid creating any misunderstanding on the part of America. It seems that Iwabuchi Tatsuo probably brought Secretary of State Dulles' attitude to Miki's attention. Miki's speech to the inaugural meeting of the new party tells us something about him. It included these words: 'Our success in rallying conservative power here today defies description. It is something for which the Japanese people who desired it so fervently and the people of the family of free nations that account for the majority of the world population should offer mutual congratulations.' I found the extent of this old man's involvement remarkable.

When Miki came to meetings he would sit very still, waiting, with his hands folded on top of his stick and his head on his hands, looking just about alive. Even when he mounted the platform, for a while, he would say nothing. He would look from right to left around the audience and quietly, gradually his mouth would begin to move. Even so, the audience, knowing a famous politician was before them, would be silent. Then suddenly a stream of witticisms would be let fly. When he made attacking speeches, the old man, whose very breath was faint would become animated and his body would seem to be about to emit flames. Sometimes he would tease, sometimes lavish praise, and then at the end, abruptly, he would knock you over the edge, down into the abyss. The audience moved their bodies as one with Miki, shifting to left and right, completely bewitched. It was just like witchcraft.

In his last year it is probable that he knew he was near death. He used Kōno, Kishi and others as his hands and feet and, having prevailed on the veteran big shots Ōno and Ōgata and added them to the battle line, he succeeded in the once-in-a-lifetime job of merging the conservative parties and, in doing so, establishing the basis for conservative stability. No one else could have done it.

Helping the course of 'Love in Parliament'

Every morning the sound of ritual clapping could be heard from someone in the inner courtyard as he turned to face the sun. It was Arafune Seijurō. This noise acted as the reveille for the Diet members lodgings in Kudan, near Yasukuni Shrine. Before long we could hear Arafune's voice calling up his constituents. This too was a daily routine.

The Diet lodgings were built in 1952 and I took a room there. It was not like the high-class apartment style of today, but a plain, wooden, two-storey, building. My room was on the ground floor. Above, and to the right, on the second floor, was Yamanaka Sadanori. I had a puppy and Yamanaka had a little monkey and our wives used to joke that that was why we were always at loggerheads.[2] Nikaidō Susumu and Setoyama Mitsuo lived on the ground floor and all our children played nicely together in each others apartments. Arafune's wife would bath my daughter and later, my daughter baby-sat for Tamura Hajime's children. We men, including people like Sakata Michio and Ezaki Masumi, fraternised at the bath house.

It was about that time that the good news came that a beauty parlour in Chikujō, Hachibancho in Ushigome, which belonged to one of my supporters, had developed an effective hair restorer. We were all worried about having things done to our hair so I went along first to investigate. It seemed quite good so we dragged along Sonoda Tadashi and had him treated, but he complained that it was totally useless.

Before we moved into the Diet members lodgings I used to stay in a room at the old First Diet Members Lodge, in Building 6, with a blanket and an electric ring on which I cooked for myself. It was the sort of building that was used during the war as a billet for soldiers or as a military hospital, and I cooked rice in an army canteen, made *miso* soup and broiled sardines in a small, anodised aluminium pot and drank Japanese *shōchū* wine.

The March Doll's Festival with our second daughter, Mieko

From the day I entered parliament I almost always wore a black necktie because I felt that Japan under the Occupation was in a state of mourning. Looking back now this might seem a little affected but it was very straightforward. The Kyoto representative, Ogawa Heiji, thought it would be clever to give me a western army tie and I gave it to a sympathiser in my constituency.

At the end of 1949, a number of objects that didn't seem to be the sort of thing for an office: a dresser, small boxes and a trunk, had started to pile up in Sonoda's room on the ground floor of the same building. I thought that they were things he was looking after for a supporter but he confided that he was going to live with the Labour-Farmer Party (*Ronōto*) Diet member, Matsutani Tenkōkō.

Sonoda had a wife and two children, and he and Miss Matsutani were at opposite poles both ideologically and politically. Matsutani's father was naturally strongly opposed. Nevertheless, Sonoda said he was going to leave his wife and that Matsutani would leave home. When I heard this heroic decision I wished them luck saying, 'If two politicians have taken responsibility and have made up their minds to that extent, then so be it'.

At early dawn on 11 December, Mastutani escaped from her father and reported this fact to her late mother's grave, then she sought refuge with Mr and Mrs Yokota Tadao, their go-between. Only Kawasaki Hidekazu, Sakurauchi Yoshio, Shiikuma Saburo and ten or so friends and school friends of Matsutani attended the ceremony, but in fact, it was a dignified affair. There was an attack in the evening papers on what they were calling, 'Love in Parliament'. I helped them to escape. Secretly, I got a room for them at a Japanese inn belonging to relations of mine in Ikaho hot springs and, suspecting that they would be discovered if they boarded a train in Ueno, I took them to Omiya by car and put them on the train there.

This shocking marriage was much talked about in the sense that human love and human reality had broken the bounds of politics. It was my belief that the essential thing was to pursue reality and not betray it.

Tenkōko served her husband sincerely; when she first went to his constituency, Kumamoto, she said, ' I am a sinful woman. I will not come to the constituency unless the supporters can forgive me,' and she was careful to lodge outside the prefecture and not to step foot inside the constituency until she received an invitation from the supporters club. With this kind of attitude, she soon won great popularity in the district and helped her husband to success.

At about the time I moved to the Diet member's lodgings, draught beer hit the market. I fancied a drink in Ueno on my way back from Takasaki but having taken stock of my financial situation I desisted and went home with blocks of chocolate for my three children.

An argument for the public election of the prime minister

[Prime ministers and lovers are a
matter of individual choice]

On 13 April 1956, a 'song festival for constitutional revision' was performed at the Takarazuka theatre, sponsored by the Diet Members League for Drafting an Independent Constitution. I planned the concert, wrote the lyrics to the 'constitution' song and got Akemoto Kyōsei to set it to music. We did not have a venue and I was racking my brains when someone whispered in my ear, 'Kobayashi Ichizō at the Tōhō is a man of discernment and courage, and is public spirited so why don't you go all out for it and see him.'

I got an introduction from Takasaki Tatsunosuke and called on Kobayashi at his home in Takarazuka. I seem to remember meeting Harada Ken there when he had yet to become a Diet member. When I had finished my explanation, Kobayashi said, 'Right. I will lend you the Takarazuka Theatre free of charge'.

Emboldened, and afraid that no one would turn up if there were no attractions, I got the Takarazuka's Amatsu Otome to perform her Chinese lion dance. In addition, we prevailed on Kawakami Yasuko and Funakoshi Eiji from the Daiei Movie Company; Takarada Akira from Tōhō, and Kagurazaka Ukiko and Miura Kōichi from Victor to perform for us and the concert sold out. The constitution song itself was sung by the 'Aunty of song', Anzai Aiko.

> Ah, defeated in war and occupied by enemy soldiers,
> Coerced by an Occupation constitution on the pretext of pacifist democracy,
> The plan was to enervate our native land.
> The war had been over for half a year.
>
> Ten long years drag by, but now freedom returns,
> We must make our own constitution to build the foundations of our country,
> If we fulfil our historic duty
> The decision will swell our hearts.

This song was put out by Victor as a track on the B-side of the record 'Songs for National Independence' and I received more than 3,000 yen in royalties.

When the Constitutional Research Board was set up by the Kishi Cabinet, I immediately became a member and participated in its deliberations until it made its final report in 1964. On Professor Yabe Teiichi's recommendation, I took on Kamiwada Yoshihiko, a younger graduate of my own *alma mater*, Takasaki Middle School to help me with my work on constitutional reform When Kamiwada married one of the women involved in the movement for drafting an independent constitution, a talented graduate of Tokyo Women's University, I acted as go-between. Strangely enough, the connection deepened.

Until then I had gone at the question of constitutional revision like a dog with a bone, but with the Security Treaty, and the related Anpō riots and so on, even I began to reflect deeply on the issue. Before and during the war, people's freedom had been grossly restricted and they had suffered greatly. Under the new constitution, equality had been achieved between men and women and the people had finally acquired freedom. They were then frantic lest they should deprived of this good fortune. Such were the walls and bed-rock of civil society.

As a naval officer, a bureaucrat and a politician, I had always been on the side of the rulers and had not been accustomed to take account of the feelings of the ruled. I realised that, with whatever good intentions we professed to be defending freedom, democracy or human rights, the people were afraid and had no wish to shift from their present state. Such reflections caused me to change the position I had held up to then, and to spell out some new ideas. 1. To work to achieve common agreement among the leading political parties and to move forward through co-operative action. 2. To restrict reform to only those things which would be likely to be welcomed by the majority of the electorate. 3.To have the flexibility to proceed not all at once, but step by step.

One reform that I insisted upon as something the majority of the people would welcome, was the election of the prime minister by public vote. The first constitutional reform would address only this issue and would bring in public polling. A wide ranging debate ensued.

In the academic world, opponents included professor Yoshimura Tadashi of Waseda University and professor Tabata Shinobu of Dōshisha University, whilst among the supporters were Ukai Nobunari, President of International Christian University and Ko-bayashi Shōzō a professor at Hōsei. Professor Tsuji Kiyoaki of Tokyo University recognised the sense of such a move but, 'doubted whether there was such urgent necessity for it to be done immediately that it necessitated such drastic action as constitutional reform.' Anything which would entail constitutional reform was anathema to left-wing scholars, irrespective of the fine detail.

Subsequently Shōriki Matsutaro, Takasaki Tatsunosuke, Miyazawa Taneo and others secured the participation of a number of members of both Upper and Lower Houses and formed the 'Prime Ministerial Electoral System Study Group' to study the issue and to take practical action. In the Autumn of 1961, at a Japanese restaurant called Hikaritei in Shinanomachi, I met with these three senior colleagues and with two Socialist party members who were in favour of public elections, Sasaki Kōzō and Yamamoto Koichi, and we discussed ways forward. There were a fair number of people within the Socialist Party who were in favour of this particular reform, but they remained wary of our interfering in other areas and about whether constitutional reform could be limited to this one area.

Organisations sprang up one after the other. There was 'Prime Ministerial Public Election Press Study Group,' consisting predominantly of journalists and sponsored by Miyazaki Yoshimasa and Wakamiya Kotarō. There were those set up by students of Tokyo, Hōsei, Keiō, Chuō and Takushoku Universities and so on such as the 'Prime Ministerial Public Election System Student Study Group' and the 'Prime Ministerial Public Election System Combined High Schools Study Group'. A supporters group was formed in the financial world with such elders as Matsunaga Yasusaemon and Imazato Hiroki at the heart of it. Even within the leadership of the labour groups, people began to emerge who supported the idea of public election of the prime minister, people like Ōta Kaoru, President of Sōhyō, and Takita Minoru, Chairman of Dōmei.

At the same time as these various Diet member, journalist and student supporting organisations were being formed, I was getting a national movement off the ground to erect bill boards with the slogan 'Let's choose the prime minister by popular vote.' These billboards were about two-thirds the height of a telegraph pole and the slogan was written in white letters of fifty centimetres square on a dark blue background. I made pilgrimages all over telling people, 'Prime ministers and lovers are a matter for individual choice.'

Matsumura Kenzō declared that, 'politics is deeply emotional' and indeed it was as if something that had been sleeping in the hearts of the people had come awake; a new beat had begun and there was of feeling of vitality regained. In local assemblies all around the country, decisions were passed pushing for public elections at an early date. Developments thereafter were unsatisfactory however. First of all, Prime Minister Ikeda opposed constitutional reform, and then more

Erecting billboards across the country
in support of popular election of the
prime minister

142

cold water was poured on the movement by the next administration, the Satō Cabinet, which announced that it would not touch the constitution during its lifetime. During my own period as prime minister I had the major business of administrative reform to contend with and I announced, 'I will not put constitutional revision into the political timetable'. My conviction that there must be a proper re-examination of the constitution was not extinguished, and I regret deeply that I side-stepped it politically.

On September 19, 1983, twenty-seven years after the release of the 'constitutional reform song', and when I was prime minister, a Socialist Party member of the Lower House Budget Committee, Ishibashi Masashi, used that platform to declare all-out political war and challenge me in committee. It was a long-standing fundamental dispute between fellow party leaders about defence. It had been around since Ashida Hitoshi disputed defence with Prime Minister Yoshida and Kōno Ichiro confronted Yoshida over the handling of the GARIOA-EROA funds,[3] and the old atmosphere boiled up.

In the middle of his question, Ishibashi suddenly brought up the fifth verse of the constitutional reform song.

> While this constitution remains, unconditional surrender persists,
> Defending the MacArthur constitution, we are servants of the Commander in Chief,
> The destiny of our fatherland is to be a colony
> and we will lack the spirit to make the country prosperous.

Ishibashi pressed me to say whether I would defend or criticise the constitution. For a moment I was caught off my guard and then suddenly, I remembered the fourth verse and counter-attacked.

> Loving our country sincerely, we must ourselves stand forth and defend it,
> We must carve our constitution on freedom and democratic peace.
> Keeping up with the nuclear age we shall carve too the ideals of the country.

At this, everyone there laughed and no further response was necessary.

In the present era we must change our style from Max Weber's, 'Nation of reputable party men' to that of 'Nation by plebiscite' in a high information society. Prefectural governors and mayors of cities, towns and villages are publicly elected by direct vote and the stability we see there suggests that public election of the prime minister would not be impossible and would, moreover, be more in keeping with the doctrine of democratic sovereignty.

In recent times there have been calls for political reform through the introduction of a small district electoral system for the Lower House in order to eradicate the evils of factional politics and foster two strong parties. This would be one way, but whatever system we have will have its pros and cons. If we are thinking about ways to eliminate political corruption, and promote the activities of the two big parties so that transfer of power becomes possible, then public election of the prime minister is a quicker way than the small electoral system and more in tune with public opinion. I would like to see a broad debate on whether the people would prefer the small electoral system or the public election of the prime minister.

The participation of the Self Defence Forces in the United Nations has become the focus of the present day constitutional problems of Japan. I think that the time has come when, without committing ourselves in any way to constitutional reform, we should set up a 'Special Investigatory Committee for Constitutional Issues' in the cabinet, disinter all constitutional issues, and place them in the public arena where they belong.

CHAPTER SEVEN

BECOMING A MINISTER OF STATE

First Cabinet post as Director of the Science and Technology Agency

On 18 June 1959, I was given my first cabinet post as Minister of State and Director of the Science and Technology Agency in the Kishi Administration. At the same time I became the chairman of the Committee for Nuclear Power. When I came into the presence of the Emperor Showa, and his majesty said, 'Thank you for assuming this responsibility', I felt braced for what was to come.

Prime Minister Kishi's aim when he was re-elected was the revision of the Security Treaty with America, and when he remodelled his cabinet, he tried to have Kōno Ichiro take up a senior ministerial position. In a bid to remove Satō from the post of Finance Minister, Kōno countered by making it a condition of his acceptance that the whole cabinet, except for Foreign Minister Fujiyama, be changed. However, Kishi eventually refused and the Kōno faction became anti-mainstream. When I was asked, nevertheless, to join the cabinet, Kōno said, 'You have your constituency to consider so don't say anything, just take it.' I was forty-one.

The first Director of the Science and Technology Agency had been Shōriki Matsutaro, and the fourth, Takasaki Tatsunosuke. Both were well-respected incumbents and I felt it a privilege to serve after them. Since the end of the war I had consistently promoted science and technology and the development of a nuclear power policy, and my appointment to this post was like coming home. At that time I used to say, 'The second half of the 20th century belongs to the imaginers', and I travelled to various areas making speeches saying, 'The imaginers are those people who can combine vision with technology. Come on youth and be imaginers.'

In October 1957, the Soviet Union launched the first man-made satellite, Sputnik One. From that point, world interest shifted from nuclear power to space science and technology, and the United States and the Soviet Union threw themselves into a furious race. Even then, the academic world in Japan, fearful of the prospect of military usage, had what almost amounted to a taboo about calling for the development of space science and technology. Professor Itogawa Hideo of Tokyo University was studying the development of what were then very elementary rockets known as 'pencil rockets', but the learned institutions looked askance and development of space science and technology stalled.

Soon after I took up office, on July 10, 1959, I formed a Preparatory Committee for the Promotion of Space Science and Technology. Dr Kaneshige Kankurō, President of the Science Council of Japan, Wadachi Kiyō, Director of the Weather Bureau, Fukui Nobuo, Director of the Tokyo University Aviation Research Centre, Horikoshi Teizō, Secretary General of the Federation of Economic Organisations (*Keidanren*), and Itogawa were among the fifteen members. On 4 February, the following year, the committee put together an interim plan for space science and technology development. When the plan

Putting on a morning suit for my first
appointment to the cabinet

was published, the press once again made a fuss, and when I said, 'At any rate we will get a satellite bearing the Japanese flag into orbit', the left decided this would be 'developing rocket weaponry' and opposed it. However, in the end, on 16 May 1960, after a number of preparatory stages, a Space Development Inquiry Commission was set up in the Prime Minister's Office, and before long we got one launched.

The second project we undertook was to determine our policy toward typhoon research. On September 26, 1959, a typhoon in Ise Bay resulted in unprecedented disaster with over 5,000 people killed in the Tōkai district. I immediately set up a special Typhoon Scientific Policy Committee and undertook a variety of measures to ascertain the scientific character of typhoons and to report and interpret weather forecasts accurately.

An American military plane flew in the eye of the storm and sent back weather reports for us but Japanese aircraft were incapable of performing such functions. Straight away we gave concrete form to a budget guarantee to enable direct observation by Japanese aircraft of the eye of the storm. We readied personnel, increased the number of ocean observation ships and fixed observation points, and set up a system of prompt reporting using radio and television. I also encouraged research into man-made rain as one link in understanding the structure of typhoons. The question of whether it might be possible to divert a typhoon from its path by scientific methods was a matter of great concern and interest to me. Unfortunately, that question remains unresolved.

I asked researchers in the Science and Technology Agency and experts in government and private organisations how far world science and technology would advance by the year 2,000. The scope of their inquiries ranged from space through to transportation, agriculture and biotechnology and the results were compiled into a book called, *Steps to the Twenty-first Century*. This book, which began with, ' The Microscopic World in the Palm of our Hands', and ended with, 'Embracing an Infinite Space', addressed issues such as the electronic brain, organ donation, the creation of substances, solar power and peaceful coexistence. When I look back at it now, almost everything in it has been achieved already. Progress in the fields of computers and high-tech has already exceeded predictions.

In his ceremonial address on the occasion of the opening ceremony of the Fifth National Diet in March 1949, Shidehara, the Speaker of the Lower House, called for the refurbishment of a totally

Making a reply in the Lower House Budget Committee as Director General of the Science and Technology Agency

anomalous science and technology policy. These words were the testament of a senior politician who had dispassionately observed the weak points of Japan before and during the war and, at the time, I was very moved by them.

Even the President of Tokyo University, Kaya Seiji, once said to me, 'American and European science and technology have brought forth flowers rooted in the soil, but Japan does no more than put the cut flowers in a vase and enjoy them'. Japan is known as a major world economic power, but there is work to be done before we can be called a major world science and technology power.

Diary of the 1960 Security Treaty Riots

May 25, Wednesday
Announcement toward the end of the cabinet council meeting.

1. This important announcement to be secret. From Prime Minster Kishi down, everyone nervous. Finance Minister Satō stared. He probably expected calls for a general resignation.

2. At present political stability is a big topic. 19 June, the day that the new Security Treaty will automatically come into force is a bad day because it is the same day that President Eisenhower arrives. We will fall between two stools. We must postpone the visit by the President of the U.S.A. now, whilst there is time.
3. There is no absolute guarantee of the safety of the American President and the Emperor. If anything were to happen it would have an enormous impact on American-Japanese relations.
4. We must not involve the Emperor in the whirlpools of political battles such as this. We must have him there, symbolic and transcendental. All the Cabinet Ministers listened carefully. The Prime Minister answered that the issue was important and he could recognise the need to consider what I had said, that he would think seriously about it.

May 27, Friday
Was surprised to see in the evening paper that five ministers, Prime Minister Kishi, Foreign Minister Fujiyama, Finance Minister Satō, Minister of International Trade and Industry Ikeda and Deputy Prime Minister Masutani had made a decision on the visit to Japan by the President of America. When I found that the cabinet members responsible for public security, Minister of Justice, Ino, and the head of the National Public Safety Commission, Ishiwara, were not included, I inferred that it was a quick political decision encouraged by Yoshida to whom Finance Minister Satō had spoken by telephone in Washington. Unbelievably worried.

May 28, Saturday
Called the chief of the guards section of the Metropolitan Police Department to the room of the chief of the Science and Technology Agency in the Prime Minister's residence and asked him about the deployment of guards at Haneda airport and in the vicinity of the American Embassy. He was not confident.

1. The exits and roads from Haneda are narrow and therefore very dangerous. [There was no highway at this time.] It would be difficult because it is a factory belt to stop traffic.
2. If 2,000 people were to sit down in front of the American Embassy [main entrance] there would be problems. It would take more than an hour to remove them.

May 30, Monday

Noon, met with Economic Planning Agency Director, Kanno and Transport Minister Narahashi. Talked to them about the significance of the presidential visit to Japan and related the views of the authorities concerned. Showed them a map of the road situation around Haneda and, because I am bringing the matter up again tomorrow in Cabinet Council, I asked for support. Both men felt exactly the same and consented.

May 31, Tuesday

Cabinet Council Meeting. Spoke again about ways of postponing the visit of the American president to Japan and requested that this be done. Reasons:

1. Lack of confidence amongst the authorities responsible for public safety. Showed a map of the route to Haneda and the situation in front of the American Embassy. Prime Minister Kishi looked away, but looked surreptitiously over Justice Minister Ino's shoulder. A chill fell over the gathering.
2. The current situation will be troublesome for the Emperor. The Emperor must be the Emperor for the Socialist Party as well as for the Liberal Democratic Party. If the Imperial car were to be stopped for a long period, there would be grave implications for the future prospects of the emperor system.
3. If blood flows and people are left dead, or injured, it will be put out that the blood of Japanese youth was spilt for the sake of Americans. It would be stupid to get caught up in that.
4. Will they be happy if the American president addresses a Diet from which the Socialist Party is absent? I asked the ministers responsible for public safety if they were confident. Ishihara, Chairman of the National Public Security Commission replied, 'We cannot afford to be worried' Justice Minister Ino replied, 'To the extent that the roads are narrow, they will be easier to police'. Transport Minister Narahashi said, 'What Nakasone says is right. If anything happens the Cabinet will have to resign collectively'. Another cabinet member said, 'Let us give him a big welcome and overwhelm the demonstrations. If we postpone the visit of the President of America to Japan the international repercussions will be enormous.'

Prime Minister Kishi answered: 'This has already been decided once so we will stick with our previous decision and just make absolutely sure that everything is right. I want to overwhelm them with a positive welcome'.

June 10, Friday
The Haggarty Incident

When Press Secretary Haggarty landed in Haneda to make the arrangements for the president's visit, he was surrounded at the exit of the airport by demonstrators from *Zengakuren* and *Sōhyō*[1] and his car was destroyed. He made a narrow escape by American naval helicopter.

9.30 p.m. extraordinary cabinet meeting

There were many voices arguing that this was a violent conspiracy by international communism and that it should be vigorously put down. MITI minister Ikeda, Finance Minister Satō, Construction Minister Murakami, Welfare Minister Watanabe and Director General of the Defence Agency Akagi, all insisted on invoking the crime of rioting and the Subversion Prevention Law. Education Minister Matsuda said he was not giving in to violence but we should stand aside and think before we act; that strength alone would not be effective. He had changed his position. The faces of Ishihara, Chairman of the National Public Security Commission and Justice Minister Ino blackened.

June 15, Wednesday

Demonstrators broke into the Diet. One dead. Then a 'wall of people' was formed. The death of the woman student Kanba Michiko has caused the public debate to become noisy and excited.

June 16, Thursday

Extraordinary Cabinet Council meeting at eighteen minutes past midnight. Called because Minister of International Trade and Industry, Ikeda, demanded a meeting be held concerning loose talk by Chief Cabinet Secretary Shiina. Once again Prime Minister Kishi and Finance Minister Satō, adopted an unbending position and wanted to put out a firm statement to the effect that this was an internationally supported communist plot which would be put down through the mobilisation of police power to its limits.

Education Minister, Matsuda said it was necessary to take political steps to soothe public feelings. Director General of the Defence Agency Akagi, was of the hard-line faction. Transport Minister

Narahashi stressed the use of the Subversion Prevention Law. Minister of International Trade and Industry Ikeda, said we should bring in as many police officers as were necessary from around the country and make doubly certain of our defences regardless of cost. He argued that the government must repeat its statement. Construction Minister Murakami, and Welfare Minister Watanabe, were in agreement. Chairman of the National Public Security Commission Ishihara, regretted that there were limits on the strength of the police and that the situation would be untenable if they did not receive political help. He finally said what he really thought.

A big national funeral is to be held on the 19th, the day the President of the United States comes to Japan and tens of thousands of people will gather. If they then get stirred up, the demonstrations where the funeral ceremony is conducted will turn into a riot. Who knows what sort of incidents the American President and Prime Minister Kishi will become involved in. I strongly agreed with Chief Ishihara and made known my support. With my statement a pall descended and the meeting broke up.

2.00pm met with Kōno Ichiro to ask for his understanding. If Prime Minister Kishi doesn't call for a postponement of the President's visit to Japan I am going to tender him my resignation. Plan to do so in the evening.

Notice comes at 3.55 p.m. of an emergency Cabinet Council meeting and I go to the Prime Minister's residence. Prime Minister Kishi opens by saying that he wants to postpone the President's visit to Japan.

Opposed: Labour Minister Matsuno, Justice Minister Watanabe. In favour: Nakasone. Can't be helped: Minister of Agriculture Fukuda, Director General of the Defence Agency Akagi, Minister of Posts and Telecommunications Uetake, Chairman of the National Public Security Commission Ishihara, Minister of Construction Murakami. Very regrettable but can't be helped: Foreign Minister Fujiyama, Minister of International Trade and Industry Ikeda, Finance Minister Satō, Justice Minister Ino, Deputy Prime Minister Masutani.

Thus the visit was postponed. Prime Minister Kishi emphasised the menace of international communism and ordered Commission Chairman Ishihara to [1] increase the number of armed police by 10,000, [2] enact legislation against group violence, [3] strengthen technical equipment.

As the meeting closed, Deputy Cabinet Secretary Matsumoto tapped me on the shoulder and agreed: 'Its just as you say; if this had been settled on the 24th of last month, there wouldn't have been these riots. They do such stupid things these people'.

◆

This was my diary at the time of the Security Treaty Riots in 1960.

The revised Security Treaty that Prime Minister Kishi had so earnestly craved was signed in Washington on 19 June by Foreign Minister Fujiyama after fifteen months of negotiations. The 34th National Diet was convened immediately and the Treaty put before it, but public opinion was split. Five years after the conservative merger and the union of the Socialist Party, the two big power blocs of the Japanese right and left were polarising around defence issues. Fifteen years after the end of the war and eight years after independence left and right-wing nationalism, which had been bottled up under the Occupation, was now dissipating its energy in internecine clashes as the Cold War progressed.

The procedure for approving the date of the visit by the American President was rushed through the Diet session by the Government and the ruling party. The way this was done caused unnecessary instability and suspicion among the general populace. Demonstrations continued day after day around the Diet building whilst, inside the Diet, the opposition prevented discussion by use of force and the proceedings stagnated.

The content of the revised treaty was reasonable and, compared with the old treaty, restored to Japan the independence and equality which we had demanded. For that reason I was a strong supporter. However there was then little of the daily commentary on issues that we get today on radio and television, and the government was careless about disseminating information. Most students and workers demonstrated without knowing the contents of the Treaty.

As a Minister of State I was fearful that the disturbances might cause a serious obstacle to the exchange of courtesies and good will between the two heads of state, the visiting American President and the Japanese Emperor. I was extremely worried that it might leave an ineradicable source of trouble for the post-war emperor system and for the history of American-Japanese relations.

This fuss was about fear, not of something real, but of the phantom of a revised treaty. The fact that demonstrations raged in the vicinity of the Diet but the Kōrakuen professional baseball grounds were full, was evidence of this. Nevertheless when it was announced that Prime Minister Kishi, the same Kishi who had been a cabinet minister in the Tōjō Cabinet at the start of the Pacific War, was to conclude a new treaty which touched the fundamentals of Japan's defence, the popular nationalism which had been unable to find its voice during the occupation was skilfully fanned.

If the authorities had taken into account that the revised treaty was being debated in this sort of political arena, and within this sort of social atmosphere, and had thought about the timing of the vote on the revised treaty in the Lower House, and the timing of the President's visit, this tragedy could probably have been averted. When the resignation of the Kishi Cabinet was announced, the tide turned and peace returned abruptly to public affairs. If the content of the revised treaty had really been bad, this wouldn't have happened.

The new Ikeda Cabinet advocated 'patience and forbearance', and assumed a completely opposite political posture to that of the Kishi Cabinet. It would have been difficult to predict this from Ikeda's statements in the Cabinet Council meetings on the treaty, but politics changes from one minute to the next. Perhaps the people understood that when it is a matter of national prosperity, 'A wise man may change his mind, a fool never.'

In 1967, Nakasone became Minister for Transport in the Satō Cabinet.
In 1970 he became Director-General of the Defense Agency, and in 1972, Minister of International Trade and Industry.

Negotiating JAL flights to Moscow

When the telephone rings, the heart of a Minister for Transport beats faster. His head is invaded by the uneasy feeling that there's been a plane crash, or a train crash. He is particularly afraid of the phone call that comes when he has left the office and is at home. The first thing I did was to stop driving a car. Until then, I had always driven myself to the golf course on my days off. But for the Minister for Transport to cause an accident would be unforgivable.

The decade of fast economic growth in Japan in the period which started in the mid-fifties, caused glaring disparities to emerge between the advanced industrial facilities and outdated transport facilities. This rapidly became a bottleneck to further growth. The Ministry of Transport was moving forward quickly with land, sea, harbour and airport facilities but the lack of an overall, co-ordinating power was evident. The loss to the national economy caused by this lack of harmony and balance between the various departments had become striking.

The first thing I wanted to do, therefore, was to transform the Ministry of Transport from a government office based on divisional authorisation to one based on integrated planning. I sought the opinions of the backbone of the Ministry, the young officials, and started the Transport Economics Discussion Group with Nakayama Ichiro as Chairman, and Ōkita Saburō and Tsuru Shigeto as assistants. Next, I established a Minister's Secretariat planning division with a Minister's Secretariat Deliberative Office at its head. At a stroke I fashioned an organisation of just two sections in one room into a large structure consisting of eleven individuals at the level of section chief, with two councillors above them. As far as the provision of staff for this planning department was concerned, our attitude was that we wouldn't take no for an answer, and strong orders were sent to each department by Vice Minister Hori's assistants. For those days this was quite drastic treatment, and this division produced research which led to massive structural reform.

The second major issue was the purchase of land for the international airport at Narita. Purchasing the land was extremely tough going, but Nemoto Shinsuke, who was a trusted friend of

My father at the desk of the Minister of Transport

Tomonō, the governor of Chiba, made desperate efforts to woo the people on the ground and to find a solution. It was through his good offices that I was able to have secret discussions with the farmers' representatives and negotiations with the Narita City authorities. As a result, a farmers group known as the Fourth Faction, consisting of those who were prepared to sell their land if certain conditions were met, was set up, and on 6 April 1968, a 'memo concerning the sale of land' was finally signed between this faction and the Airport public corporation at the Ministry of Transport with Governor Tomonō and myself in attendance. The selling price was 1,500,000 yen per 0.245 acres of farmland. At the time this was a surprisingly high price and necessitated the co-operation of Finance Minister Mizuta.

With this, roughly 89% of private land, that is 597 hectares, was secured and progress toward the construction of the airport took a great step forward. Unfortunately, however, because of the armed struggle taken up by the Third Faction *Zengakuren* and others, further progress was brought to a standstill.

The third major issue was the negotiation of a new Japan-Soviet Aviation Agreement. Under the Agreement of 3 March 1967, flights between Tokyo and Moscow were operated by Aeroflot and Japan Airlines in co-operation, using Soviet aircraft leased from the Soviet Ministry of Aviation with flight crew attached. The Japanese, for their part, were against operating solely with Soviet planes like this, but the Soviets argued that while the Vietnam War continued, they would take special steps with regard to flights over Siberia, and they would not give way.

However, the agreed record of proceedings expresses Japan's desire for independent operations within two years and the Soviet recognition of this strong desire. I watched this time limit of 4 April 1969, approach and in a reply in the Diet in autumn 1968, said, 'If they do not approve flights to Moscow by Japanese planes we will abrogate the commercial affairs agreement in April next year and ban flights by Soviet aircraft from Moscow to Tokyo.' In the past the Soviet Union had avoided answering Japanese demands, but when I just kept on reiterating my reply in all seriousness, the Soviets began to get very concerned.

Soon, the Soviet Ambassador to Japan Troyanouski, and the head of the Aeroflot office in Japan got in touch. I conveyed to them in the strongest terms the same message I had given in my explanation to the Diet. The result was that the Soviets indicated their willingness to negotiate further, and I visited Moscow with President Matsuo of

Japan Air for talks with Minister of Aviation Roginou for four days from 24 October.

However the Soviets made no attempt to comply on the matter of flights by Japanese aircraft. I asked for a meeting with Premier Kosygin. At that meeting, I got this reply from the Soviet premier, ' If we can agree conditions between us, the Soviet Union will respond positively, but the Soviet Union has not hitherto allowed international flights over Siberia. This will be the first time for such a route to be set up so there is the question of third parties, and I would therefore ask you to be careful with announcements in the press.' I affirmed that 'We will divide the results into issues which will be made publicly known and those which will not, and will issue a joint communiqué on just those results which can be made public'. Kosygin agreed with this.

In the middle of these talks a memo was delivered to Premier Kosygin, and when I asked him to, 'make efforts to achieve peace in Vietnam', he declared, 'We have seen certain advances in negotiations for peace recently and particularly yesterday. The Soviet Union is also making every effort to achieve peace. I can't say much, but we may be near a solution.' The Premier's face, when he read the memo, had been suffused with happiness, and I guessed that the Soviet Union had invested a considerable amount in the Vietnam war and had sacrificed much in terms of its people's livelihood. But on the question of the Northern Territories he answered coldly, 'There is no territorial problem.'

In a further meeting with Minister of Aviation, Roginou, we discussed matters broadly, and had officials negotiate through the night to formulate the prose for those issues on which we had reached an understanding. However we still had not reached agreement when the time came for our plane to leave. This route was Aeroflot's dollar earner and if it were scrapped, it would be a big loss to the Soviet Union. Consequently I judged that in the end they would have to listen to what I had to say, and I took my leave for Japan and set off for the airport without accepting any irrational demands. As expected, the other side rushed out to the airport with a draft that incorporated our demands, and we signed it in the VIP lounge.

Such were the realities of negotiations with the Soviets at that time. Soon after I gave up the post of Transport Minister a new formal agreement was concluded by my successor, Harada Tadashi, and JAL flights to Moscow became a reality.

Whilst I was Minister of Transport, there were a number of large earthquakes; among them the Matsushiro earthquake in Nagano

Prefecture, the Ebino earthquake in Miyazaki Prefecture and the Tokachioki earthquake in Hokkaido. The Tokachioki quake alone left 52 dead or missing and 330 people injured. As a consequence we decided at a Cabinet Council meeting that earthquake measures should be strengthened, the land observation network enhanced, and highly sensitive underwater earthquake meters developed. Thanks to the new, efficient, underwater earthquake meters the network for predicting underwater tremors in the seas off Tōkai and Bōsō was remarkably improved. Eighty percent of all earthquakes in Japan begin under the sea.

There were two big accidents as well. One was the train collision inside Tengachaya station on the Nankai electric railway in which ten people were seriously hurt and 229 received lesser injuries. The other tragedy was when a charter bus plunged into the River Hida killing 104 and injuring three. The cause was inadequate planning on the part of the organiser, but the fact that there had been a landslide was also the responsibility of the government administration and I felt deep anguish. I was particularly worried because the organisers were financially weak and might be unable to pay compensation to the bereaved families. The argument that automobile accident compensation insurance could not be applied in this case, occupied a number of people in the government, but in the end, we set a precedent, and took steps to disburse 3,000,000 yen per person. Even so, when I think about the sorrow of the bereaved families my heart breaks

'Volunteer' Director-General of the Defence Agency

Through a friend of mine, Yoshitomo Yoshitaka, I let it be known to Prime Minister Satō that, if I were to join the Cabinet, I would like the post of Director-General of the Defence Agency. At that time the post of Director-General of the Defence Agency was a lowly one where it was easy to cause problems, and it was common for new entrants to the cabinet to be given that job. Naturally, an inquiry came from Prime Minister Satō, 'Why'? My answer was, 'The basic axis of relations between America and Japan is security. Right now when friction is great, I would like to find out where the tenuous line joining America and Japan is, and what the relationship is at bottom, away from view.' Satō understood this. I was a 'volunteer' Director General of the Defence Agency.

I was appointed Director-General of the Defence Agency on 14 January 1970, and my first job was to form an advisory body on the defence forces. I called on ten people including Hosokawa Ryūgen, Endō Shūsaku, Morita Akio and Satō Aiko to write a prescription with the business diagnosis in mind. The setting up of a defence medical college was one product of this diagnosis.

My second task was to begin holding a regular Three Ministers Conference which brought together the Chief Cabinet Secretary, the Foreign Minister and the Director-General of the Defence Agency. In order to ensure civilian control, I quietly made some contacts with business and, with Prime Minister Satō's approval, I opened the first conference on 3 February. My other aim in setting up the conference was to bring together diplomacy and defence.

Next I met with the U.S. military and enlarged the independent administration of bases and even suggested the return of bases and co-operative management with the Self Defence Forces. My favourite saying was, 'The Japanese Self Defence Forces will defend the sky over Tokyo', and I flew it like a flag in my negotiations. On 6 March, the Commanding Officer of the American Forces in Japan, Graham, came to give notice that, 'From July next year, almost all American troops in Japan will be pulled out. The bases will be handed back and the naval base at Atsugi will be turned over to the Self Defence Forces as soon as possible'.

Before long, on 4 September, the United States airforce withdrew from the air defence command centres of seven radar sites. There was even notice of the closure of the biggest powder magazine at Yamada in Northern Kyūshū. Four days later, I went to America, and it was decided by Secretary of Defence Laird, Commander-in-Chief of the Pacific Army Mckeen and others that four bases, including the firing range at Mito, and the bases at Tokorozawa and Tachikawa, would be handed back along with the naval repairs facilities and the rest of the facilities at Yokosuka. The bases at Misawa, Itsuki and elsewhere were to be used jointly.

The return of the bases inevitably increased lay-offs of Japanese labourers at the bases. Japanese base workers at that time totalled 39,544 people of whom 8,431 were dismissed between the end of 1970 and the following spring. I worked hard to find ways of dealing with this.

I also tried to tackle the revision of the 'Basic Policy for National Defence' BPND[2] This had been set down in the First Defence Build-up Plan in 1957, and its fourth clause stated, 'Concerning invasion from abroad, until such times in the future that the United Nations shall have the ability to effectively prevent this occurring, we shall deal with this on the basis of the security system set up with America'.

The result of this was that the Japanese people came to lack the will to defend their own country, and their dependence on the United States and the United Nations grew to unacceptable levels. It was my belief that we must change our aim to 'Concerning invasion, first, we shall fight to repulse it ourselves with all the strength we possess nationally. Where necessary we shall deal with this with the co-operation of America.' Nor was there anywhere any provision for enforcing the principle of civilian control, and I pointed this omission

On 23 March 1971, in response to a question by Haniyū Sanshichi of the Socialist Party in the general interpolation of the Lower House Budget Committee meeting, I put forward my personal view on the five principles of independent defence.

1. The protection of the constitution and the defence of the country.
2. The unification of diplomacy and defence, and the maintenance of harmony between those and other national policies.
3. Civilian control.
4. Support for the three non-nuclear principles.
5. U.S.-Japan Security Treaty system used as a supplement.

In the Lower House plenary session which followed, Prime Minister Satō confirmed his approval with the words, 'These five principles are entirely appropriate'. Foreign Minister Fukuda backed him up saying, 'It is appropriate to include a balance to each policy as a brake on the excessive growth of defence expenditure.'

In the National Defence Council meeting of 24 March, the proposed revisions were considered by the Deputy Chief Cabinet Secretary, the Vice-Minister for Foreign Affairs and the Deputy Director-General of the Defence Agency, and it was decided that the draft would be polished if necessary. Meetings between the three began on 19 August, but the start coincided with my retirement; time had run out. However, one reform was made. I protested the fact that telegrams originating with a resident military official in overseas legations were sent initially to the Foreign Minister in the name of the Ambassador and arrived belatedly with the Director-General of the Defence Agency, and I proposed that, 'When something is put on the desk of the Foreign Minister, it should be put at the same time on the desk of the Director General of the Defence Agency'. This was done.

There is a tendency in the Ministry of Foreign Affairs to monopolise anything related to foreign policy in the name of diplomatic precedence. Even during the Gulf War in 1991 they still seemed to want to keep participation by the Defence Agency and the Self Defence Forces at arms length. It seems that the old faults have still not been cured.

At the time I was Director-General, the LDP defence *zoku*[3] could often be heard recommending raising the status of the Defence Agency to that of a Ministry of Defence. Successive Director Generals of the Defence Agency had also pledged their efforts to realise this aim, but I rejected it out of hand. I did so because I believed that the priority for defence policy was to set up a standing committee on security in the Diet and only then to go on to deal with the question of a Ministry of Defence.

On the grounds that either way civilian control was paramount, I published the first Defence White Paper. The Defence Agency had previously shown a desire to publish, and had produced a trial run, but it hadn't seen the light of day. This was partly because it had not been possible to get a firm and unified opinion among the various Ministries and Agencies on how the defence of Japan should be secured, and partly because of deeply entrenched voices of caution which said that to publish would be to provide the Opposition with material, and to put the government at a disadvantage. I recognised the significance of the Defence Agency taking the positive step of making its beliefs known in the public arena and, with the agreement of the leaders of the Liberal Democratic Party, I pushed actively for publication.

The first presentation of a Defence White Paper was made at the Cabinet Council Meeting of 20 October and this was then published. This became the regular pattern.

In the midst of all this activity, the deadline for the U.S.-Japan Security Treaty came and it was automatically extended without any fuss. Compared with the Security Treaty riots of 1960, the transition was like a dream. However it seemed as if almost every day telegrams poured in from China and the Soviet Union identifying Satō and myself as leaders of Japanese militarism.

The Director-General takes to the skies

But it was not a matter of 'ploughing the field and forgetting the seed'. The most important thing for the newly created Self Defence

Forces was the promotion of front-line morale. The things I had been taught during my time with the navy had remained with me. I knew too that American commanders always say 'Let's go. Follow me.' So I had the idea of flying in a fighter to inspect the units around the country. All the leaders, from Obata, the Deputy Director-General of the Defence Agency on down, were opposed.

This was because the carefully cultivated prestige of the Self Defence Forces would be lost in an instant if by any chance there were an accident. It was a question of 'Chief, defend thyself'. But I argued that front line pilots took their lives in their hands daily scrambling as a precaution against aircraft invading the country's airspace, and I insisted that it was perfectly reasonable that the Director-General should put his life on the line too.

In order to fly in a fighter I had to go to the experimental aviation forces in Tachikawa to be tested for my ability to withstand thin air and oxygen in case it should prove necessary to escape by parachute from 1,000 metres. On 21 January 1971, I went to Tachikawa and took the examination. The biggest obstacle was the low pressure room. Captain Yokobori Sakae was greatly concerned and had a medical officer who specialised in aviation physiology accompany me into the room where the tests were being carried out.

The tests consisted of three essentials. The first was to climb to 5,000 feet and then return to ground level to habituate the body and particularly the ears. After that there was a climb at the rate of 3,000 to 4,000 feet per minute reaching 43,000 feet in about 15 minutes. If an error in the flying operation caused the aircraft to lose speed and fall abruptly, it would fall 25,000 feet in one second. We flew level at that height for 20 minutes and intentionally took off the oxygen masks to experience the symptoms of oxygen deprivation. In more concrete terms, we had to solve a sequence of easy calculations, addition and subtraction, and check the answers later.

At first my answers were properly written but, as I was gradually deprived of oxygen, my figures became like worms wriggling across the page. Before long the doctor who was accompanying me suddenly began to feel ill and excused himself and left the room. Finally I did the high speed lowering of pressure which corresponded to escaping from a plane. There was an almighty bang accompanied by the appearance of a white mist and I felt a tremendous pressure all over my body. The temperature immediately fell by 25 degrees and I felt a chill. That was the worst part.

162

In a T33 jet trainer en route to Hokkaido

However, everything finished well and I went home with my large, peach-coloured certificate showing I had passed. It was very useful. Afterwards, when I went with friends to bars in the Ginza I would pull out this certificate and say, 'I still have a lot of life left in me' and beautiful woman would gather round to look.

I flew from Iruma base to Hokkaido in a T33 jet fighter. In Kyushu I flew in an anti-submarine patrol plane and in F104s and travelled the length of Japan. I stayed in barracks buried in snow, scrubbed the backs of members of the company in the bath, nibbled on rice crackers and chatted with them, and gave up the top berth to a cadet and slept in the bottom berth of a bunk bed. The cadet was so excited he couldn't sleep, and I too found sleep difficult. I was putting into practice what I had learned about leadership as chief paymaster in the supplies unit in the Pacific War.

In a haiku competition for the Defense Agency about this time, the poem which won the Director-General's prize read:

> *We seldom shoot, but when we need to*
> *Find no bullets left.*
> *A fly in the ointment, you could say.*

The public did not, at that time, look altogether warmly on the Self Defence Forces, and, for that reason, I felt it was important to become one of them, and to boast their self-respect. I was also keen to root out the so-called anti-war camp among Self Defence Force officials.

In the budget compilation at the end of the year, I stressed three things: respect for the person, strengthening the intelligence function and developing prospects for the future. In this context I advocated improvements in Self Defence Force salaries, changes in the warrant officer system, an increase in the number of resident overseas military officers and expanded intelligence function facilities. Changes in the warrant officer system increased the opportunity for promotion for the cadet class and was greatly welcomed. The budget for the technical research headquarters was also increased by more than twenty percent.

I built a network from the Director-Generals office to all the units and talked with their members. I brought representatives of units from across the country together and held *karaoke* festivals at the Ground Self Defense Force school in Fuji which were used as a springboard for similar ventures with the Maritime Self Defense Force in the Yokosuka base and the Air Self Defense Force in the base at Hamamatsu.

It was said that I was playing to the gallery, and perhaps the senior officers were tense and it was an imposition. But it was from spending time with the members of the units that I learned for example that they bought their own toilet paper. It goes without saying that this was then provided.

The poem that received the Director-General's prize the following year was as follows:

> *Toilet rolls are now standard issue!*
> *We wipe our bottoms with this tissue,*
> *With great thanks.*

The Mishima Incident

Just after 11 o'clock in the morning of 26 October 1970, I was in my office in the Sabo Kaikan building in the Hirakawa district, changing out of the morning suit I had worn to the opening of the 64th Extraordinary session of the Diet in the presence of his Majesty the Emperor in my capacity as Director-General of the Defence Agency. Suddenly an urgent telephone call came from Takeda Tsugushaku, executive staff officer in the Ground Self Defence Force.

'At about 11.00 a.m. today, the writer, Mishima Yukio, went with four members of the 'Shield Club' (*Tate no kai*), to a meeting with the

Inspector General of the Eastern Area in Ichigaya. He has now occupied the Inspector General's room and has tied him up. Several members of the unit who went in to help the Inspector General have been wounded with swords wielded by Mishima and the others.'

I asked him to confirm that it was indeed Mishima and gave the immediate order to, 'Arrest all of them immediately. The Self Defences Forces will encircle the area and, if necessary, will deal with it themselves but, insofar as possible, violence should be avoided and the police should be to the fore.' What Mishima did was undoubtedly a crime of conviction and, if the Self Defence Forces were to kill or injure Mishima, a famous artist nominated for a Nobel prize, the social impact would be enormous. Consequently, I wanted to deal with it quietly and, insofar as possible, to put the police in the front line and leave use of the Defence Forces until the last.

At 12:13 p.m., as I arrived in the Defence Agency, a call came direct from Inspector General Masuda Kanetoshi, who had been imprisoned, saying, 'I am sorry to have caused so much concern. Mishima and one of the students have committed suicide; the others have been arrested. There is no disturbance within the unit.' I called the officers together and announced, 'Disrupting law and order, and killing and injuring people, are actions which deviate from the proper course and we must denounce, absolutely, conduct which breaks down democratic order in this way.' Before long, I had a directive drawn up, and passed down the word through the various chief staff officers that the members of the Self Defence Forces should hold themselves in readiness.

The directive read, 'Members of the Japan Self Defence Forces, who bear the burden for national peace and independence, must not be distracted by these events. Attempts to destroy law and order through violence are a direct denial of democracy and will not be recognised in any form. Members of the JSDF, make sure you are as a body mentally prepared, be persistent in the execution of your own duties and worthy of the people's trust.'

I also had the Director of the Defence Academy, Inoki Masamichi, make a personal statement refuting Mishima's manifesto. This read: 'For someone arbitrarily to use the Self Defence Forces for a specific political purpose would be to turn them into a private army. However pure the motives, and no matter that the actions put the perpetrator's own fate on the line, such a destructive philosophy must be firmly rejected.'

I dealt with the incident particularly expeditiously because I remembered how in the February Incident in 1936, the initial ambiguity of Army Minister Kawashima Yoshiyuki, had caused uncertainty within the Army and had delayed the resolution of the incident. After the Mishima Incident I felt it necessary to lose no time in making the rights and wrongs of the situation clear to the members of the JSDF.

That night, after I had gone home, the telephone rang non-stop and the protests poured forth: 'I thought you were supposed to be a friend of Mishima.' I had read many of Mishima's books, but in fact I was not particularly close to him. I had only met him two or three times: once when he came to lecture at a study group for my faction, once when we dined together at a study meeting with a small group of friends and again for a newspaper dialogue. It was because I was a proponent of constitutional reform that I was taken for a sworn friend of Mishima.

We last met at this small, study meeting in the spring of the year before the incident happened. When I think about the things he said on that occasion, I realise that the words he spoke were, in fact, a leave-taking. Of his last four works, it is in the hero of *Wild Horses* that a trace of Mishima dwells.

On a personal level I could understand Mishima's feelings. I experienced a sense of regret at the loss of a person of importance and a feeling of loneliness. I felt Mishima's death neither as an aesthetic event nor as artistic martyrdom, but as a philosophical protest, a death in anger at the nature of the age.

Nevertheless I was a public servant in charge of the Self Defence Forces and so I could not stand silent while its members were being injured and vilified. Nor could I accept the Self Defence Forces being used for private purposes and being incited to do things contrary to its proper purpose. Just as in the Chinese classic, it was time to, 'Show strict fidelity without violence', not a time to indulge in personal emotion.

Inspector General Masuda, dragged into this incident by events beyond his control and forced against his will to be present at the scene of the ritual suicide and beheading of Mishima and the others, had shown outstanding talent as a student in the 46th graduating year of the Army Officers school. He had received the Imperial Military Sword on graduating and had served as a staff officer in the Imperial Headquarters during the war. Directly after the fall of Saipan, Lieutenant Commander Haruki Makato, staff officer for the Saipan region, and a colleague of Masuda, disembowelled himself, also at Ichigaya, and was discovered in the act by Masuda.

It is hard not to feel a sort of karma in the fate of the inspector general who, twenty years later, when he was in charge of Ichigaya, once again observed a second tragedy. Masuda resigned and took early retirement Living up to his reputation as a deep-thinking military man, the Inspector General made the following statement. 'It will probably sound as if I am making excuses but both staff officers and members of the JSDF have truly acquitted themselves well. They dealt with the problem prudently and without causing any injury. I had met with Mishima on three occasions but had not thought him to be brooding to such an extent. I think that if I could have talked to him quietly, on a one-to-one basis, things might have worked out very differently. When public opinion will allow it, in the future, I intend to meet with the bereaved families and ask them to let me visit the spirits of the dead.'

I tried hard to dissuade him from resigning, but in the end I understood his feelings. By chance, I had received some wild duck meat from the Emperor and I gave it to him. He accepted it reverently and took it for a last dinner with his subordinates, the Chiefs of the 1st and 12th Divisions.

CHAPTER EIGHT

KILLING TIME

My friendship with the Kennedy brothers

In the summer of 1960, directly after the Security Treaty riots, when the Kishi Cabinet resigned and I left my post as Director of the Science and Technology Agency, Miura Kineji of the Asahi newspaper came to me and said, 'If you've got your sights set on being prime minister then you've got to keep away from ministerial jobs and party posts for the next ten years. Just concentrate on making speeches for your friends and on digging out new people and getting them elected.'

My colleague Inaba Osamu also said, 'You don't get large trees thriving underneath other large trees, Nakasone: you have to play for a while.' Probably he had watched my delicate relationship with Kōno and that was why he warned me.

Though I hesitate to say it, whilst Kōno was popular among the professionals, I was more popular with the amateurs and the students. There are always going to be those in the number one slot in the party who are not entirely pleased when a number two emerges. Inevitably, a subtle sense of rivalry arises toward colleagues in the same faction who are of the same or longer standing. Probably what Inaba meant was, 'Once a Kōno Cabinet is formed you can stretch your wings to your heart's content. Until then, go back to the country and think only of Kōno.' There must have been something in the air at that time because Ishii Mitsujiro also advised me, 'Nakasone, you need to kill time for a while. They even have an expression for it in English.'

So for the next seven years I held no ministerial post, I chaired no Diet committees, I didn't even hold a party post; I left it all to others and killed time. I enjoyed a variety of interests, bore in mind what would be useful in the future, and left the main track for the sidings.

In January 1961, I was invited by Takasaki Tatsunosuke to attend the inauguration of President Kennedy. He said when we were leaving, 'I will introduce you to my friends in U.S. As my successor so you must inherit it all.' On the JAL flight across the Pacific he said something that was to become a motto of mine: 'We are Asians; let us stick with Asian morality, not do what a lot of Japanese are doing these days, that is go to Peking and badmouth America, then go to Washington and badmouth the Chinese.'

When we arrived in Washington, Takasaki wrote on the back of a postcard of the Lincoln Memorial the address, 'His Excellency, Premier Chou En lai, Peking, People's Republic of China', and mailed it as a New Year's card. He grinned and said, 'I wonder if that will get it there?' At that time relations between America and China were at rock bottom and Takasaki's breadth as a politician amazed me.

The presidential inauguration ceremony was held on 20 January. It was a bitterly cold day and everybody was shivering. The figure of President Kennedy his left hand on the bible, his right hand aloft, swearing the oath is seared on my memory. I was greatly influence by Theodore White's great work *The Making of a President: 1960*. Reading White's book, I learned that Kennedy had built a brains trust known as the Kennedy Machine. I felt very keenly that in the future, politics in Japan would also have to undertake its policy planning, propaganda and fund raising within this kind of rational, scientific system, and I got together with Watanabe Tsuneo and Ujiie Seiichirō of the Yomiuri newspaper, and Waseda University professor, Kobayashi Shōzo, to look into forming a 'Political Science Research Group.'

After the inauguration ceremony I toured Central and Southern America with Yabe Teiji and the rest of the investigatory group dispatched by the constitutional investigation body. From there I went independently to visit Castro's Cuba, returning to Washington on 6 March. I had a hunch that America might move decisively to launch an amphibious assault on Cuba, so I had deliberately gone to meet Castro.

I met with President Kennedy's younger brother, the Attorney General Robert Kennedy, for an hour and a half. He took off his coat and rolled up his sleeves and, keeping his shoes on, rested his feet on the desk, put his hands behind his head and talked. I too took off my coat and loosened my tie, leaned back in the chair, and stretched out my legs. This was the first time that I had assumed such a posture in my discussion with an American VIP.

The Attorney General questioned me closely about conditions in Cuba and offered his own assessment, 'There is no guarantee that America will win even if we launch landing operations, and if we make a half-hearted attempt we will probably fail. President Castro has already deployed a fair number of troops in the coastal area.' Just one month later, America attempted to land in Cuba with a joint force of private volunteers and Cubans under the guidance of the Central Intelligence Agency [CIA] and failed badly.

On 6 February the following year, Robert Kennedy responded to an invitation I had made during my American visit, and came to Japan. Just before that, he had surprised the Japanese people with the ordinary familiarity of his performance in the presidential elections; with the way that he kept formal events to a minimum and how he threw himself into parties and lectures with students and young people and visited factories and primary and middle schools. This was the first the Japanese people had seen of an American style campaign and American politics. On 6 June 1968, as I arrived in Niigata airport on a electoral campaign visit, I learned of his assassination. That both brothers should be killed like this filled me with despondency.

Cheering on Ozawa Seiji

The headlines on 11 December 1962 read, 'Clash at NHK, Ozawa performance halted.' The articles referred to the boycotting of a performance by certain members of the NHK Symphony Orchestra who were unhappy with the style and personality of the up-and-coming conductor. I had a connection with Ozawa. He had become the conductor of the first regional symphony orchestra, the Gunma Symphony Orchestra, set up in 1955 in my home town of Takasaki. He came frequently to Takasaki, travelling on congested steam trains. The Gunma Orchestra toured the primary and middle schools throughout the prefecture and brought the sound of real violins, clarinets and cellos to the children of a savage post-war society.

Ozawa's father, an explorer, was a private volunteer in the ground-breaking enterprises undertaken when the old nation of Manchukuo [Manchuria] was being founded. In the process he quarrelled with the Kwantung Army and returned to Japan. When I met him then I had asked him what the situation was really like in Manchuria.

I thought the boycott was an arrogant attempt by a group within the NHK to take advantage of its weight of numbers to preserve its privileges, and I felt it unfortunate that the future prospects of such an outstanding talent should receive a set back like this. Accordingly I rallied the troops with a 'help group' at the Golden Dragon restaurant in Akasaka. The producer Asari Keita was there along with Abe Yasushi, the music critic, and the film director Teshigawara Hiroshi. The overwhelming majority was critical of the musicians for conspiring together and refusing to perform, and agreed that the fault could be laid at the door of a limited group in the NHK Symphony Orchestra, and should be investigated.

The argument seethed over whether the artist could recover from this blow. Some people there called for the newspapers and weekly journals to take the matter up, but Miura Kineji argued that, 'In art, we must be artful in our opposition' so, in the end, it was decided to have Ozawa direct the Japan Philharmonic, fill the house for a spectacular performance and let that be the telling reply.

Everyone knew of the incident. Ozawa's direction of Tchaikovsky's Fifth, and Berlioz at the Tokyo Bunkakaikan in Ueno in January the following year, was truly dynamic. When the baton fell, the audience rose to their feet and clapped as if possessed. Ozawa's face crumpled but this was not with simple pride. I had only been able to act in this way, without reservation because I had no official position.

Standing at the South Pole

At 6.10 in the afternoon of 20 November 1963, I stood at the South Pole and raised the Rising Sun Flag. It was 37 degrees below and Hasegawa Shun was with me. Travellers in their own country, surrounded by a like-minded society, become poets; those who cross the sea and travel abroad, are touched by different cultures and become philosophers. When I ventured into the raw nature of the South Pole, I was touched with a religious feeling.

There, at the South Pole, there was no 'night', no 'women', and no 'bacteria'. When I said this in a speech in my constituency later, I was rounded on for, 'Putting bacteria and women together'. In the face of nature's vastness, sexual desire seems insignificant.

Near to the American base at MacMurdo on the Ross Sea, there is a small hut which the hero of south polar exploration, Captain Robert Falcon Scott, built in 1902, before he set out for the South Pole. Scattered about on the bare rocks are the bones of the Siberian ponies they used. There are bricks, manila rope, a bench, the barley that was food for the horses, and in a small box underneath the eaves there is desiccated bread left as it had been sixty years before; the result of the cold and the lack of bacteria no doubt.

Scott's last words, written just before he died, are inscribed on the base of a stone statue in a park in Christchurch in South Island New Zealand.

Had we lived, I should have had a tale to tell of the hardihood, endurance and courage of my companions which would have stirred the heart of every Englishman.

I'm told that the entrance exam for Christchurch primary schools often includes the question 'What were Scott's last words?'

When I visited the laboratory in a tunnel 8 metres below the ice at Bard base at the South Pole, the first room I entered was the sanatorium where there was a strong smell of carbolic acid. It reminded me of the more powerful smell of human society I had left behind in Japan. The next room was a chapel. A white cloth was draped over a big table in the middle of a room of about 48 square feet, and on the table was a large wooden crucifix. I thought of the people who quietly bowed their heads under that sunless winter blizzard and was touched by the solemnity of the occasion.

We were also taken aboard an American navy support ice breaker. When I asked the captain for the secret to steering a ship successfully in the Antarctic, he smiled and replied without hesitation, 'Patience, patience and more patience.' If you are locked in by the ice you must take it very gently, stay where you are and wait till the ice moves and a water channel opens. It occurred to me that it is the same in politics. You must wait, wait and wait some more.

The stone monument at Ashinoyū in Hakone

The owner of the Matsuzakaya Inn at the Ashinoyū hot spring in Hakone, Matsuzaka Yasushi, was a laudable man. The competition between the Matsuzakaya Inn and the neighbouring Kinokuniya became the model for Shishi Bunroku's novel *Mount Hakone,* about the struggle for supremacy in Hakone between Tsutsumi's Seibu and Gotō's Tōkyū.

Matsuzaka and I became very close when my father-in-law, who was a geologist, drilled for a new water source when the hot spring at the Matsuzakaya became exhausted. In 1960 some stone-age implements were discovered at Mount Benten, a hill to the east of Ashinoyū.

They were uncovered accidentally by Matsuzaka and a friend. He undertook to maintain the site and since then has advocated the philosophy of '*asu*'. The following is an outline of the '*Asu* primitive man philosophy' co-authored by Matsuzaka and myself.

> The mother language since the time man first stood upright and began to hunt, the language which developed into all other languages, was '*asu*'. That is to say, human pronunciation began with the simple sound 'a'. 'A' and 'asu' referred to the things necessary to life: energy, light, the east. The word '*asu*' developed to become '*ashi*', meaning food and then '*ashia*' meaning Asia.
>
> However, when man began to farm, he learned to store food and because it was then necessary to protect that store of food, passwords, spoken only by friends, developed, bringing word differentiation which developed into cultural differentiation. The end result is that mankind is now on the verge of mutual destruction by atomic weapons.
>
> But in the world of the senses the same human intuition that existed in the old era of symbiotic coexistence remains. It is manifested in happiness at the birth of a child, sadness when a mother dies, and the fear of the night. That such intuition and sensitivity overrides race, is apparent in the drawings of very young children; drawings which cannot be bettered by Picasso. Similarly, jazz, which has its roots in African folk music has become ubiquitous throughout the world.
>
> Man must now rid himself of nuclear weapons and return to his spiritual homeland of the past. Primitive man had no nations; he worshipped the sun, brought up his family and lived in peace. The United Nations should create a symphony of human life based on such primitive sensitivity and when violence threatens, it must call a halt and play that music in the defence of peace.

The theory made a deep impression on Shishi Bunroku and the hero in *Mount Hakone* is made to discuss it.

I talked to Matsuzaka about holding a discussion evening with like-minded people, and on 31 May 1964, Shishi Bunroku, Munakata Shikō, Kaya Seiji, Tominaka Saburō, Miyata Shigeo, Yamamoto Gaen, Masuda Yoshinobu, and myself gathered at the Matsuzakaya with our wives. Yamamoto is a mountain priest in Hakone. I learned how to play the trumpet shell from him and later when President Reagan came to Japan, I introduced him to it.

Everyone agreed on two things: that, ' We should get rid of nuclear weapons' and 'We should protect the natural environment of Hakone'. In order to leave the '*Asu* primitive man philosophy' for posterity, Matsuzaka and I worked on the *Asu* Declaration and through the good offices of Tsutsumi Yoshiaki, we raised the '*Asu* Declaration monument ' on Mount Benten.

With respect to the protection of Hakone's natural environment I should also mention the Hakone Kempel Festival held on 23 November every year. Engelbert Kempel was a Dutchman, born in Germany and known as a philosopher, doctor and historian, who came to Japan around three hundred years ago. Kempel met with the fifth Tokugawa Shogun, Tsunayoshi, at Edo castle. His *Nihonshi,* [Documents on Japan] which chronicled the circumstances in Japan at that time, became the most important book introducing Japan to Europe. Kempel praised Japan for the beauty of its scenery, the politeness of its people, the fineness of their human feelings and their faithfulness of character.

In the Taisho period the Kobe merchant Cyril Montague-Barney, had a retreat in Hakone and, loving its natural environment and the simplicity of the villagers, he built a stone monument to remind the Japanese of the importance of preserving their environment.

> *To someone who will stand on this spot,*
> *Where old and new highways meet:*
> *Pray, ask your descendants*
> *To make this glorious motherland of yours;*
> *Even more beautiful and admirable.*

Through the endeavours of a friend of mine, Andō Atsuyoshi, and the town tourist association, a Barney festival is now held beneath the stone monument in conjunction with the Kempel festival where we vow to protect the natural environment of Hakone. My secretary, Iwamatsu Mutsuo, who died young, published a book in 1984 called *The Big Green Corridor,* in which he mentions this monument.

A life of solitude in a mountain hut in Hinode

It was during this period of 'killing time' that I acquired a derelict farmhouse in Hinode village in Saitama, Tokyo. The headman of Hinode village, came out of the blue to my office and asked me to buy it. Apparently, emotional difficulties had arisen between the vendor and the purchaser, and for some reason, both sides wanted me to have it. The headman took me first to Hinode village and then, just as if he were fishing with decoys, tried to lure me using my friends.

When I went to look, it was like the hideout of the Takeda samurai, an isolated house on a remote mountain. The sloping land was situated on a mountain stream; it was not particularly big, but the surrounding scenery it overlooked was a truly grand spectacle; on rainy days the landscape flowed mysteriously, like a painting by Kawai Gyokudō and delighted my eyes.

To the south-east there was a plot of grassland which caught the sun and later, I cleared it and cultivated vegetables there. I ordered *konnyaku* and gourds from Gunma and transplanted citrons from Tokushima. It was in this way that the 'Hinode mountain retreat', which became the stage for top-level discussions with President Reagan and President Gorbachev, came into being.

I knocked down a small hut that had been used for agricultural tools, and built a hermitage of two twelve by nine foot rooms and slept there. I thatched it with cryptomeria bark and because it was covered with plywood, it only cost ¥350,000. This was the 'Tenshin Tei', which was the stage for the Ron-Yasu dialogues. Because there were only two rooms, I had to share with my secretary. I read and wrote. There were no confidential telephone calls about what was going on in politics. After I retired as Prime Minister I built more study space on the vacant land to house the materials from my time in office.

Working up a sweat on the farm at Hinode

I was satisfied with my life there. A pair of big blue-green snakes lived in the stone wall below the hermitage, and as they passed through in the middle of the night, foxes and badgers would keep an eye on us drinking around the fireplace. Sometimes pit vipers would appear and the caretaker, Mr Hara, would catch them and preserve them in a bottle of low-grade rice wine for us to drink.

I wrote a lot of *haiku* here.

Mountain-like summer clouds
Make vulgar opinions from below
Fade like the sound of waves.

Cicadas are singing in the autumn,
Taking their last breath of ephemeral life,
Even though it is already dark.

Long have I been branded
A wily old fox.
I carry on peeling sweet chestnuts.

The Milky Way
Flows
Into my home village.

Tonight again,
I sleep on the grass,
Embracing the Milky Way.

Politicians need solitude occasionally. Banquets and Mah-jong are important, but you also need time to be alone. Solitude leads a man to reflect on his own arrogance, and to look with awe and caution on Nature. It informs man's existence and gives rise to the strength of mind which lies behind originality and moral bravery.

Later, after I became a cabinet minister and prime minister, I faced difficulties and problems at home and abroad, and it is only now that it comes home to me just how valuable the solitude at this hermitage was.

CHAPTER NINE

THE YEARS OF POLITICAL POWER

The youngest faction leader

In December, 1966, the *Shunjūkai*, the old Kōno faction following Kōno's death, split over the re-election of Prime Minister Satō. It divided into two factions. The first had eighteen members, including Shigemasa Seishi, Mori Kiyoshi and Sonoda Sunao, and saw its future as a mainstream faction under Satō's leadership. The second boasted twenty-six members including myself, Nakamura Umekichi, Noda Takeo and Sakurauchi Yoshio, and intended to abide by Kōno's dying wishes and oppose Satō to the bitter end. I became the representative for this group, the *Shinsei Dōshikai*. I was forty-eight years old.

Kōno had been given the cold shoulder by Prime Minister Satō, who he had challenged for the leadership when Ikeda resigned as leader in November 1964. Kōno had recommended Sonoda and Mori for posts in the cabinet reshuffle in June the following year, but Satō insisted on having Kōno remain in office as Minister of State without portfolio and on appointing Nakamura Umekichi as Minister for Education. Kōno was livid and refused the request that he remain in office and took up a non-mainstream position. One month later, he died suddenly. Those of us who were left moved to a system of group leadership consisting of Mori, Sonoda, Sakurauchi and myself, with the more senior Shigemasa as representative. It was not long before we split.

Just at that time, there was a pall cast over the political world by what was known collectively as the 'Black mist' incidents:[1] the Kyōwa Sugar-Refining scandal, the Tanaka Shōji Incident and the Fukuhara Incident. Prime Minister Satō responded by carrying out a radical cabinet reshuffle, but the new cabinet too was preponderantly mainstream Satō people. I criticised the cabinet for 'flying with only a right wing', and I joined up with a group which included Akagi

Munenori, Ezaki Masumi and Fujiyama Aiichirō, to launch the 'Clean up the Party Council'. When we were suddenly thrown into an election, we all wore white roses on our lapels to campaign.

However, it was only a scant fourteen days before the dissolution of the Lower House that I became the youngest ever faction leader. With no experience as Finance Minister, let alone in any of the top three party posts, there was no possibility of gathering funds even though I now headed a faction. It was with considerable difficulty that I covered the election expenses. This feat was achieved with the support of the '*Sankinkai*' which consisted of people who had been close to Kōno, people such as Kawai Yoshinari, Nagata Masaichi, Hagiwara Kichitarō and Hiratsuka Tsunejirō. I also benefited from the good offices of the director of the Nuclear Power Industrial Council Hashimoto Seinosuke, and of Maeda Hajime, the managing director of the Japan Federation of Employer's Association [*Nikkeiren*] who, in the past, had sponsored meetings of company directors in charge of labour management on my behalf.

Maeda picked me out and arranged a monthly breakfast meeting where he introduced me to the various up-and-coming directors in charge of labour management by saying that, although the Kōno faction had a poor reputation within the financial world, 'Nakasone is an exception'. Among the breakfast guests were Miyazaki Kagayaki of Asahi Chemicals, Shinojima Hideo of Mitsubishi Chemicals, Ōtaki Yoshio of Furukawa Mining, Nagata Keisei of Hitachi Shipbuilding, Iriye Torao of Nihon Transport and Kawahara Ryosaburō of Toshiba. These people subsequently rose to the top of their industries or were appointed to public bodies and became stout champions of Japanese capitalism. Hashimoto Seinosuke of the Nuclear Power Industrial Council was in sympathy with my policies on nuclear power and got the leaders of the electricity companies together for me. These people were my benefactors during the early years.

In the election the Clean Government Party [*Komeitō*] fought a good first-time fight, whilst the Democratic Socialist Party [*Minshatō*] and Communist parties made advances. This opened the curtain on a multi-party period. The number of seats held by the LDP fell substantially from the time of the dissolution, and my *Shinsei Dōshikai* lost two seats, but I had my electoral baptism and consolidated my base as a faction leader. However it was not until two years later, in December 1968, that I was made the actual leader of the faction. I was young and could wait for the right moment. I practised the rule of patience I had learned at the South Pole.

A faction is a group of people and, just as in any Japanese household, balance and linkage are necessary between young and old. It is especially the case with a new faction that it is vital to have a senior man to add weight and counterbalance any lack of watch-fulness on the part of a young leader. Such a figure must also be on the look-out for any jealousy or disrespect by those who had known the leader as an equal. Ikeda Hayato and Satō Eisaku had Masutani Hidetsugu and Hori Shigeru; Tanaka Kakuei, Fukuda Takeo and Takeshita Noboru had Nishimura Eiichi, Kishi Nobusuke and Kanemaru Shin respectively. In my case it was Nakamura Umekichi and Noda Takeo who gave me their backing.

The other essential is the presence of leaders among the young; men like the baseball pro, Akiyama, on the Seibu team, or Ikeyama, who plays for Yakult; men who will be a pulling power that will galvanise the team and instil enthusiasm into the members. Orators who speak well and can draw an audience are necessary too. Once, not long after he had been purged, I asked Ōasa Tadao, 'How did you manage to keep faith whilst the *Kenseikai* [later the *Minseitō*] ate the cold fare of opposition for ten years during the latter part of the Taisho period and the early Showa years'? He answered, ' I led the glittering existence of party leader and toured the provinces with good speakers to attract the crowds like popular show girls.'

In the *Shinsei Dōshikai* we had our clean-up trio of Inaba Osamu, Yamanaka Sadanori and Watanabe Michio and show girls like our so-called three crows, Kuranari Tadashi, Yagi Tetsuo and Minato Tetsuo. It is one of the functions of a faction leader to search out and nurture members like these who will make a strong impression on the public.

Victory or defeat by the reach of the sword

In November, 1967, Prime Minister Satō went to America and had talks with President Johnson. They agreed that the reversion of Okinawa would take place within 'two or three years' and issued a joint statement acknowledging a consensus of opinion that the Ogasawara Islands would revert in the near future. Not long before, Prime Minister Satō had visited Okinawa and announced his conviction that, 'Until Okinawa is returned, Japan will not emerge from the post-war period.' The war in Vietnam was still in progress and the U.S. Army evaluated the strategic capacity of Okinawa highly so it was thought unlikely that they would cede the rights easily. Consequently, it was widely believed that Prime Minister Satō's resolution was just lip service to the people of Okinawa prefecture. Personally, Personally, I was surprised by his boldness, but at the same time I was of the belief that he fully intended to achieve reversion during his period in office.

Prime Minister Satō's country house in Karuizawa stood on the opposite side of a stream from the country house belonging to the main branch of the Nakasone family, and was no more than about a hundred metres from the mountain hut of the rented summer house I had inherited from my late father. As a result, although we had differences of opinion, we were close neighbours, and we took in deliveries of fruit and vegetables for one another and very occasionally called in for a gossip.

In November 1967 Hori Shigeru said he wanted to meet me. He brought the message that, 'Prime Minister Satō is determined to achieve the return of Okinawa and would like the whole party involved so he would like your co-operation. Will you meet him and listen to what he has to say.' I promised to listen to the Prime Minister's opinions and then consider my position. A few days later, I got a telephone call whilst I was attending a study conference in Tsukiji with representatives from the financial world. The message was, 'Will you come after the reporters have left, without letting anyone see you?' I went to Satō's house after 10.30 that night and was met at the door by the Prime Minister and his wife. I was surprised to find the Prime Minister was dressed formally in *haori hakama*.

The Prime Minister explained that he was putting his political life on the line for the return of Okinawa, and that he would like to have the whole party act as one, and was very keen to have my co-operation. Listening to what he said, it struck me that although people said of him, 'This man might be sugar, but he is black sugar'[2] and, 'He is a false-bottomed bureaucrat who never speaks honestly', in fact, he was awkward and naive. I promised him, 'We will co-operate sincerely in the efforts to secure the return of Okinawa. Please do your very best'.

There was a reshuffle shortly after and I recommended Noda Takeo, from my faction, for a cabinet post. However, at the entreaty of Prime Minister Satō who wanted a gesture of party unity, I, myself, entered the cabinet as Minister of Transport. This was controversial. I had expected attacks from the left-wing who, during the Vietnam war, stirred up public opinion against the war, against America and against Satō, but the conservative camp too stuck me with the labels 'turncoat' and 'weather-vane'. They demanded to know, 'Why this sudden turn by those in the anti-Satō vanguard on the pretext of the reversion of Okinawa'.

Early on in the run-up to the San Francisco Peace Conference, Prime Minister Yoshida paid a sudden visit to Tomabechi, the chairman of the Progressive Party which had been very critical of the way the Yoshida school was pushing for peace, saying he wanted to attend the Conference as a supra-partisan group. This was the start of Tomabechi's participation in the group of plenipotentiaries. I would say that my mental state at this time resembled Tomabechi's in some respects.

At the time I feigned indifference and said things like, 'A man must be a hero to understand a hero,' and 'Politics doesn't shift with the yelp of a dog. You can't win if you don't get in striking distance of the sword.' In fact, I did it because I understood that a supra-factional, supra-party movement for the reversion of Okinawa would add weight to the cabinet in its negotiations with America, but there is no denying that it was also a political strategy with the aim, at some time in the future, of becoming Prime Minister and party leader. It was also a factional strategy intended to increase the strength of the faction. To become Prime Minister it is vital to have experience as an economic minister or in one of the top three party posts, and one way to maintain a faction is to put its bright young talent in good positions.

This time even the Nakasone faction, which had been out in the cold for a long time, obtained the posts of vice-minister, deputy secretary-general and deputy chairman of the policy research council and we put in our finest talent. My friends thought they could see light at the end of the tunnel.

By this time, I had begun to gather a number of backing groups. The *Kōkikai* [Broad Base Club], for example, was launched by the so-called financial main current centring on Nagano Shigeo, Inayama Yoshihiro, Hiyūga Hōsai, Miyazaki Kagayaki, Iwasa Yoshizane and Tajitsu Wataru. Supporters' groups were set up in Osaka and Nagoya under a variety of leaders. The Sannō Economic Study Club, which was to become a long term source of support, was formed under the guardianship of leading industry representatives such as Tabuchi Setsuya and Tsuboi Higashi, with men like Kamiya Kazuo, Matsumoto Seiya and Mochida Nobuo in pivotal positions. Even in the world of journalism, the young troops joined in, and men like Miyazaki

Yoshimasa, Watanabe Tsuneo and Togawa Isamu formed a study group called the Matsubara Club that continues to this day.

Later I realised that, although power relationships within the party are important to an aspiring prime minister, support groups formed by discerning people outside of the party are valuable too.

Becoming the President of Takushoku University

On 13 September, 1967, I took up office as the 12th President of Takushoku University. I felt some hesitation about a serving politician and faction leader, taking up the position of director of a university. However, this particular university was unique in that it had been set up by a politician, Katsura Tarō, in 1900, and since then had had among its presidents such men as Gotō Shimpei, Shimomura Kainan and Ugaki Kazushige. Since my mentor, Yabe Teiji, had also been president for a long period, and there was the sense of having his mantle fall on me, I decided to take the job on. Besides myself, the deputy leader of the Liberal Democratic Party, Kawashima Shōjirō, was also a director and president of Senshū University.

In the Takushoku University song are the words, 'In our system there is no discrimination by colour or by border.' In accordance with this spirit, the university had a long history of educating men of ability who were predominantly active in Asia and South America. Takushoku University is generally thought of as right-wing but this was largely because of Waki Kōzō, a student of Russian at the university at the time of the Russo-Japanese war. Waki applied to join the army and was sent to the theatre of war in what was formerly Manchuria, where he joined special operations. Caught trying to blow up an iron bridge in order to impede the advance of the Russian army, he became famous as one of three heroes who died at their posts. The university has a tradition of casting in its lot with the state.

I wanted to follow the educational principles of Yabe which emphasised liberalism and internationalism and, at the same time, to encourage learning by bringing the energy of living politics to the education process. There was an outcry from journalists, but the students were curious and welcomed me, while the faculty members were divided between those who made me welcome, those who felt suspicious and were antagonistic, and those who just looked on. There were complicated ripples too, among the alumni. Most welcomed me very warmly, but some central figures kept me at arm's length as if I were something alien. I came to understand the difficulties of dealing with old universities.

In my inaugural speech I referred to the traditional characteristics that set Takushoku apart from other private universities. My argument was that, 'Where Waseda stands for freedom and Keiō for independence, Takushoku stands for the breaking of new ground' and I suggested that the path to be taken could lead to an international, people's university. I then pointed out that, 'Student life is first about ability, secondly about friendship and thirdly about serving the country' and declared that, 'An indifference to appearances is fine and students should not go in for putting on a show without soul. People who excel, be it in a science or a language or in physical education, will be allowed to graduate even if their credits fall a bit short'. My goal was a practical, field education that would be useful when they went out into society.

As a general rule we got all the students together in a lecture theatre once a month and the president addressed them. I addressed them twenty-two times in all, and distributed pamphlets of the content of the lectures. I established an industry education course and invited special lecturers. His Imperial Highness Mikasa Nomiya Takahito, Inayama Yoshihiro the president of Nippon Iron and Steel Corporation, Watanabe Tsuneo the chief of the political section at the Yomiuri newspaper and the rocket scientist, Dr. Itogawa, all took part. Because this course conferred credits it became very popular and the students spilled over from the hall. With Dr Akamatsu Kaname as chairman we invited people like the Japanese economic historian Dr Tsuchiya Takao, the international relations theorist, Itagaki Yoichi, and the constitutional lawyer Dr Kiyomiya Shirō, and succeeded in establishing a doctoral course in the graduate school.

But in 1970, there was a scandal at the university. A first year student in the politics and economics department died as a result of bullying in the karate club. As a result, the university came under attack for being right-wing, and student activists from outside invaded what had, up until then, been the last peaceful university, and demonstrations began in the grounds. For the university in Japan authorities this was an inexcusable incident and for me as president and as the serving Director-general of the Defense Agency, it was the most dreadful anguish.

I took the advice of my secretary, Ikeda Katsuki and went immediately to the home of the victim in Tochigi Prefecture to apologise to his parents. I also sent out a long, hand-written letter of apology to all the students and their parents, spelling out the measures we would take and the path we would follow in the future. It was round about this time that my father was taken unconscious to the national hospital in Takasaki, suffering from a cerebral haemorrhage. I shall never forget sitting by his bedside writing that letter. We brought forward the summer holidays and suspended the courses and, in desperation, at the end of August, I held a meeting of everyone concerned to explain the reforms. Fortunately our sincerity was recognised and when the next term started on September 1, the campus was quiet once more.

I was a complete amateur as far as student education was concerned but I believed that we should speak out against the stereotypical nature of Japanese higher education, the laziness and peace-at-any-price attitudes of some of the lecturers and the faculty, and the lack of individualistic aspirations among the students. My personal incantation was: 'Education of the whole man, not only intellectual education; "A" grades are not a passport for life; let us be men of passion and emotion, men who can be relied on'. At the entrance ceremony, I took off my morning coat and taught the school song to the freshmen myself. On the occasion of the University Festival I drank fresh snake's blood to encourage them.

The purpose of education is to stir the youthful spirit and to instil the power to act on the basis of moral courage and ideals. I felt that this was the soul of education and I followed this belief. How successful I was, I still don't know. In March 1971 I gave up the presidency due to pressure of work and became honorary president. Even now this period in my life remains as a bitter-sweet, sometimes painful, memory.

The last days of the Satō administration

On 5 March 1970 I addressed the Foreign Press Club in Marunouchi as Director-General of the Defense Agency in the Satō Cabinet. When we moved to the question and answer session, Samuel Jameson, who was then a reporter with the Chicago Tribune, knowing that the Liberal Democratic Party [LDP] presidential election was being held back till the autumn and that there was a problem with Satō seeking a forth term, put a provocative question.

One year ago you said, "For the Showa men its good morning, for the Taisho men its good afternoon, for the Meiji men, its good night." If the Meiji men decide on a fourth election will you say "good afternoon", or will you say "good night"?

The conference room held its breath and pricked up its ears as I answered, in English, to cheers from the audience of journalists, 'In Japan the twilight is very long'.

There is nothing so difficult as dropping the final curtain on an administration. Caught up in it, you taste the thrill, you are anxious, you feel a little ashamed. I didn't just watch the dropping of the curtain from the wings. As Chairman of the Executive Council in the Satō Cabinet I was intimately involved and learned from it.

I became the Chairman of the Executive Council on 5 July 1971, in the shifts in party personnel that accompanied the last cabinet reshuffle of the Satō administration. The new Secretary General was Hori Shigeru, and the Chairman of the Policy Affairs Research Council was Kosaka Zentarō. According to Hori's notes of a meeting he had with Satō in January, they agreed that Satō would retire when the Diet had approved the arrangements for the return of Okinawa. Twilight was nigh.

The Secretary General at that time was Tanaka Kakuei, and it seems probable that Satō talked only to Hori of his decision because Tanaka was expected to be one of the candidates for the presidency. By the time of the reshuffle in July he seemed to have worked out the personnel plans for the ending of his administration The appointment of Hori as secretary general was generally seen as being pre-arranged for that purpose, but my appointment as Chairman of the Executive Council attracted some attention.

This shake-up split the cabinet posts, four to the Satō faction, three to Ōhira, two each to the Fukuda, Nakasone and Funada factions, one each to the Ishii, Shiina and Miki factions and three to the Upper House, thereby preserving the factional balance. The Miki faction had been reduced by one to just one cabinet member, and the Sonoda and Murakami factions had been cut to zero but, from the point of view of power, it was the only possible arrangement. Seen as the best arrangement for soothing the party, the plan had as its premise that Fukuda was Satō's heir, whilst at the same time it provided kind treatment for the Ōhira and Nakasone factions and a balance of power between Fukuda Takeo and Tanaka Kakuei. However, with hindsight, Prime Minister Satō made a serious error.

On parade in the Diet: The Satō Cabinet

Tanaka had been building up his strength as Secretary-General in the Satō administration. Now Satō failed to restrain him by giving him the post of chief cabinet secretary, and instead let him go to the Ministry for International Trade and Industry. At the following year's presidential election this was to become a matter of serious regret for Satō, who had his eye on Fukuda to succeed him. The problem was that Satō thought that no one but Tanaka could manage the US-Japan textile negotiations, which were his biggest source of concern at the time, and Tanaka himself boasted: 'I'll show you; I'll sort it out'. It is easy to imagine he got the post of Minister of International Trade and Industry through force. It was in this way that the plot for Fukuda's dominance was cleverly upset.

Management of personnel is a terrible business. If you are chief cabinet secretary, living together in the prime minister's residence, following his instructions, then you are busy all the time and it is very difficult to extend your influence in the party. Often you must lunch with the prime minister and he has every opportunity to control you. However, for the Minister of International Trade and Industry there is frequent contact with Diet members of the ruling party who are seeking the assistance of the financial world and the small and medium sized industries. Making Tanaka Minister for International Trade and Industry was like loosing a tiger in a field.

It could be that even Satō, renowned for his expertise in personnel management, had been in office for too long and had lost his touch. Toward the end of his administration the cabinet had become weakened and the public estranged. This led to unexpected complications. Between July 1971, and January of the following year, four cabinet ministers were obliged to resign as a result of unexpected incidents or for making untoward statements; a phenomenon known commonly as, 'cutting the tail off the lizard'.

The first squall came in the regional elections in April when an increased number of reformist governors were elected or re-elected. With the addition of Kuroda as governor of Osaka, Asukata as governor of Yokohama, and Minobe, with his 'Stop Satō' slogan, as the governor of Tokyo, alongside Ninagawa, who had been elected previously for Kyoto, the Tokaidō megalopolis became a reformist camp. In metropolitan Tokyo and the prefecture of Osaka, the numbers of reformist mayors grew dramatically and the Communist Party made great strides in the regional assemblies.

Then, in the June Upper House elections, the number of seats won by the LDP fell yet again to 63, from 69 in the previous election and from 71 in the election before that. Against this, the Socialist Party went up from 35 to 39 seats, the Social Democratic Party from 2 to 6 seats and the Communist Party from 3 to 6 seats. These results made the party realise just how fragile the long-term Satō administration had become, and a mixture of boredom and irritation created the conditions for an early retirement.

The second squall was the resignation of the Speaker, Shigemune Yūzū, who provided a stronghold of support for Satō in the Upper House. Shigemune, Prime Minister Satō and former Prime Minister Kishi were known as the 'three Chōshū families'. From 1962 onwards, Shigemune had served as speaker and led the largest LDP faction in the Upper House, the eighty-member *Seifū* Club. He was bruited to be capable of gathering a hundred votes in an election for party president. It was known as the Shigemune kingdom. A 'Tarafuku party'[3] was organised to celebrate Shigemune's birthday; Moriya Kamejirō brought the cod from his home in Ishikawa prefecture and Shigemune the blow-fish from Yamaguchi prefecture. The party, on 11 February in the Speaker's residence, was a great success; the guests numbered around two hundred and sixty and almost the only people who didn't attend were myself and Shiina Etsusaburō. Four months later this kingdom was destroyed.

Out of the blue, Kōno Kenzō announced his candidature in the July election for speaker. There was a difference of twenty-one seats between the government party and the opposition party and only twelve members of the LDP needed to turn against the establishment for Shigemune to lose. Kōno sent a draft of proposed reforms of the chamber to all the members of the Upper House and the opposition party took them up. Even from within the LDP there were twelve people who were unhappy with Shigemune's dictatorial organisation, and people like Sakomizu Hisatsune, Aoki Kazuo, Kennoki Toshihiro and Shintani Torasaburō became strong supporters of Kōno. Kōno himself had grown up in the Green Breeze Society (*Ryōfukukai*) and was against factional activity in the Upper House. He revealed his thinking to his friend Ino Hiroya: that he was determined to overthrow Shigemune and he was not demanding the position of Speaker.

Nevertheless, Shigemune, who withdrew his candidacy when he saw he would not win, criticised Kōno for, 'Having joined with the opposition to leave a stain on the constitution.' This upset Kōno. Secretary General Hori, who was talking to the Upper House and making the final arrangements for the third candidate, Kiuchi Shirō, met with Kōno and asked him to support Kiuchi, but Kōno refused with tears in his eyes saying 'When so much has been said, I cannot pull out.'

At Hori's request, and since Kōno was somebody with whom I had had connections since the time of the Kōno faction, I met with him in a hotel room to talk, but there was nothing to be done. Kōno, his nephew Yōhei, and his relation Tagawa Seiichi were extremely agitated and in tears saying, 'Please allow us to do what we want to do.' The early morning results of the election made Kōno speaker by ten votes. The sudden emergence of Kōno, who disliked bureaucrats and who was close to both Tanaka Kakuei and Ōhira Masayoshi, gradually changed the situation in the Upper House to Tanaka's advantage.

How to be Prime Minister

At the same time as Kōno's dramatic emergence as Speaker, the Satō Cabinet was buffeted internationally by the two Nixon shocks; the Sino-American rapprochement which took place on 15 July

1971, and the suspension of the gold-dollar exchange one month later on 15 August. These decisions were taken, without prior consultation with Japan, despite the agreement reached between Foreign Minister Aichi and American Secretary of State Rogers in Paris, as recently as 12 May, that, 'Following the reversion of Okinawa, diplomatic issues will, as far as possible, be agreed through prior consultation'. People were beginning to whisper openly about the end of the administration when, at the beginning of September, the question of Chinese representation in the United Nations General Assembly came up.

Ever since he had become Prime Minister, Satō had taken great pains over what he believed to be the two major diplomatic issues: the reversion of Okinawa and the restoration of diplomatic relations with China. Latterly, the return of Okinawa had become intertwined with the textile negotiations between Japan and the United States, but had progressed comparatively smoothly. When he had visited America in November 1969, a joint statement had been negotiated agreeing reversion of Okinawa, free of nuclear weapons and with mainland status, by 1972.

Because of the inclusion, in that joint statement, of the so-called Taiwan clause, making 'The maintenance of peace and security in the region of Taiwan an important element in the stability of Japan', the Chinese government began to attack the Satō cabinet violently. They went so far as to make accusations of a revival of Japanese militarism, and relations between the two governments grew frosty. At the time, the two birds of Okinawa and China, could not be killed with one stone.

Nevertheless, looking back at the stance that Satō took, I believe that he hoped, albeit belatedly, to resolve the China problem and that he hoped to set something in motion during his administration. He was called 'Double bottomed' for his extremely careful character and that was how he was with the China question. Satō, like a lot of people when they drive, would turn the steering wheel to the left when they wanted to go right. He didn't tell lies, but he often played that sort of trick on newspaper reporters. He was famous too for being tight-lipped, to the extent that it was said that his family home was known as 'No scoop in Awashima'

In public Satō declared, 'We must repay Chang Kai-shek for his kindness to our defeated country directly after the war ended', and indeed, he stuck closely to Yasuoka Shōtoku's advice. But in private, he also believed that, insofar as was consistent with good faith as the

Prime Minister of Japan, he had to play his cards in such a way as to achieve the normalisation of relations between China and Japan.

One manifestation of this was his decision to send the deputy Prime Minister, Kawashima, to the tenth anniversary ceremony of the Asian African Conference, and to have him contact Chou En-lai on the spot. In 1971 he suggested, in the Diet, that someone of cabinet rank be sent to China, and he asked Noda Takeo, LDP Chairman of the China Issues Committee, to go as well. China sent a large group to Japan for the thirty-first world table tennis competition which opened in Nagoya at that time and the so-called Ping-Pong diplomacy developed.[4]

Even as Satō was under attack for being '*musaku*' [without policy] rather than '*Eisaku*' [his given name], there was one famous incident when secretary-general Hori entrusted Tokyo governor Minobe with a letter for China's Premier Chou En-lai, and Chou would not receive it because, he said, 'I cannot trust this letter'. Foreign Minister Fukuda cited this incident as one example of the 'duck-paddle' hidden diplomacy of the Satō administration. However there was another example of such sustained diplomatic activity away from the public gaze in which Eguchi Mahiko played the part of secret messenger.[5]

In September 1971, Japan became a joint proposer, with the United States, of the reversal concept relating to China's membership of the United Nations. According to Eguchi, Satō had earlier written a letter to Premier Chou, dated 7 September, which he had signed and handed to Eguchi. The gist of the letter was, 'I would like to visit China and exchange views with Premier Chou for the purpose of normalising diplomatic relations between Japan and China and of resolving the problems for long-term peace. Please give this matter consideration'.

Because the letter lacked clarity on the matter of the relationship between China and Taiwan, the Chinese would not accept it. Whereupon Satō wrote again on 12 September including the words 'I have told the Japanese Diet that the Chinese government is the representative of all Chinese people and that the problem of Taiwan is a domestic political problem for China and that is my belief.' However, this was just at the time when the question of China's representation at the United Nations was about to come up, and Japan acted as a proposer for the reversal concept. In the end, therefore, the letter was never delivered to Chou.

Even then, Satō did not give up and entrusted Eguchi with a letter dated 4 April 1972 offering to talk with Premier Chou. The letter was handed over by Eguchi in Hong Kong on 17 June, to China's representative to the Hong Kong Chapter for China-Japan Normalisation. On 18 June, Eguchi was given one original and one copy of a reply addressed to Satō from Premier Chou but, he says, 'I handed over the copy to Satō at the official residence on June 22 but, as it happened, there were reports about Satō resigning and the original was taken back to Beijing'. The purport of the letter was that, 'Premier Chou will meet with Satō in Beijing to discuss Sino-Japanese issues.'

While these negotiations were underway, I learned by chance what was happening from Imai Hiroshi, chairman of Japan Soda, who was helping Eguchi, and when I checked with Satō, he confirmed what I had heard. Satō indicated that he would give a confidential briefing on the negotiations to the candidates for the presidency of the party and, accordingly, I heard the explanation on 5 April. Eguchi told me he had explained the situation to Minister of International Trade and Industry, Tanaka, on 9 February, and to Foreign Minister Fukuda on 6 March. The people in the Japan-related manoeuvrings in Hong Kong were Huang Zhiwen the former Indonesian ambassador, and Ye Tong and Ke Zhengren, temple brothers of Ye Jian-Ying. On the Japanese side there was Satō Ichirō of the Upper House, and Kogane Yoshiteru and Hatta Sadayoshi of the Lower House and I confirmed these facts with them too.

In November 1991 I was shown a copy of the letter Satō had entrusted to Eguchi. When I checked the signature and mark at the bottom, 'Satō Eisaku', with Ōtsu Tadashi, the top private secretary, through Satō's son, the Diet member Satō Shunji, he confirmed again that it was authentic. Satō used Eguchi as an emissary, forging an opening for a breakthrough in Sino-Japanese relations and probably hoping, if things went well, to visit China himself during his period in office.

While he was pushing hard, he would also offer soft words in what was probably a deliberate two pronged technique. In this incident I could not help feeling that I had caught a glimpse of an unexpectedly bold side of Satō who was more usually known as 'Satō the watchful'. There is no doubt that Satō was very disappointed when his period in office came to an end. The Tanaka cabinet was formed in July and, at the end of September, Tanaka went to China and the joint declaration of the restoration of diplomatic relations between China and Japan was announced It seems likely however that the groundwork for this had been done during the Satō administration.

I was instructed in how to be a politician by Matsumura Kenzō, and in how to be a party man by Kōno Ichiro, but I was initiated into how to be a prime minister by Satō. Yoshida Shigeru's secret of success was political longevity and innate disposition; Satō's was an eagerness to learn and determination. People were apt to see him as a careful, powerful bureaucrat, but he was also an amiable, shy man with a strong sense of duty who took good care of others. He was a Confucianist and his goal was to be a Confucian prime minister.

His wife, Hiroko, reminisced about him. 'When he was at high school, all the family would gather at his parents' home in Tabuse City in Yamaguchi prefecture. His older brother, Nobusuke, was good with words and sociable and would sit in the centre at such gatherings, but on occasions like this, Eisaku, the younger brother, would sit alone by the stream out back and stare at the surface of the water. He looked so pitiable like that ...'. It is the sort of story that makes one wonder.

Heaven finally blessed the politician who had devoted himself to the art of being prime minister. His formidable opponents Kōno Ichiro and Ōno Banboku both died and Prime Minister Ikeda resigned because of illness. Satō steered the administration with 'the politics of waiting' and by being 'Satō the manager', and he managed an excellent stable that included Kawashima Shojirō, Hori Shigeru, Fukuda Takeo and Tanaka Kakuei. In this way, he contrived to run a long race.

Prime ministers Yoshida, Ikeda, Tanaka and Ōhira all concentrated on economic policies, while Hatoyama, Kishi, Satō and Miki paid comparatively greater attention to Japan's independence and individuality. I am probably of Hatoyama's lineage. Satō's negotiation of the return of Okinawa and his establishment of the three non-nuclear principles are historically significant post-war achievements.

The first oil crisis and the secret messenger to the Arabs

It was Sunday, November 20, 1973 and the middle of the night when the president of Arabian Oil, Mizuno Sōhei, came rushing to my home. At the time I was Minister for International Trade and Industry in the Tanaka cabinet.

Six weeks earlier, the fourth Middle-East war had broken out and, unbelievably, the Arab states had designated Japan a non-friendly state and had cut oil supplies suddenly. This was the first oil crisis.

From October our supplies were reduced by five percent and the threat was of a further cut of five percent each month. The price of oil and gas rose suddenly, at a stroke, to more than six times the previous level. Inflation intensified and housewives began to hoard detergents and toilet paper. We had about 80 days worth of oil stored but the situation was worsening and it was predicted that by March we would fall below the minimum level for stored oil (60 days), and the engines of the Japanese economy would stop across the country.

An economy is powered by perception and psychology. If we were about to enter a crisis in March, the chances were that we would be paralysed from January. To avoid this, we had to get the Arabs to designate us a friendly state and ensure the oil we needed. Our deadline, counting backwards, was the end of December.

Mizuno was anxious about this situation and visited Saudi Arabia to have an audience with King Faisal to petition him to classify Japan as a friendly state. In particular Mizuno made the appeal that, 'If things carry on as they are, Japan's production of fertiliser will suffer a sharp decrease; this will cause great problems in the production of foodstuffs in Asia and Africa which depends on it, and there is a danger that the ravages of famine will occur.' The King accepted, but on the condition that the Japanese government accept resolution 242 of the United Nations Security Council and speak out in support of total self-determination for the Palestinian people.

Mizuno negotiated with the Saudis and, armed with the draft of the statement of understanding, he hurried straight from Haneda airport to my house. My feeling was that the first priority was to break out of the state of panic we were in and, having made adjustments to the draft, I called Prime Minister Tanaka on the telephone and asked him to adopt it. Tanaka's answer was, 'Persuade Foreign Minister Ōhira.' But the Foreign Ministry and Ōhira disapproved the draft and would not accept it. They were afraid of America's reaction.

The following Monday I worked without a break in the Diet defending two emergency bills on oil policy and economic stability. In between, the chief secretary to the Foreign Ministry came and went with various amendments proposed by the Foreign Office. My feeling was that, if we carried on in this vein, it would be the Saudis who would get angry. The third time it happened I flew into a rage and sent him off saying, 'What are you moaning on about? You have no idea. You just tell the Foreign Minister that if you bring a Foreign Office draft to the cabinet meeting tomorrow, I shall rip it up and throw it away.'

In the end, the draft was announced informally in the cabinet meeting by Chief Cabinet Secretary Nikaidō and Japan, as promised, was awarded the status of friendly nation. At the end of December ships importing oil were arriving in a steady stream in Japan. In my long political career nothing has made me so happy.

Some time before this, the American Secretary of State Henry Kissinger, who had been in the Middle-East working for a cease-fire agreement, came to Japan via China. I showed him in figures indicating that unless the supply of oil to Japan recovered before the end of December, the Japanese economy would be panicked. I emphasised three points: 1. Part of the reserves of the world's majors should be sent to Japan. 2. Oil for use in the U.S. bases in Japan should be sent from America, Japanese oil for civilian use should not be used. 3. Peace in the Middle-East should be realised as soon as possible.

Kissinger rejected my argument saying, 'I will see what I can do about the matter of the American troops in Japan, but I can't give instructions to the major oil companies about transfers. Putting a time limit on negotiations for peace in the Middle-East would be stupid. We don't want an easy compromise with the Arab states'. I replied, 'If the Japanese economy crashes, the Security Treaty will

In the Middle East as Minister for International
Trade and Industry

194

cease to function, and the American army will be unable to move. This will create a crisis in the whole liberal bloc. If such a danger were imminent, Japan would have to take suitable steps to preserve the state.' Kissinger asked, 'What would these suitable steps be?' I kept Mizuno's secret activities to myself and answered only, 'They would be suitable steps taken after consideration of the totality of the international and domestic situations pertaining at the time.' I didn't tell him about the conditions King Faisal had presented to President Mizuno.

Kissinger and I had known one another since an international seminar at Harvard University in 1953 and so we were able to speak bluntly to one another. On this occasion Kissinger was silent and for a while we glared at each other without speaking. There were large numbers of reporters in the corridor outside so by prior arrangement we made a performance of leaving the room together smiling, but in reality it had been a heavy conference.

Because of what had happened, Prime Minister Tanaka and myself were identified as pro-Arab and lost our good reputation in the United States. In the conference of oil importing nations in Washington the following year Foreign Minister Ōhira explained the situation and tried to correct the misconception about us. The episode was an example of successful collaboration between Tanaka and myself.

After that episode, whenever there was an economic or a security crisis in Japan, I was particularly aware that the government needed a comprehensive crisis management policy. This was the case in 1983 on the occasion of the shooting down of the KAL plane, and again in 1991 at the time of the Gulf War.

Same class struggles with Tanaka Kakuei

Someone once said, 'Marx talked of "Class struggle", but more than half the fighting is "Same class struggle"'. In companies and government offices contemporaries always jockey for position and try to survive by pushing their way through. On the other hand, it is one of the subtleties of Japanese society that men are protective of those at a different stage from themselves, and when someone outstanding at the same stage emerges, everyone lines up firmly behind him.

The political world is, of course, no exception to this rule. The relationship between former Prime Minister Tanaka Kakuei and myself was exactly this. We were both born in May 1918. We were both strongly intuitive and self-willed; we both gave free play to our tongues and were very assertive. On the other hand, whilst I was theoretical, he was emotional. I joined the navy, he was in the army. In the election for president of the Democratic Party [*Minshutō*] immediately after we were first elected, I supported Ashida Hitoshi while he gave his backing to Shidehara Kijūrō. I agreed with, while he strongly opposed, the bill for state control of coal mines.

In meetings of Diet members, both of us would be on our feet and there would be great debates. On my side would be Kawasaki Hideji, Sakurauchi Yoshio, Sonoda Sunao and so on; supporting Tanaka there would be people like Hara Kenzaburō, Nemoto Ryutarō, and Kosaka Zentarō. In those days, the party and the Diet were the forums for discussion and talk and persuasion were part of the job of the politician. The prevalence of behind the scenes negotiations and deals, the so-called *nemawashi* [digging round the roots to lay the groundwork] meant a corruption of traditional constitutional government in Japan.

In truth, the two of us were the new men of the post-war political world and were the centre of attention. Later, when the Democratic Party split, I remained with the opposition party faction while Tanaka joined Yoshida's Liberal Party. I stayed in opposition, fought the Yoshida cabinet and held back from being overtly active in Diet or radio debates until the time of the Hatoyama cabinet's restoration of diplomatic relations with the Soviet Union. Tanaka was buried away in the sheer numbers of the party in power and did not appear in public either, but was quietly building his base in both business and politics. Eventually the Kishi cabinet was formed and he distinguished himself in the conservative mainstream while I continued to eat cold rations in a small, conservative tributary.

Kōno Ichirō died suddenly and, in 1967, I formed the Nakasone faction with a number of sympathisers. I was five years ahead of Tanaka in becoming a faction leader. With Fukuda Takeo and Hori Shigeru, Tanaka was one of the head clerks of the Satō cabinet: he served as Secretary General and as Minister for International Trade and Industry and in time he had more than half of the Satō faction in his grasp. This was the case when, in 1972, the problem of who should succeed the long-lived Satō administration began to bubble up.

I had three reasons for supporting Tanaka at this time. First, Tanaka was a new face; a self-made man of the people, decisive, a man of action. He was the right man for the job.

Second, the normalisation of diplomatic relations between China and Japan had become an urgent issue on the political agenda. Of course, Fukuda Takeo was the most eminently well-qualified person for the task in terms of outlook and experience but, as Foreign Minister in the last days of the Satō cabinet, he bore responsibility for the reversal concept defending Taiwan and so didn't fit the bill. I was asked by Prime Minister Satō and by members of the financial world, both directly and indirectly, to support Fukuda and there was also a fair amount of pressure from my electoral district. However after mature deliberation I felt that the statesman-like thing to do was to put national interest above personal feelings and so I decided to support Tanaka.

Third, the vast majority of the people in my faction felt as I did and asked me to support Tanaka's candidacy. Their position had been formulated as a result of top-secret talks among the members at about the time of the summit talks in San Clemente in 1972, between Prime Minister Satō and President Nixon. What they wanted was a ticket to the post of president and the prime minister and they tried for a time to have me stand. It was also a means of avoiding the faction becoming a hunting ground for other factions. Ultimately the question of whether or not I would stand for election myself was left for me to decide on the basis of the situation at the time.

Sometime around February I received an invitation from Sei Ikudo of the Ryūen Chinese restaurant and met with Dr. Lee, a fortune-teller from Hong Kong. When I had him tell the fortunes of the various LDP leaders of the time, he told me, 'Tanaka is 100% certain to become Prime Minister whereas Fukuda has almost no chance at all'. I don't particularly believe in fortune telling, but as it coincided with the direction we were going, I felt very reassured. Confucius said, 'Do not trust in your own distorted vision of superhuman strength' and I had recourse even to such things as this as a staff with which to keep my footing.

Ultimately I made the establishment of Sino-Japanese diplomatic relations a condition for supporting Tanaka's candidature and withdrew as a candidate for the presidency. This was to ensure that Tanaka ranked top in the first-round vote. As a result, Tanaka came top by six votes. Ten years later, when I stood as a candidate to succeed the Suzuki cabinet, Tanaka supported me totally; a manifestation of the subtle interplay of competitiveness and co-operation between contemporaries.

Our political techniques were quite different. We were similar in our intuitive ability, in our ability to size things up and to unify, but I was no match for him in terms of compassion, smoothness and ability to win people over. He was terrifically active, keeping an eye on local friendships and neighbourhood association festivals, and everything from the tax office to the road safety association, and was blessed with the kind of worldly wisdom which is able to take over a private shop and end up with big listed company. This was something he was particularly good at. It was this kind of power that built his sort of massive group and I didn't go in for that kind of emotional way of operating. For the most part, I would put ideas up front, use advisory groups to develop policy, decide on a course, and rely on theoretical knowledge to persuade the electorate. He searched for the main issue through the concrete theories, while I tended to develop concrete theories from main issues.

Very few people are aware that, though I often met and talked with Tanaka, there was never any occasion when he asked me for any personal favours. To sum him up in a word, he was a liberal. He made up for a lack of early education through passionate individual study,

Shaking hands on an agreement to support
Tanaka for president

he always held a pencil in his hand and would have a piece of paper ready to write down the numbers and explain concrete policies. In this he was a genius, and this was the reason that he was criticised as 'the computerised bulldozer.'

The fact that more than half of the so-called 'intellectual Diet members' who belonged to the Satō faction shifted to the Tanaka faction was a huge surprise to me at the time. I believe they were attracted by the fact that he possessed what they, the intellectuals, lacked.

What we had in common was a keen sense of nation-state consciousness. Occasionally our viewpoints differed, but as members of the conservative camp, we worked together to share our fate with the state. We were anxious for world peace and worked hard for the well-being of the state. We expressed our mutual respect for each other's ability, and were always staunch friends who understood one another. There were things we forgave each other because of our mutual understanding. People involved in political life have to take a long term view of things and not be overzealous about those things immediately in front of them. I often tell young Diet men this, 'Politicians are like whirligig beetles; sometimes they are swimming with the current, sometimes against it. Then after a time they are back in the flow. But everyone gets carried along by the major currents. Today's enemy is tomorrow's ally. At the macro level, one governs the nation; at the micro level one is only a single member of 512 in the Diet. There are no absolutes in politics. You must leave yourself space to manoeuvre in your relationships.'

In the second post-war election, in 1947, roughly one hundred and twenty new members were elected from the conservative camp. In addition to Tanaka, there was Sakurauchi, Nemoto and Sonoda while from the Socialist party there was Suzuki Zenko Sasaki Kozō and Katsumata Seiichi. Now the years have passed, and I am the only one left who has been elected seventeen times in succession.

Even the remarkable talent of Tanaka Kakuei has withdrawn from the front line. There are four seasons in a man's life. I sincerely hope that the rest of his life will be peaceful.

CHAPTER TEN

APPOINTMENT AS PRIME MINISTER

Dokō's tears

The Second Ad Hoc Commission on Administration [Second *Rinchō*] had run its course, and the First Advisory Council for the Promotion of Administrative Reform [First *Gyōkakushin*] had not long been set up when Nakagawa Kōji, now Director of the Peace Institute, went to see Dokō Toshio and explained how financial reconstruction could be achieved without tax increases. When he produced the numbers to back up his case, Dokō was overjoyed, and when Nakagawa left, Dokō, in a highly emotional state, made a point of accompanying him to the elevator. He was in tears. Whilst Chairman of *Rinchō*, Dokō had consistently pressed for 'financial reconstruction without tax increases', but clearly even he, in his heart of hearts, had not been certain whether it would be possible, and this incident suggests the extent of his concern.

On New Year's Day 1981 I had been standing next to Prime Minister Suzuki in the Plum Room [*Ume no ma*] at the Imperial Palace waiting, in my capacity as Director of the Administrative Management Agency, for the Showa Emperor to appear. As we waited I said to the Prime Minister, 'I would like Dokō to become chairman of *Rinchō*, what do you think?' The Prime Minister agreed he would be very stable. With this, I asked Sejima Ryūzo and Hanamura Jinhachirō to intercede and it was arranged that Prime Minister Suzuki and myself would make a formal request in March. Dokō, when approached, laid down four conditions.

First, the report would definitely be implemented. Second, there would be financial reconstruction without tax increases. Third, there would be regional administrative reform. Finally, there would be radical reform of policy on rice, railways and health insurance,[1] and the private sector would be comprehensively revitalised.

In fact, at the time we began to tackle administrative reform, there were two major issues. These were financial reconstruction, and the privatisation of the two public corporations: the Japan National Railways and Nippon Telegraph and Telephone. Each was a challenge worse than the climbing of Everest, and it was questionable whether we could succeed in such a major enterprise. Resistance from the opposition parties and the labour unions was expected to be intense. When General MacArthur had reformed the national railways, the body of the JNR president had been found on the tracks. Even Kishi Nobusuke said, 'You know, Nakasone, the only times administrative reform has succeeded in Japan were during the Meiji Restoration and the MacArthur reforms. Short of a revolution or a coup-d'état, it can't be done.'

I was deeply impressed by the fact that Dokō made his acceptance conditional. It was the first time a private person had set conditions of this nature, and my doubts and uneasiness disappeared in the light of his determination and sense of responsibility. I took a solemn vow to push through administrative reform.

However, when Rinchō first began, Dokō didn't trust government officials and seemed to believe that politicians were a shady lot who tried to evade their commitments. In fact, according to the people who worked closest to Dokō in the *Rinchō* office, deputy chairman Yamamoto, and head of the general affairs section Shigetomi, no sooner did Dokō meet them than he asked, 'Are you with us or against us?' They were angered by this. From August of the previous year, the two of them had worked frantically to formulate the bill to set up *Rinchō*, to prepare the budget and to sort out personnel and public relations. Dokō changed his mind afterwards when he saw how persistent they were despite the pressure they were under from all sides.

One day, when the opposition from the various ministries, agencies and interest groups was particularly dreadful and the committee members began to talk of compromise, Yamamoto went to Dokō's room and said, 'We will never agree a plan for fiscal reconstruction without increased taxes under these conditions. We have to be more strict.' Not long after he returned to his own desk, he was surprised by Dokō appearing in front of him to say, 'I will support you in whatever you want to do, so go ahead and do it.'

This was an eighty-odd year old man who had gone out of his way to go, in person, to his subordinate's room in order to show how determined he was, and to be encouraging. From then on, they would do anything for him. Dokō, the *Rinchō* committee members and the office united and closed in on the enemy camp in a frontal attack and a single-minded drive forward that lasted five years.

In order to fulfil the commitments made to Dokō and to withstand long-term austerities, it was necessary to get off to a running start. To this end, I thought the budget compilation in July 1981 for the following fiscal year would be a good opportunity to find out rough estimates of the requests each ministry and agency would be making, to ascertain what the basic government keynote plan based on these would be, and to use this as an impetus for administrative reform. I was aware that if we didn't act resolutely and we ended up with some half-cocked compromise, then administrative reform would run on broken rails and would not be successful. The time had come to show the courage and determination to deliver financial reconstruction without increased taxes, to disavow swelling budgets, to curtail government subsidies and grants and to carry through administrative reform.

Shortly before the beginning of July, I had *Rinchō* put out an emergency report on the basis of which we made drastic cuts aimed at realising 'small government'. On this occasion, committee member Sejima Ryuzō formulated several useful principles: that if we did our best we would succeed; that we would not be mischievously hostile to the ministries and agencies and that we would proceed with the co-operation of officials.

Over a period of forty-five days between May and July, we began an operation of unprecedented scope. The responsible people in each

Chatting with Dokō at a *Rinchō* Party

ministry and agency were sent for and were pressed to take a knife to their budgets so that they would fall in with the basic keynote plan of *Rinchō*. The opposition from ministries and agencies was unbelievable and there were even eruptions of pressure and rumbling criticism from LDP support groups. After a joint meeting of the Policy Affairs Research Council [PARC] divisions and the *Rinchō* committee members in the Akasaka Prince Hotel, Dokō and the Rinchō members were downcast about the future. The people who broke the deadlock were the deputy chairman Enjōji Jirō, one of the committee members Sejima Ryūzo; the chairman of the LDP Council of Administrative and Financial Research Hashimoto Ryutarō and the Deputy Chairman of PARC Katō Mutsuki.

We also set up a 'shadow' *Rinchō* whose meetings were separate from the formal daytime meetings; a group comprising myself, Horiuchi Mitsuo, Nakamura Yasushi, Kaji Natsuo, Hashimoto, Sejima, Akazawa Shōichi, Katō Hiroshi, and Umemoto Junsei. The shadow *Rinchō* met fifteen times on Friday evenings at a restaurant in Akasaka where we prepared moderate drafts and refined strategy for supporting them.

I had enormous support from the friends I had made in my days on short-term active service with the navy and from my colleagues and successors in the Ministry of Home Affairs [MHA]. Because the MHA had not had one of their own as prime minister since the war, Murata Gorō, Imai Hisashi, Kashiwamura Nobuo and Kobayashi Yosōji formed the *Sakafunekai*, a club to debate national policy, on my behalf. At the critical moment for administrative reform Kataoka Seiichi used his influence to start the Naiyūkai club with forty-seven Diet members.

Machimura Kingo, Furui Yoshimi and Nadao Hirokichi, the three most senior members, would be in the centre with Saitō Kunikichi, Okuno Seiryō and Hara Bunpei taking up positions to each side. They would spread into the sitting room and sit, cross-legged, in discussion. They too were a powerful engine propelling administrative reform. Ultimately though, such reform was a massive undertaking which could not be achieved without the long-term and lasting support of the nation. I argued that, 'Administrative reform is the work of three cabinets and ten years', 'Administrative reform is a glider, if the wind of support from the people stops blowing, it will crash' and, 'It is the Japanese version of Mao Tse-tung's long march.' I was surprised when the eighty-five year old Dokō responded by saying, 'Then let's start a people's movement'. We already had the promise of total support from the leading economic associations but, more than that, Dokō wanted to get the nation-wide backing of the people. 'One-day *Rinchōs*' and administrative reform rallies flourished nation-wide and Dokō himself travelled all over the country.

Just at that time NHK television broadcast a programme about the simple life led by Dokō and his wife where they were shown eating a simple dinner of dried sardines. The programme made a deep impression on the country. The wind of support strengthened and the glider climbed.

There were three watersheds. The first was when, in response to severe opposition from the ministries and agencies, I announced in a cabinet meeting that officials who refused to cooperate in administrative reform could be demoted or relocated without it being necessary to wait for them to resign. Another was in November 1983, after I had become prime minister. Following the first trial of Tanaka Kakuei and the Lockheed affair we had compromised with the opposition parties in order to pass bills connected with administrative reform. However, since we expected to be defeated, I decided to dissolve the Lower House. In the subsequent general election we suffered a set-back and survived by co-operating with the New Liberal Club. The third watershed was when the president of the National Railways, who had agreed to the division and privatisation of the railways when he took up office, suddenly became negative toward it under pressure from the deputy president and union members. I accepted his resignation and this became a decisive springboard in promoting reform.

These Japanese reforms have been given historical recognition alongside the reforms of President Ronald Reagan and Prime Minister Margaret Thatcher, as the political reforms of 'the new conservatism' which began at the end of the 1970s. By relaxing labour regulations the reforms addressed the stagflation created by Keynesian managed economics and an excessive stress on welfare. Essentially forms of economic liberalism, they promised revitalisation of the private sector, and 'small government' by means of allowing the 'free hand' of the market to operate unhindered and through privatisation, deregulation and the reduction of subsidies.

The new conservatism emphasised the regeneration of national morality and the strengthening of the family, education and national identity. Its aim was the enrichment of the middle class. It sought, even at the expense of pain and sacrifice, to rebuild the spiritual order which had been destroyed in the 1960s and to correct the reckless policies of those years.

The scale of the undertaking was unprecedented. During the five years and three months, the 1,980 days of *Rinchō* and the Advisory Council for the Promotion of Administrative Reform which followed, the material distributed to the committee covered 2,446 cases. There were 16,000 topics investigated, replies and opinions were given thirteen times, formal meetings were chaired by Dokō 313 times, and sectional meetings and sub-committee meetings took place 914 times.

In the spring of 1987, Dokō received the Order of the Rising Sun, First Class, with Star and Ribbon. I will never forget the scene. When he came before the Emperor in his wheelchair, he raised up the medal presented to him by the Shōwa Emperor and sat with his head bowed, unmoving. He stayed like that for close to a minute and I began to think there was something physically wrong and was about to go to him. At that precise moment he slowly raised his face and his eyes were full of tears. The Emperor too seemed relieved.

Birth of an entrepreneurial cabinet

How far
Have I come
To this meadow of bush clovers!

On 27 November 1982, I was deeply moved by my appointment as Prime Minister. It was thirty years since I had entered the Diet and fifteen years since I had become faction leader. The son of a timber merchant, I had made the journey from the northern district of Jōshū where the dry winds blow: my teeth gritted, I had weathered the storms. This was now the promised land.

From about September of that year, political tension increased as Prime Minister Suzuki's term of office as president drew to a close. It was taken for granted that Suzuki would be re-elected so I wagered my political life on administrative reform and devoted my days to that. I told Suzuki I would support his re-election. My feeling was this. If you want to be Prime Minister, you can't do it solely through your own efforts. When destiny and the needs of the time combine, the door opens. If you have made it as far as deputy prime minister the only course open to you is to work hard and refrain from worldly ambition. The rest is in the hands of fate.

But unexpectedly, at the end of September, before Suzuki visited China, I had notice from a friendly newspaper reporter that, 'The Prime Minister will probably drop hints to the journalists accompanying his party that he might not run for re-election.' After the cabinet meeting on 6 October straight after his return, Suzuki called me back and explained, 'It is' possible that I might not stand for election as prime minister, so make preparations.' I reiterated my absolute support and urged him to stand for re-election. I did not leak the information to anyone; I kept it to myself and watched the situation unfold. On 12 October, Suzuki suddenly announced his intention to resign. This was a complete thunderclap to the Suzuki faction.

Suzuki had devoted himself to the affairs of state and had made 'harmony' his watchword. When his period of office expired he decided, in his calm way, to use the opportunity to leave the path clear for the younger generation and so to avoid stagnation in the national administration. The dissolution of the Tanaka cabinet had resulted in a period of 'grudge politics' and the end of every administration had brought great confusion. Consequently, Suzuki's decision to resign whilst he still had some political strength remaining made a favourable impression on the public.

The task of sorting out the succession was entrusted to the top four officials in the party and there were meetings of the top advisors. However, the discussions foundered and on 16 October, the day of notification for the primary election, four candidates came forward: Kōmoto Toshio, Abe Shintarō, Nakagawa Ichirō and myself. We were in the midst of a recession in the aftermath of the oil crisis, and national finances were facing a crisis. Diplomatic relations with both America and Asia were at an impasse, and within the party the general feeling was that this was not the time for a primary election.

So, although the candidacies were accepted, the election campaigns were frozen for one week and negotiations continued. The job was entrusted to Suzuki, Former Prime Minister Fukuda and Secretary General Nikaidō, but no conclusion was reached. Then an in *camera* conference was held overnight from the evening of the 22nd to the morning of the 23rd, and, as a last resort it was proposed that the posts of president and prime minister should be divided and myself appointed prime minister whilst Fukuda became president. The four candidates were called and were pressed for a definite reply. The others reluctantly agreed but I rejected the proposal saying, 'This violates the normal course of constitutional government and I will not accept it under any circumstances.' We hurried into the primary elections that same day.

Luckily I had the support of the Tanaka faction, the Suzuki faction and a section of the independents and at 1.00 p.m. on 24 November, I was elected amidst a fantastic commotion in the ballot counting hall.

The results were:

Nakasone Yasuhiro – 559,673 votes
Kōmoto Toshio   – 265,078 votes
Abe Shintarō   – 80,443 votes
Nakagawa Ichirō   – 66,041 votes.

On the following day, 25 November, I was nominated 11th president of the LDP in a special general meeting of the party, and on the 26th I was nominated as the seventy-first prime minister by a plenary session of both houses.

On the night of the nomination, as I waited for the designation as prime minister in the Diet the following day, I turned off the light in the room of the Director of the Administrative Management Agency, leaving only the desk lamp burning, and sat alone, quietly absorbed in the personnel plans for the cabinet. Two hours passed like that. Afterwards my chief private secretary recalled that there was an unearthly air about me.

First I reduced the number of posts assigned to the Nakasone faction and allocated them to other factions. The only members of the cabinet who came from the Nakasone faction were Yamanaka who was Minster of International Trade and Industry and Higaki who was Minister of Posts and Telecommunications. I broke the precedent whereby the chief cabinet secretary was a member of the prime minister's own faction and decided to approach Gotoda Masaharu. I had discussed my plan with former prime minister Tanaka from the time of the Suzuki Cabinet, but even he did not appear to think I would actually implement it.

I had two reasons for nominating Gotoda. The first was that the successful implementation of administrative reform required both a quick decision and the selection of someone who could control the bureaucracy. The second was that there were warnings of a big earthquake expected in the Tōkai region and I believed that, were anything like that to happen, there was no other politician who was so adept at crisis management. I had met with Gotoda, who was deputy chairman of LDP Council of Administrative and Financial

Designation as Prime Minister in the Lower
House plenary session

Research, in September, and had asked him, in the strictest confidence, to accept a post when I formed a cabinet.

My political philosophy was, 'A politician is what he achieves, government is a job.' Even a cabinet that looks good disappears without a trace if its work leaves no concrete results. A seemingly less impressive cabinet will, if it gets on with the job, win the support of the people and leave an historical legacy. Political power for me came hard won at the end of a period of difficulties and I was determined to make free and exhaustive use of it so that I would have no regrets. Once you have grasped political power, it is yours; there is only the judgement of history for those who hold public office.

When he looked at the list of candidates for cabinet posts drawn up on the basis of this policy, Secretary General Nikaidō was at a loss for words. Then, when some moments had passed, he suggested a rethink saying, 'Prime Minister, are you serious? This won't do at all.' Nikaidō was one of the chief executives in the Tanaka faction but when he saw the line-up which took six members of the Tanaka faction into the cabinet and even gave them the post of chief cabinet secretary and put Hatano Akira, known as pro-Tanaka, into the post of Minister of Justice, he was surprised. In addition, in the column for the director of the National Land Agency and the Hokkaido Development Agency there was the name of a man long left in the shade, Katō Mutsuki.

I told Nikaidō, 'Tomorrow's newspapers and television reports will probably be critical. We will get the sort of big headlines you would expect if a Greater East Asia War had broken out or there had been a Great Kantō earthquake. I am resigned to that. More than anything I am putting together a group of able men who can get the job done. I will take full responsibility for it.' Nikaidō replied, 'If the Prime Minister says so.'

It was thus that the 'entrepreneurial cabinet' came into being.

When I got home I said, 'There will be a huge storm tomorrow, I'm going to sleep under the covers.' As I had feared, the newspapers the following morning jumped with abusive and back-biting headlines like, 'Tanaka Puppet Cabinet', 'Tanakasone Cabinet', 'Right-angle Cabinet' and, 'The Docking of Financial Influence and the Right.'. I made a decision, that the Nakasone Cabinet would make a furious dash off the blocks and if it fell in six months, so be it.

Home-made diplomacy moves the world

The moment the Nakasone administration began on 26 November 1982, I called President Chun Do Hwan of Korea, President Reagan of the United States and the heads of all the ASEAN countries to greet them. This, too, was a historical first. President Chun answered warmly, 'I would like us to cooperate in opening a new era in relations between Japan and Korea.' I thought that this had potential, and I decided to visit Korea first, before going to America. To this end I had to break the disagreeable deadlock between Japan and Korea, and Japan and America within the year.

On the third day after the cabinet was established, I called Sejima Ryūzō and asked him to come secretly to the prime ministerial residence that evening. I entrusted Sejima with the co-ordination of normalisation. At the same time I began conferring with the various ministries and departments about the matter of economic co-operation with Korea. The sums under discussion totalled about four billion dollars and had been pending since the Suzuki Cabinet.

I entered into talks with the party about reducing customs duties on tobacco in an effort to improve relations with the United State, but violent resistance from the party led me to cut short the debate, and leave the question with the two party men responsible, Ozawa Tatsuo and Hidaka Hirotame. I also planned to reduce the duty on chocolate and to increase the volume of imports. These were things that influential members of the U.S. Senate had requested. The big problem, as it had been for successive cabinets, was the issue of providing military technology to America. In the past, the Cabinet Legislation Bureau had always taken the line that export of military technology was not possible, but I explained that, 'In this respect, we must treat the Security Treaty preferentially. The export of arms would be improper, but it must be constitutionally possible to provide technology for the purpose of mutual co-operation and help.' This resulted in a change of interpretation.

In parallel with this Sejima visited Korea twice in December and met with President Chun for talks. If he had left from Narita he would have attracted attention so he went from Osaka by KAL, and from Fukuoka, through Pusan, to negotiate with the special envoy for Chun, the Secretary General of the ROK ruling party. On 29 December, I had a secret report from Sejima that an agreement had been reached on a visit to Korea. I prayed to every conceivable God that there would be no leak before it was officially announced on 3 January. The whole of Japan drew in its collective breath with surprise as it heard the news under the influence of the New Year *sake.*

On 11 January 1983, I made the first official visit of a Japanese prime minister of Korea since the end of the war. For the first time since the war, the Japanese flag was flown in Kimpo Airport, and the Japanese anthem was played.

I had been studying Korean since the previous year and in my speeches at the opening and again at the end of the official banquet in Seoul, I spoke for about a third of the time in Korean. The Korean VIPs were very surprised, and many of them were moved to tears. Even when the banquet was over, there were further parties in the Korean style reception hall. President Chun and I joined forces; I sang, 'The Yellow Shirt' in Korean and President Chun sang, 'Sentimental Journey to Shiretoko' in Japanese.

The new turn in relations between Japan and Korea appeared to cause a shock wave in America. I touched down in Washington one week later carrying this achievement with me. The next morning I was

Greeting President Chun Do Hwan during the visit to Korea

invited to a breakfast meeting with the publisher of the Washington Post, Katherine Graham. I remarked that 'Japan is what I would call an unsinkable aircraft carrier and as such will not allow incursions by foreign military planes'. This comment shook both Washington and Tokyo. The expression, 'unsinkable aircraft carrier' was without doubt an inappropriate translation, but with this one shot, all of Washington's pent up feelings of mistrust at Japan's negative attitude toward defence, were blown away. It was an enormously effective shock treatment that changed the gloomy atmosphere between Japan and America completely.

That night the then Vice-President, George Bush, held a banquet in my honour. I rose and greeted the guests.

'My second daughter Mieko is here this evening. When she was eleven, she took part in an American International Summer Village [CIVS] camp and was looked after by a family by the name of Winski in the town of Michigan in Indiana. Through that connection we had the daughter of that family to stay in our house. Since then, the two families have kept up a relationship for twenty years. When they heard I was visiting this time, they brought the whole family to Washington so that we could embrace. When I sent Mieko to America, it was my heart's desire that if I ever came to the U.S. with my wife, as the Prime Minister of Japan, Mieko would act as interpreter for me.

211

Now we have crossed many mountains and forded many rivers, and that dream has become reality and my heart is filled with great emotion. The American and Japanese nations must, like our two families, build on a basis of friendship and trust.'

A number of times I stumbled as I spoke. Vice President Bush, Secretary of State George Shultz, Secretary of Defense Caspar Weinberger all pressed handkerchiefs to their eyes. It was said that Mrs Reagan, hearing this from Shultz also blinked away the tears.

The following morning my family was invited to breakfast with the President in the private quarters of the White House. It was an unusual honour. The President asked me to call him 'Ron' and asked my first name? I told him, 'Yasu'. What became known as the 'Ron-Yasu relationship', began with this exchange.

Thereafter the President protected me; I helped him, and we co-operated regardless of the downside for our own administrations. At the Williamsburg Summit I was able to help President Reagan, in his capacity as Chairman, by intermediating with President François Mitterand of France. Later, in the arms reduction negotiations with the Soviet Union, the President pressed his reluctant officials, and secured the removal of 140 Soviet SS20 medium range missiles deployed throughout Siberia which had constituted a great threat to Japan.

Establishing the Ron-Yasu relationship

I told the President, 'You be the pitcher and I'll be the catcher. Sometimes the pitcher has to listen to what the catcher has to say.' And when the foreign press corps asked, 'Why do you support the President to such an extent?' I answered, 'Because I like John Wayne.'

Diplomacy truly is hand-crafted. Now, more than ever, the world moves in response to the hand-built trust that exists between statesmen, and as a result of their leadership.

World leaders

At the Williamsburg Summit in 1983, when the commemorative photograph was taken, the fact that I was photographed in the middle, standing next to President Reagan, became a topic of conversation. It was not that I had particularly planned to stand in the centre. When I arrived in Williamsburg I was greeted by the host country, to the tune of the 'Battleship March' The critical response from a section of the Japanese press who condemned it as militarist, worried the State Department, but I reassured President Reagan, 'There is no need to worry. In Japan it is a famous piece of music and presents no problem at all.' As I walked beside him explaining this, we came to the place where the photograph was to be taken and I stayed where I was, by his side, and that was the extent of it. But there were two occasions on which Reagan took my hand and made space for me to sit beside him; the first was at the Williamsburg Summit, the second was at the emergency summit in New York before the talks at Rekyavik between President Reagan and President Mikhail Gorbachev. This closeness was a direct result of the Ron-Yasu relationship.

Reagan always had the air of the captain of the western team. He carried jokes and stories with him in his pocket, and he would fish them out from time to time and make us laugh. Amongst them were some risqué stories, and these he would only tell when the Prime Minister of England, Mrs Thatcher was not there. Margaret Thatcher was known as 'the Iron Lady,' but this concealed a certain refinement and womanly shyness. As a chairman she was decisive in winding up discussions and taking a vote: the manner in which she brought discussions to a close was truly splendid.

At the London Summit in 1984, Prime Minister Thatcher asked me the secret of economic growth in Japan, and I replied, 'One of them is the development of robots and their large-scale use.' I continued, 'In your country you probably think of robots as strange iron

213

World leaders at the Williamsburg summit

Frankensteins, but in polytheistic Japan, we regard them as siblings and on special occasions we say, "have a drink" and pour them a beer.' She made me laugh when she flashed back, without missing a beat, 'When that happens I want you to make it a Scotch, not a beer'.

In my talks with China's Paramount leader Deng Xiaoping I avoided practical business as far as possible and asked him his views on life, and about his experiences. When I asked him, 'In almost eighty years as a member of the Communist Party, what has been the most difficult thing for you?' he answered very frankly. 'The Cultural Revolution. At times, when I was put in the cattle barn, I thought that it was the end. My philosophy was optimism, and I held out through force of will, in the belief that such stupidity could not last. When I am asked to write a Chinese character, I write "optimism"'. To the question 'What made you happiest?' he replied, 'When we chased the Kuomintang army across the Plain of China and crossed the Yangtze. Our strategy worked precisely as we had predicted and nothing brought me as much pleasure as that.'

I have vivid memories of a three hour talk with President Mikhail Gorbachev of the Soviet Union in July 1988. I pointed out that, 'The present Cold War came about because the West acted to contain the expansionism and hegemonic intentions of Stalin. If you correct Stalin's mistakes, the West will probably reduce its opposition. The

Northern Territories issue is another of Stalin's mistakes and you must return them to us. The time has come for planning world reconciliation'. Gorbachev replied, 'I have a great interest in that way of thinking. Let us talk again.'

On the same occasion I made a speech to the Soviet Science Academy World Economics International Relations Centre, [IMEMO] on the same lines as the conversation I had with Gorbachev. Afterwards, when I went to speak at the Royal Institute of International Affairs at Chatham House in London, I learned that the English translation of my speech had been sent from the Soviet Union. The ideal of world reconciliation was thereafter enshrined in my new diplomacy.

Amintore Fanfani, the Italian Prime Minister, was a great politician, mature and highly cultured. He was a man of mild appearance but he had a loud voice and was surprisingly resolute as chairman. He reminisced once, 'I went from being a university professor of politics to being a politician, but real politics was a series of frustrations and disappointments. When I talked to the Pope about withdrawing from politics, the Pope said, "That is up to you. But when you are faced with two roads, you should take the more difficult." That made me take up the challenge of the political path.'

We exchanged oil paintings painted by ourselves and those I received from Prime Minister Fanfani were hung in my office in the Prime Minister's residence. When I guided the Showa Emperor around on the occasion of the 100th anniversary celebration of cabinet government held in the Prime Minister's residence I showed him the pictures.

I am grateful that on two occasions during summits, I achieved the support of all the leaders for proposals I made. One was a proposal for a 'conference on life sciences and mankind' that I made at the Williamsburg Summit. The purpose of the conference was to have the members – scientists, philosophers and men of religion – discuss such ethical questions as whether, genetic manipulation carried the danger of a loss of human dignity. Each country held conferences and the results were circulated to universities and research organs in each country.

The other was a proposal I put to the Venice Summit in 1987 for a 'Human Frontiers Science Forum.' Each country made co-operative studies into how far it might be possible to substitute computers or mechatronics for the human brain and biological functions. Japan gave substantial amounts of capital to such basic studies and built an international foundation with its headquarters in Strasboug in France. It was a small effort but it grew from the feeling that I would like to begin to change the impression of Japan as a country concerned only with economic affairs.

I took part in five summits as Prime Minister. The summits are important conferences for Japan. The other countries which participated were the constituent countries of NATO and the EC, whose leaders met frequently each year to work for mutual understanding. By contrast, the Prime Minister of Japan is left out in the cold, only meeting up with the leaders of Europe and the U.S. once a year at these summits. Now the Soviet Union has dissolved, the Cold War is over and the UN has gained importance, Japanese prime ministers must understand the importance of summits as an opportunity to take action and to show leadership in a world context.

CHAPTER ELEVEN

WHITHER JAPAN THE FATHERLAND?

Toward the 'Third Opening' of Japan

The world has entered a new era. Historical changes are afoot: structural changes in the world order which generally happen only once or twice in a century.

The first of these historical changes is the collapse of the Communist Empire of the Soviet Union. The 'Red Star' which had threatened the world ever since the revolution of 1917, has been extinguished, and the constellation of white stars continues to grow. The Cold War is over. As Cold War structures collapse, instability spreads and problems break out across the globe. The world is facing new, widespread instability and confusion.

The second development is the growing success of collective security through the United Nations, and the burgeoning role of the U.N. The League of Nations was set up following World War I, but before it was functioning properly, World War II was upon us. Following WWII, the United Nations was set up but barely functioned during the period of the Cold War. Now, with the end of the Cold War and the outbreak of the Gulf War in 1991, the system of U.N. collective security has become effective and there is hope for the future.

The third structural change is the appearance of the European Community. The group of sovereign nations which was born following the Vienna Conference in 1815 has now put aside some portion of that sovereignty, and is again attempting to integrate into one large community. The creation of this vast political and economic dome which stretches from the Atlantic to the Urals is about to influence Asia, the Americas and other regions.

The fourth is the International Peace Conferences between the Arabs and the Israelis. These conferences, which were held successively in Madrid, Washington and Moscow, were major historical events which sought to transcend an Arab-Israeli conflict that had lasted for 2,000 years. The future will not be easy, but the fact that long-standing mortal enemies are at the same table looking for peace seems to me like a sign of a new era.

Faced with historical changes on such a global scale, each country is beginning to feel its way toward a new world order. There is the integration of the European Community on the one hand, and the collapse of the Soviet Empire on the other. At the same time, new nation states are continually being created through a process of disintegration. The flames of nationalism are everywhere set to burn fiercely once again. With the disappearance of its long-term enemy, the Soviet Union, the United States, too, is experiencing a weakening of its own unity. Having wearied of arms expansion, it is on the verge of losing its leadership role.

The U.N. is the joint international body man has idealised for many years, but it is still just an ideal to look up to; we do not yet know its true capacities. We need an aggregate of nations which will take this ideal and use it to push forward the frontiers of history.

There is a suggestion that the five permanent member nations of the United Nations Security Council; the United States, China, Great Britain, France and the former Soviet Union [P5], might take up this mission, but there is no real hope that they have the power to unite or to take agreed action. Moreover, neither Japan nor Germany participates in this group.

It is necessary for the countries which comprise the summit nations, those countries who share a common belief in liberalism and the market economy, that is the U.S., the U.K., Japan, Germany, France, Italy and Canada, to participate from the three poles of Europe, America and Asia. Acting under the collective mantle of the U.N., they must use their unifying power and their influence to cooperate with China, the CIS and other countries, and with their various regional co-operative organisations. At the same time they must assist in maintaining order now and creating order in the future.

The new world order should be founded on a *pax consortium* [peace through co-operative administration] enforced through a group guidance system with the U.S. at its head. Summits have an important role to play in bringing together the leading nations to pursue the original aims of the United Nations in the spirit of the U.N. Charter. I believe that Japan and Germany have the qualifications to become permanent member nations of the U.N. Security Council but that this can not be achieved suddenly. We must use the summits to try to solve the problems we face, be they political, economic, environmental, problems of security, or North-South issues. The summit, which began life as a means of securing economic adjustment, must now cut its cloth to suit the season and become a 'general summit' which will tackle all major world issues.

We have entered a period of world-wide historical change, and we have reached the stage where we must revise and extend the scope of Japan's foreign policy. Japan's previous international stance must be changed step by step. The path that Japan follows internationally will determine her destiny. The strength of Japan's economy and her technological strength has shocked the international community and caused unease abroad to an extent we find difficult to imagine. The leaders of Japan must be sure at all times to explain to its people where the ship of state is on its international voyage and what the prevailing weather conditions are. They must make no errors in that voyage. At the same time they must secure co-operation and alleviate international unease by telling the world clearly where Japan is heading.

Japan is facing massive reforms; a 'Third Opening' which will stand alongside the Meiji Restoration and the MacArthur Reforms. It is hard to imagine how Japan can prosper in the 21st century without it. People talk of 'Japan, the fragile blossom', and such descriptions are apt. For Japan to try to isolate itself within the Far East would be to sail very close to the wind.

We must realise that the enmity harboured by the nations who suffered from invasion and from the imperialist expansion of Japan, will be with us for three generations, until the war has been over a hundred years. So, for the next fifty years we must continue to tread the path of self-control and humility. In light of the mistakes and the tragedy of the Second World War, there are five principles to which Japanese diplomacy must adhere. These are:

1. No action must be taken abroad which exceeds the power of the nation.
2. Diplomacy must not be a gamble.
3. Policy must be both based on a full knowledge of the facts and transparent.
4. Diplomacy must not deviate from the orthodox current of world history.
5. Domestic politics must not become a weapon of diplomacy.

The Cold War is over and the social-economic structure of Communism has collapsed. What will be the future for liberal democracy and the market economy? Contrary to what Francis Fukuyama, the author of *The End of History*, suggests, what follows is not a dull consensus, but an intensification of the problems of narcotics, crime, the North-South issue, racial struggles, environmental destruction, religious confrontations, stagflation and discrepancies in wealth within nations.

Liberal democracy, having survived, is the legitimate path of world history. What sustains this at a domestic level is conviction based on co-operation and good sense. These in turn are accumulated in the traditions and conventions of races or populations forged by a long history. In liberal democratic societies good sense is born of balance and historically accumulated knowledge. Without this, our lives would be constantly plagued by relativism. Too much equality led to rigidity and finally to defeat: the result of a perversion of equality and of the power of privilege which supported it. Liberalism too, when it loses its good sense and balance, becomes mob rule.

For some time the trilateral relationship between the U.S., the CIS and China has been very unstable. The ideological conflict between Beijing, now the chief temple of Communism, and Washington, is worrying. Perhaps the long-term aim of Japanese diplomacy ought to be to have America and China face the Pacific and join hands as Pacific states.

When Socialist economics failed, economic friction occurred in the surviving market economies between Japan and the U.S. Following the fall of Communism, we may well see a similar outbreak of economic struggles between the advanced and the non-advanced nations. As a nation which has risen to become an advanced nation, Japan has a duty to make the necessary adjustments. Some aspects of the current political situation in Japan show a notable lack of ideas, philosophy or religious spirit. Politics is degenerating into a business, or a technique for getting on in life, and it is difficult to perceive any grand ideals. I would like to see politicians work together to leave a legacy of 'good politics' and 'a good Japan', for our children and grandchildren.

The role and qualities of Japan's prime minister

In Japan, the Emperor has symbolic authority, and actual power is wielded by the prime minister. It is a dual structure with transcendence on the one hand and secular life on the other. The Emperor is the symbolic focus of traditional authority and national integration. The prime minister is the focus of actual national power as manifest in the checks and balances of the legislature, the judiciary and the administration. This dual structure is a unique characteristic of Japan and is wonderfully functional.

Politics fluctuates between blarney and matters of life and death importance. If you don't do the rounds and dispense the blarney, even to the extent of making the mistake of bowing to the stone statue at the roadside, then you will not get elected in the popular democracies of today. It is a worldly business, but the Diet member elected in this way has a serious duty to deal with the important issues affecting people's lives.

To sum up, the prime minister exercises political power from a position at the centre of the clash between the government and opposition parties, at the centre of journalistic attack and at the centre of public praise and censure. Those who, having come so close to power, try to use it to achieve their ideals are 'veterans among the worldly'. The prime minister, who, of course, is one of the worldly, is in the thick of the battle and frequently, is wounded and falls. For politicians, disgrace and glory are inseparable.

In Japan, even if the administration is disgraced and falls, there is still the Emperor who exists transcendentally. The spray from the secular world does not reach the Emperor: nor should it. We should recognise that through this dual structure we achieve a harmony of Japanese tradition and democracy, and that liberal democracy in Japan is maintained through the balance of centripetal and centrifugal forces, by the effect of historical wisdom so to speak. Since the war, a number of administrations have fallen because of graft or maladministration, and the fact that Japan's liberal democratic system has been maintained until today is actually, I believe, the result of its dual structure.

When I became prime minister I was open about my conviction that, 'The prime minister of Japan should be a presidential style of prime minister', and I ran my administration accordingly. Some people objected either because of a lack of understanding of Japan's constitutional structure or because they were still swayed by the habits of the pre-war political system.

The prime minister under the old, pre-war constitution, and the prime minister under the new, post-war constitution are completely different creatures. Before the war, the prime minister's position was that of advisor to the emperor; the prime minister appointed cabinet ministers in a personal capacity and did not have the power of dismissal. The prime minister today selects his cabinet ministers without hindrance and dismisses them as he sees fit. He names judges to the Supreme Court in Cabinet Council and is also Supreme Commander of the Self Defense Forces.

In Japan, the executive and legislative are, in principle fused and the leader of the majority party in the Diet becomes prime minister. Consequently the prime minister's influence over the Diet is far greater than that of the U.S. president over Congress. The prime minister, by exercising his powers under the present constitution, can occupy a stronger position, within his country, than the U.S. president. The prime minister bears ultimate responsibility; he does not play a supporting role to a power bearing emperor. He is in a position to manage both state affairs and diplomacy through the exercise of leadership powers considerably stronger than those he enjoyed before the war.

The main task of the prime minister is to lead. Now that television allows immediate access to events both at home and abroad, what people most want to know is how the government is reacting. Politics must not lag behind the tempo and the rhythm of the people's 'desire to know'. Leadership is the power to control both. But people have continued to find it difficult to rid their minds of the way prime ministers used to operate before the War, and have rejected the Anglo-American style of leadership. The press is essentially 'anti-power', and so is apt to be suspicious of prime ministers who show strong leadership and to attack, or ridicule them.

In this kind of political culture, and faced with strong, if discreet, resistance from the bureaucracy, the prime minister is sometimes tempted to take the easy way out and go along with what officials and journalists want. It goes without saying that beneath all leadership must be concealed a wealth of careful study, investigation and policy. Leadership can not be complacent. It must be persuasive and comprehensible.

Above all, at times like this, when there is deep confusion and no long term political visibility, either domestically or internationally, the best leader must have three attributes: good judgement, powers of unification and a facility for persuasion. Passion, courage and historical insight are also necessary: nowhere more so than in present-day Japan. 'Good judgement', is an ability to forecast ways of dealing with problems. 'Powers of unification' implies an ability to bring together expertise, men of talent and proper funding. Finally, a 'facility for persuasion' is a talent for effective communication of one's policies known at home and abroad. In the television era, this has become most important.

As for governmental structure, we must reassess the present constitution. Unfortunately, the Japanese people have no personal experience of drawing up a written constitution. Not only was the Meiji Constitution a gift of the Emperor, but the present constitution was written to accommodate the demands of the Occupation army in the confusion following defeat in the war.

No constitution is perfect. Contradictions are exposed by the passage of time and defects become apparent. The major weakness in the Meiji Constitution, the 'independence of the high command' which led to opposition between the army high command and the cabinet, became obvious in the Taisho period. For so long as the Genro, Itō Hirobumi, Matsukata Masayoshi and so on were alive, government and military were unified by their personal force and opinions. However, when the Genro disappeared, this human unifying force was lost. The military authorities put military affairs under the direct control of the Emperor in the name of the independence of the high command, came into conflict with the cabinet and split the national administration. This became a major factor in bringing about the Great East Asia War. If the Meiji constitution had been revised at the start of the Taisho period so that the subordination of the military to the cabinet had been clarified, the tragedy might have been averted.

The pretence that there were no serious faults in the Meiji constitution brought ruin to pre-war Japan. The present constitution also has its defects and contradictions. These have been exposed, and we have reached a point where they are becoming increasingly difficult to ignore. Re-examination of the constitution is now becoming a national issue.

Navigating the 'sea of politics'

Government is a kind of human symphony. A drama woven by men, it results sometimes in tragedy, sometimes in farce. Politics is an act of state. It is the great mandala which weaves together the various aspects of human nature: joy and anger, ideals, platonic love, scheming, devotion, betrayal, malice. In the end, for politicians, all politics comes back to 'How can I form a cabinet, and how can I bring the cabinet down.' The quest to seize and retain power is something extraordinary and formidable.

Human society, since primitive times, has comprised four elements: the leader, the hunter, the jester and the shaman. My own experience in the vortex of politics has taught me that the jester and the shaman are more necessary to the functioning of human society than might be expected. Perhaps this should not be surprising given the strong tragic element in politics.

Hamaguchi Yūko was one of the Prime Ministers I admired the most. He was a master in meditation and was known as a fastidious and well-bred man. I heard the following reminiscences from his secretary, Nakajima Yadanji.

'When the Wakatsuki cabinet fell and a successor was being sought, Hamaguchi, as the new president of the *Kenseikai*, was chosen by the Genro who came to entreat him to assume office as representative of the party. Twice, however, Hamaguchi refused. He told me, "They will come again and then I will accept." Even a great man like Hamaguchi was resourceful in this way.'

Intelligence is necessary, but without a knowledge of the world you cannot cross the sea of politics. Politics is like swimming in a sea where the hot and cold currents of pure-hearted dedication and malicious envy, mingle. There are times when the pure-hearted dedication you encounter reduces you to tears, but there are times when you are sickened by the envy. Typical of the pure hearts are people's letters and donations, especially those that are anonymous. I am often moved to tears at receiving touching, heartfelt letters of encouragement and expressions of patriotic feelings with cash or cheques for 10,000 or 20,000 yen.

When I was Prime Minister, I would spend two hours on Saturday afternoons writing simple postcards in response to letters from primary and junior high school students. I enjoyed those hours. From the time I became Prime Minister to the present day I have also had more than 290 letters of advice and suggestions from the post-war political commentator and veteran journalist from before the war, Hyakutake Isao.

Letters from the general public are not all pleasing: many are attacks, but even these can be encouraging in a way. I was inundated with truly abusive and slanderous letters and phone calls over the tax question.

Among those with whom I travelled the sea of politics, there are two people who gave me unstinting friendship. They are dead now, but I will never forget them. One of them was Miura Kineji who I got to know at the time the Kōno faction was formed. Miura gave freely of his advice and support both as a journalist and as a friend. His advice to, 'Be short, and to the point', forged my domestic politics and diplomacy. Frequently, he pressed former Prime Minister Tanaka to have me take over the administration. On the night that I was appointed Prime Minister, he came to my house whilst I was out, and gave my wife a document running to ten pages of instructions on how to act as prime minister, and concrete advice to her on being the wife of the prime minister.

The other was Tanaka Rokusuke. I cannot say that we always saw eye to eye on everything, but he burned himself out physically for the sake of Japanese politics in general and my cabinet in particular. He left a book, 'Plain Speaking on the Conservative Mainstream', and a sealed letter for me in his will. As a politician he was irreplaceable.

Even though the ultimate end of politics is no more than a struggle over the locus of power, there must be scholarly research and scientific objectivity: there must be an academic basis for politics. At the very least, this is what politicians must aim for. I have denounced the politics of drift as no more that deals between the ruling and opposition parties; bargains within the political world. And I have tried to bring learning and politics together.

For years I had been saying, 'Power must serve culture', and when, during my administration, I set up the International Research Center for Japanese Studies[1] it was a reflection of these ideas. I, who spoke of an 'International Japan', was also alive to Japan's own identity and was keenly aware of the necessity to spread this sense of identity to the people of Japan and to the rest of the world. It was obvious that the old, imperial historical view wouldn't serve the purpose and that Japanology was also unsatisfactory. I therefore I went to Kyoto to meet with the head of the Kyoto University Humanities Research Centre, where new methods were being used to study this question, and I talked into the night with Kuwabara Takeo, Imanishi Kinji, Umesao Tadao, Umehara Takeshi and Ueyama Shunpei. The result was that the LDP co-operated with me, and the International Research Center for Japanese Studies was set up with surprising speed.

Despite slow progress, the Centre was relatively successful in its goals of promoting foreign exchanges, spreading Japanese studies abroad and rejuvenating Japanology through a combination of new methods and co-operation between the universities.

The late Emperor

In November 1966, I reported to the Emperor as Minister of Transport and, as the audience was ending, I said, 'Your Majesty, this is very presumptuous, but there is something I have wanted to ask about for a number of years. I wonder if I might be so bold?'

It was unusual for a cabinet member to ask the Emperor a question, and something that even the Prime Minister did not do. Normally one only answered the Emperor's enquiries. At the time, I was forty-five and in my second cabinet post. With great respect and trusting to the Emperor's kindness, I asked,

'There is a book by Shiba Ryōtarō called "Martyrdom".[2] The author writes that General Nogi, the head of the Peers School, gathered the three imperial grandchildren together at the palace two days before his suicide and gave what was his last lecture. His discussion of Yamaga Sokō's "Facts about the Middle Dynasty", was difficult and so the younger brothers, Prince Chichibu and Prince Takamatsu, drew back the screens and escaped outside. Only the Emperor stood patiently and listened to the end. He writes that General Nogi was choked by emotion and spoke through tears. Was that actually how it was?'

General Nogi had arrived at the Imperial Palace at about 7.00 in the morning on September 11 1912, and had taken the unusual step of

The Showa Emperor on the 60th anniversary of his accession to the throne

clearing the room before this last lecture to the Princes in which he expounded on what it meant to be an Emperor.

The Emperor listened to me intently then replied quietly, 'My recollection is unsure, but if that is what it says, then that is probably how it happened.' The Emperor's character was such that he forgave such a self-indulgent question. If I had not known this would be the case, I would not have asked. I gave the Emperor the volume of 'Martyrdom' I had hidden beneath my papers. The Emperor took the book and gazed fixedly at it.

The book used in that last lecture, 'Facts about the Middle Dynasty' was hand copied by General Nogi and was said to be annotated by him. When I became Prime Minister, I asked the Director of the Imperial Household Agency, Fukuda, if the book still existed and was told that it was in the Imperial Palace book repository. When I heard this, it made me think about how the late Emperor, as the oldest child, had studied to be Emperor and how, from being small, he had shown such perseverance.

When I was a student at Takasaki Middle School there was a big army exercise in Gunma Prefecture which was attended by the Showa Emperor. It was on this occasion that the 'incident of the mistaken road', occurred. The policeman on the leading motor bike was so tense that he took the wrong road and then committed suicide in atonement. I was extraordinarily shocked, It occurred to me that small parts in large machines are fated to follow the laws of mechanics, and that machines have a juggernaut quality.

Once I went to see the Emperor take part in a ceremonial presentation of arms where he inspected the troops astride a white horse. I didn't especially regard the Emperor as a god, but I remember it being very awe inspiring. The Emperor I paid my respects to as a middle school student, and the Emperor I saw attending the opening of the Diet and awarding decorations and whom I met at investitures, all had the same majestic, dignified demeanour.

As a Cabinet minister and as Prime Minister I served the Emperor at close quarters and experienced his personality on any number of occasions. He was a soft, warm character, genuine and fastidious. I am in agreement with Grand Chamberlain, Iriye, that the Emperor he had a good memory and was skilled at giving praise. When we first met, I was nervous and stiff, but the Emperor himself dispelled my nervousness and bade me relax. As a result, I grew to experience, along with a sense of respect for the Emperor, a feeling, in some ways, like that of meeting with my father.

Usually the Emperor would say, 'Thank you for your trouble', to reports of work. But when I visited America in January 1983, and again when I reported on my return from the Williamsburg Summit that same summer, and from the Bonn Summit in 1985, in addition to his usual words he added, 'You did very well for us, thank you'. I felt braced up by these words. I could imagine how the Emperor felt, bearing on his shoulders, as he did, such great responsibility toward the people and to the spirits of the Imperial Ancestors.

On the 60th anniversary of the Emperor's reign, in April 1986, I made a speech, in the National Sports Stadium, in which I thanked His Majesty for his efforts on our behalf over the long years of his reign. As I spoke, the numerous political changes and diplomatic suffering endured by the Emperor during those sixty years from the Taisho period through the Showa years, passed through my mind like the patterns in a kaleidoscope; the Tokyo earthquake of 1923, the Depression, the upheavals, social instability, War, defeat, the Occupation, imperial tours of the regions; and I was moved to tears.

In my diary I wrote:

> Pure hearted like a child,
> Benevolent, like the sunlight,
> Transparent, like reflecting water.

The late Emperor embodied the essence of imperial learning. He was one of the great Emperors of Japanese history. Truly, as the Zen priest Yamamoto Genpō said, because there was no 'I', and there was nothing to call his own, his was a character which shone everywhere, inexhaustible, like the sun.

When, in October 1988, we were prostrated by the Emperor's ill health, I gathered the wild flowers that the Emperor so loved and sent them to him. I learned that the Director of the Imperial Household Agency, Fujimori, had taken the flowers to the Emperor, who's eye was caught by one of them, a bearded creeper [*Lycopadium claratum*] and that he asked where the flower grew. The Chamberlain answered that it probably came from northern Kanto, but in fact I recollect that it came from the Tōhoku region.

The Emperor used to say, 'There is no grass called "weed"', and even when he was on his sickbed he applied himself to his studies.

Nearing the end of a long journey

My memoirs too are finally reaching their conclusion.

During my long journey I meditated as a way of regaining and maintaining spiritual equanimity and freshness. I would sit in religious contemplation for an hour with a Zen priest in the sombre main hall of the temple and when the two of us had finished and had chanted the ten line Kannon Sutra and the four pledges, I was invigorated, as if my heart had been wiped clean and equanimity and freshness were restored. For me this was a clinic for the body as well as the mind.

My introduction to Zen meditation dates back to my graduation from Tokyo University when I tried it as a way of preparing my mind to die on the battle-field. After I left the navy, I took advantage of a connection I had continue practising, and I invited Inaba Osamu and Sonoda Sunao to go to go along.

From the mid 1950s through the mid 1960s I went to the Aomatsu temple in Shiba. A predecessor of mine at Takasaki Middle School was head priest there, and there was a Zen meditation hall underground, below the main hall. It was set up so that one could always enter from

Meditation at Zenshōan

outside and sit and meditate, so when the evening meeting finished, I would sit there alone and secluded. In the mid 1970s when that head priest left, I stopped going, although occasionally, I would sit cross legged, Zen-style, in my mountain villa at 'Hinode'. My one and only sutra was the Shōbō Genzō' of the high priest Dogen.

Then right about the time I became Prime Minister, I talked with Yotsumoto Yoshitaka and, for the five years that I was in office, I went almost every Sunday to Hirai Genkyo's, 'Zenshōan' in Yanaka. Even now I go about twice a month. If I don't go I feel agitated.

I still do not understand Zen meditation. What one knows with the head is as unreliable as bubbles; it does not permeate the body and become fixed. When you meditate, you sit in the temple hall and regulate your breathing. Quietly, you draw in your breath, up, through your back bone, from the well that lies 3,000 metres beneath your buttocks, then you send it 3,000 metres back below ground.

You try to concentrate your mind on this and to rid yourself of worldly thoughts but these thoughts keep floating to the surface. With perseverance, and by imperceptible degrees, you free your mind of worldly concerns; your head becomes light and you find yourself where it seems as though a spring stream is purling by. I have even had the thought that to understand that there is no enlightenment is, in itself, enlightenment. Ultimately, it is not a matter of thinking with the head.

Sometimes strange things happened. Once when the chief priest rang the bell for the end of one hour of meditation, my whole body seemed to disintegrate, to collapse without warning, and I was plunged into an abyss of contrition. My sense of self disappeared and everything seemed to glow with warmth. Perhaps it was an hallucination.

According to the head priest there are thousands of stages, great and small, in the process of enlightenment. Like crossing the distant mountains, there are distant places beyond the distant places, and he who arrives at last can be counted a lucky man. Though there are differences in the distances we travel, we are all on the same journey. At any rate we keep walking. And that, perhaps, is enlightenment: to keep walking and to keep sitting.

The Buddhist hymn of praise written by the high priest, Hakuin and the words of the high priest, Dōgen,[3] keep coming back to me: 'People are to Buddha, what water is to ice' and, 'To seek enlightenment through enlightened things is an illusion; true enlightenment is reached through experience of the world of phenomic reality.'

At home with my wife

Kawai Yoshinari, a man for whom I have great respect, was trained, as a student, in the Nishida School of moral education by Nishida Kitaro himself, and kept up his studies of art and ideas. Once, when I was young, he said to me, 'I can recognise God exists, yet I still can't believe in him'. He was more than seventy years old at the time, and I was deeply impressed that such an old man should still be searching so avidly after the truth. Now I too am about that same age I become increasingly convinced that I am contained within another layer. I have tried to record what is in my heart, but I fear I have expressed my feelings rather too forcefully about the way life should be, while my own real, everyday life is still prey to envy and desire.

Since the mid-1950s I have written on the last page of my notebook every year, the words, '*Ketsuen, Sonen, Zuien*'.[4]

Human life may be infinite but in the end there are at most fifty or sixty people who travel closely with us; our relations, school friends, work-mates, neighbours. Human life passes so quickly. While it lasts we must treat one another warmly, hold one another close, and at the last 'goodbye', take our leave casually, with fond memories and a sense of satisfaction.

231

Life does not stop. It moves on burying memories as it goes. Before I finally put down my pen I want to give my heartfelt thanks to my wife. Throughout the harsh political journey, she has walked silently beside me, helping me, never once voicing any displeasure. One night toward the end of my time as Prime Minister when, because of the new tax issue, I was under fire from all sides, I got back to the official residence to find my wife sitting alone in a darkened room watching the television pour vitriol on me. I watched her from behind and could not bring myself to speak.

Only when I relinquished my administration could my wife's days regain their tranquillity. It is my penance that I pray constantly for her good health.

> *Falling deeply asleep*
> *My wife's breathing,*
> *Deepening autumn*

POSTSCRIPT

Now the story is told I find myself embarrassed by the telling. I embarked on this project hoping to leave a frank record of my life in politics for those aspiring to become politicians and for the young people to whom the future belongs. Instead I fear that what I have written might be read as excuses and self-justification. I beg the reader's forgiveness for a story written with passion but without skill: my hope was to make my confession without restraint.

These pages are the footprints left by the desperate race of the son of a Gunma merchant. These footprints pass from the early years of this century, through three Imperial reigns. They traverse the shores of the islands of a Japan on the Eastern edge of Asia borne down upon by the Japan Current. Blown by the wind, washed by waves, trampled by horses, scarred by seaweed and pebbles, the beach is now storm blown. But in the course of time, those footprints, will be washed away by those winds and waves, and the seashore will be left once more in its natural unmarked state.

Life is a series of connections. From the day we are born, we begin to act: we suffer ups and downs, we endure defeats and we have no inkling of when our time will end, but everything that happens, no matter how big or how small, is woven into the symphony of life. We need not be left with malice and sadness in our hearts, though we may not necessarily be snuffed out when joy and gratitude are uppermost. Our hypocrisy and arrogance and the hurt we have caused others lurks like sediment at the bottom of our memories. This is human nature.

If the truth be told, some of the worldly ambitions and desires I have had, I will perforce carry with me to the next world, and I have thoughts which are indefensible.

In the long trail that has marked my path, the thing that has stayed most firmly in my memory is the petition I presented to General MacArthur during the Occupation. When I look at it now I see places where ambition and the rashness of youth are evident, but what

233

shines through is a wholehearted passion for the restoration of independence, a passion that I felt as a citizen of an occupied country who had himself fought the Great East Asian War. At that time, ordinary, honest Japanese were deeply fearful for the future of the country and they prayed for an early deliverance from the shame of occupation by a foreign army. From where we stand today it seems unimaginable. To me, it was a ray of hope for freedom as for the Israelites in the midst of their demoralisation and confusion during the Roman occupation.

The various avenues my feet trod subsequently are the record of one politician, a politician challenged by the times and at the mercy of fate. I have called upon my memories, read the documents and talked to the people who were involved. I hope that my research has been thorough but, if errors persist, I am open to correction.

I have no doubt that in politics, as in life, fate is important. People talk of, 'providential timing, an advantageous position, good relations', but without luck you can achieve nothing of importance. When, in the flow of history, luck is necessary, it seems that Providence graciously provides it both to individuals and states. At such times, just as Christ prayed to God in the Garden of Gethsemane, before his death, 'O my Father, if this cup may not pass away from me, except I drink it, thy will be done.'[1], people are moved in unexpected ways by desperation. Luck manifests itself to a greater or lesser extent in men's determination, their feelings of responsibility, their romanticism and insight.

But that is not to say that luck is always with us; and no matter how fine the man, there are things that cannot be done without luck.

Some Japanese politicians have written diaries like those of Hara Kei, but there are few memoirs penned in person. In contrast, prominent foreign politicians almost all leave behind memoirs or autobiographies. Perhaps this is because it is regarded as a social responsibility for those involved in public service.

I too felt great hesitation at writing my memoirs. What made me dare to take the plunge was the sense that it was both meaningful and responsible for Japanese politicians, like politicians abroad, to leave behind a personal record. In particular, I felt it was important to leave as accurate a record as possible about my personal experiences as a Diet member involved in the politics of Japan for over forty-five years from the time of defeat in the War and the Occupation.

And yet, through lack of space, though there is reasonable detail up to the Tanaka Cabinets, the later period is only briefly summarised in the present volume. I would like to write about those years again in another volume.

This publication has been made possible through the help of many people. The opportunity to write the memoirs came with an article in the Nihon Keizai Shimbun called 'My Personal History'. Since then I have received invaluable help from Mr Okazaki Moriyasu in the political section of that newspaper.

I would like also to thank my secretaries and the staff at Takushoku University and at Kodansha who gave freely of their time to make this publication possible.

May 1992

Documents

1. PETITION TO GENERAL MACARTHUR

January, 1951

H.E. Gen. MacArthur:

It is a stern fact that the recent situation in Korea and the general trend of Europe are giving delicate psychological influences upon the Japanese people to-day.

For a long time the Japanese have beguiled what they thought and felt in smiles. But their smiles do not mean that the Japanese who live amid volcanoes and typhoons are not thinking anything at all.

I have been watching silently rather sympathetically the tradition of Japanese feelings to yield silently to other's friendship – that is to say the spiritual beauty trained for long two thousand years.

To-day, however, we arrived, I believe, to a stage where, pressed by various conditions, Japan's affairs, whether in domestic politics or in national defense, should be dealt with responsibility and honor of the Japanese themselves.

At this juncture, therefore, I, while thank for your kindness of these long years, would like to inform you frankly, as one of the young Japanese and member of the Diet representing the public opinion, of what is at the bottom of our heart.

As I firmly believe that the rainbow bridge of idealism spanning over the Pacific Ocean must not be faded with clouds and mists, I dare submit this 'Frankly Speaking' to you.

If I could obtain your esteemed perusal, I would deem it highly honored.

Yours sincerely,

Yasuhiro Nakasone,
Member of the House of Representatives

Outline of My Personal History

- Born in May, 1918: (32 years old.)
- Graduated form the Law Department of Tokyo University in March 1941. Mobilized to serve in the Navy for 5 years: After demobilization, was appointed Inspector of the Tokyo Metropolitan Police Board: In April 1947 and in January 1949, supported overwhelmingly by young people, was elected twice the member of the House of Representatives from Gumma Prefecture, remaining as a Diet member till now.
- June 1950: attended as a Japanese Representative at the MRA World meeting at Caux in Switzerland. Came back to Japan after having made an inspection tour of Europe and America.

Contents

1. What are the Japanese Thinking?
    (1) On Occupation Policy.
    (2) On Peace.
    (3) On the Korean Affair.
    (4) On World War III.
    (5) On US Attitude.
    (6) On Soviet's Attitude.
    (7) On the Attitude of Other Countries.
    (8) On Rearmament.
    (9) On the Trend of Society.
    (10) On Education.
2. What are Young People Thinking?
    (1) On a Change in Occupation Policy.
    (2) On the Nationalism of Asia.
    (3) On the Treatment of the Repatriation Problem and the Families of the Deceased Soldiers.
    (4) Concerning the Police Reserve Force.
    (5) Concerning a Song Which is Widely Sung by the Youths.
3. What does the Japanese Want?
(a) Domestic Matters.
(b) Concerning Peace Treaty.
    (1) On Japan's Position in the Set-up of International Democracy in Asia.
    (2) On Immediate Abolition of Occupation and Control, and Independent Self-defense.
    (3) On a Peace Treaty to be Concluded Rapidly and Fairly.
    (4) On Participation in the United Nations and Establishment of Collective Security Guarantee.

1. What are the Japanese Thinking?

(1) On Occupation Policy

A Great majority of the Japanese people, expecting Communists, cannot help holding in esteem the sublime ideal and courageous act of Your Excellency and the gentlemanlike behaviour of the Occupation personnel. The Occupation of the past five years is a success worthy to be recorded in history. But, Occupation itself, however successful it is, is not a pleasant thing from the standpoint of the occupied.

This is especially the case with us who have never had the bitter experience of being occupied and who have observed the occupation policy faithfully with the hope of independence in the near future.

'Japan is already qualified for signing of peace treaty. Continuation of Occupation is caused, not by the circumstances in Japan itself, but by the objective conditions surrounding Asia.'

This is what stated by the authority. Then, why is the sovereignty on domestic administration and diplomacy – not to say of military defense – not yet returned to us? Are the Japanese distrusted for they are doomed being incompetent? We can hear these sad voices on the street.

For examples:

Last year a jeep of the Occupation Forces drew up to the yard of a farmer who had really no wheat to deliver to urge him to complete his alloted delivery of wheat. Japanese voices were hardly recognized in operating the police Reserve Force. Every bill sponsored by a minority party to be presented to the Diet is required to be approved by G.H.Q. and it is exceedingly difficult to obtain an approval. Japanese sentiment against American exceedingly higher living standard than ours. These sad things, though we have much to reflect upon ourselves in this connection, inviting the activities of communists, are brewing an atmosphere in this country to think over.

Democracy is repetition of trials and errors. Moreover, a man, if committed, takes discreet steps on his own responsibility. Long Occupation makes both the occupier and the occupied deteriorated.

It is impossible for a general, however sagacious, to subjugate a modern nation craving for freedom of personality under occupation for more than five years solely by his personal character.

Giving back of free will, termination of Occupation and thereby established cooperative relations, fresh, wholesome, bright, cheerful and sincere relations – this is what the entire nation is earnestly desiring for, and I believe time is ripe for it.

(2) On Peace

The nationals are not blind to the efforts for peace of the U.S. They are anxiously waiting with keenest interest for the result of the efforts of the state department, Mr. Dulles, adviser to the Secretary of State and his staffs, as reported in newspapers. However, I would like to call your attention to the fact that opinions as follows are voiced by a part of the Japanese people.

Documents

'We have been kept in vain for five years long in suspense with a peace of meat dangling right before our nose. So, no hope for this time again. It is nothing but a gesture.'

'After the World War I a peace treaty was concluded within one year. But the World War II is not yet ended, for the second global war is a fight between democracy and totalitarianism, and totalitarianism of Japan and Germany was defeated in the former half of the war, but that of the soviet Union is yet remained, and the conclusion of peace treaty is hold until that time.'

'Peace with a majority means U.S.-Soviet war. The U.S. is not prepared yet for a war, and will not choose at the last moment a peace with a majority for Japan.' etc.

What the Japanese people hope for the U.S. to do in regard to the peace issue in U.S. determination to push unhesitatingly ahead what she believes in. The majority of the Japanese are implicitly praying that the U.S. without having a regard for the Soviet Union and other countries proceed with her faith in justice in a long reaching plan.

(3) On the Foreign Affair
There is a feelings working on the Japanese people that the U.N. forces are unexpectedly weak to retreat before the ill-equipped Communist Chinese forces and that A-bomb is of no use to the man-power strategy on the continent. Thus, a minority with a sane sense are concerned over the defense of this country, most persons of economic circles are worried about the future of the special procurement demand and how to preserve their properties. This is the true picture of the present conditions.

The general atmosphere to be deplored most among the Japanese is their indifference to the Korean incident regarding it as if it were a war between the U.N., or rather the U.S.A. – a member of the Organization and North Korea and Communist China, – nothing to do with the Japanese except economically.

The people do not dance to the music of the flute, played by the Government and political parties to cooperate with the United Nations, for they do not actually realize what the war means and remains aloofly unconcerned. What is the reason of it that they behave like a third party?

I dare say it is because there is found no political responsibility and initiative on the part of Japanese under Occupation.

Another reason is that international news available for Japan are limited by all optimistic and information organs such as the press and radio echo them.

I think, here lies the basic reason.

(4) On World War III
Most of the Japanese people are thinking that World War III is inevitable and that it will come within these years in the nearest future. They are not credulous of optimistic information given by the Government. But of war to which they would be directly related all the Japanese fearing it somewhat to the extent of nervous prostration, have abhorence and for the conception of war makes them recall vividly

239

the war devastation, air raid, shortage of food, death of their family members. The people who were so eager to defend their country before the war are now astonishingly negative toward war. It is for this reason that the Constitution providing for renunciation of war is bolstered though in a vague atmosphere.

What the Japanese people who see the World War III inevitable worry deeply in such atmosphere are the following matters:

1. Will the U.S. defend Japan to the last? Is Japan worth it?
2. What international position will the U.S. give Japan in that event to make Japan cooperative?
3. Will food supply be available to the last?
4. A majority peace for Japan excluding the Soviet Union and other countries on her side might give them a pretext for World War III.
5. Prior to it, North Korea and Communist China might not fail to invade Japan, and isn't it wiser for Japan to declare neutrality from the beginning to the last and thus try to ensure the safety of life and property of the nation?

The Japanese people instinctively dislike communism. However economic difficulty, prolonged occupation and the pressure from the Red sphere in the East are making them to take a wait-and-see policy. Attention must be drawn to the fact that Anti-Soviet sentiment in Japan is not so visible as it is in the U.S.

It is urgent need for the free world to give moral courage to the Japanese people by establishing international democracy and translating it into action. Utilitarianism must be beaten by moral courage.

Servility caused by the defeat and occupation has much spoilt Japanese morals fostered in two thousand long years.

(5) On US Attitude

Japanese people are thinking that the Atlantic Charter reveals the true intention of the U.S. However, we cannot overlook a recently growing tendency that those who are pro-American are sneered at as sneaks and opportunists. This is especially so among young people. This comes probably from apprehensions of Japanese people who come to know the facts of economic activities of some of the Occupation personnel, of monopolization of civil airlines by U.S. companies, banning in Japanese territories, of no payment of interest on the fund amounting to hundreds of millions of dollars for Japanese export expenses deposited at the National City Bank, and an information that the Bonin Islands and Okinawa implicitly claimed as their own by the Japanese are reportedly going to be transferred to the mandate of the U.N.

Regarding U.S. backing on the repatriation problem, aids in goods, in social works and others, the nation are grateful for them from the bottom of their heart.

(6) On Soviet's Attitude

Against the Soviet Union who, making the scrap of the Ruso-Japanese Neutraity Treaty, meanly committed the dead-lurk and still holds 370,000 Japanese prisoners of war, are ninety per cent of the entire national bearing a potential grudge. But there are not a small number of Japanese who are being beguiled by the clever tactics of Stalin arousing the passionate fire of the natives by using Koreans in Korea, Annamese, in French Indo-China and Malays in Malaya while the U.S. is fighting in Korea, France in French Indo-China and the British in the Malay Peninsula. There are not a few businessmen who are giving financial aid to the Communist Party in fear of future troubles. Some financial persons somewhere in Osaka who are clever at being insured avows that 'I hate the Communist Party, but the Communist is not bad.'

(7) On the Attitudes of Other Countries

The Japanese people are keenly regretful for the countries in Asia and around the Pacific and Britain, France and the Netherlands whom we gave so much troubles in the war and are worrying how to express this feeling even in our difficulties. Some people even advocate to invite, if possible, Parliamentary members, young men and school students of those countries to Japan to express personally our regret. We pray that these countries forgive Japan as soon as possible and allow us Japanese to enter the international community.

Generally speaking, promotion of mutual understanding between these countries and Japan is not active, for the country directly in charge of the occupation is the United States and naturally coming and going to and from between the United States and Japan are very frequent but the relationship with these countries is indirect and the Japanese, and statesmen in particular, are too precautionary to speak frankly.

The Japanese people are desirous of improvement of their relations with these countries to enable them to exchange mutual opinions more frankly.

(8) On Rearmament

Public opinions in Japan for or against rearmament, I should think, are in reality half and half.

The rearmament, however, even if it is at all realized, is said to be unexpectedly weak in its strength, if it is materialized in the form rumored to be suggested at present. The reasons therefor are as follows:

a) A sense of honor does not allow the Japanese to be fighting forces under a foreign commander and his directions.
b) Since the occupation the Japanese have seen what cold treatment wounded soldiers, bereaved families of the war dead, etc. are receiving. The pangs in the heart caused thereby will not be easily healed.
c) The young men of today have lost their idea of serving their country and many of them either indulge themselves in hedonism or devote themselves to Communist campaigns.
d) There are many mothers and women who are opposed to war and armament.
e) Following the collapse of munitions industry, industry has been disbanded.

f) Japan lacks the power of bearing financial burden for the maintenance of armament.

Should, however, rearmament be to be carried out by all means,

a) A good span of time is required for preparation to re-educate the people spiritually. It is most important among measures to speedily improve the treatment of the war victims.
b) The secret of success therein lies in the guarantee to be given to Japan for her complete independence and equal status. The true defense of Japan is impossible of execution under the relations of occupation and the occupied or superior and inferior. It becomes possible only through combination of the liberty-loving peoples who are equal to each other.
c) The elimination of excessive concentration of Japan's economic power should be more alleviated than at present.
d) Some financial aid should be given to Japan by the lease-lend or some other means.
e) The military forces should be placed under the control of the Diet for their operation, and should not be used as a rule outside of the country. Such measures are required to be guaranteed.

Among those who are hesitant about rearmament, there are a fairly good number of them who, though they are keenly feeling its necessity, yet reserve their opinion out of a fear for giving unnecessary misunderstanding to Australia and the Philippines.

I do hope that you will also keep such a matter in mind.

(9) On the Trend of Society

After finishing my tour of Europe and America lately, I have come to keenly realize that the people who have no attachment to the culture and tradition of their own country are inferior people.

Viewed from this standpoint, there seems to be a trend in Japanese society at present for depreciating the culture of its own country more than it is necessary or even for entertaining a sense of colonial servility. It is really a matter of regret. This state of things is perhaps ascribable to the lack of morals which lies at the bottom of the national character, desperation brought about by the defeat in war, a change in the idea of ownership since the occupation, etc.

What requires our specially close attention is this unstability of ownership, which is sure to entail uneasiness in society. This is because, if the fruits of the service worker are not sure to revert to him, there will be no one who would work. In Japan, the Civil War of Ōnin threw the country into disturbances. The powerful families kept their henchmen in order to create power for safeguarding their ownership. This state of things continued until Hideyoshi Toyotomi obtained from Emperor Goyozei (towards the end of the sixteenth century) at Juraku Mansion an Imperial charter for national security measures (guarantee for propriety of ownership), by which the former barely laid down a foundation for a peace throughout the country.

The farm-land liberation measure and the labor union countermeasure, which have been taken since the occupation, have thrown a new light on Japan and have cause her to make progress. Such progressive measures have 'deprived the Communists of their nutrition'. Ironically, however, the same Communists distorted the true spirit of these measures and made an ill use thereof for depriving the people of their ownership by agitating them. They wrongfully disseminated such ideas as 'Take other's things without working' or 'Other's possession is yours.' It is really beyond all imagination how much such ideas have resulted in demoralization and have tended to disrupt social order.

Such trend of society is responsible for the embezzlement of public money by Kōdan employees, politicians' scandals, or offenses against sexual morality.

Of course ownership has something of public character in it. It is reactionary to protect ownership unnecessarily. Consequently, with reference to ownership in general, a clear demarcation line is to be drawn between the public and the private ownership in order to give a criterion to social order. This is considered most important for appeasing the agitated mind of the people and for encouraging labor.

(10) On Education
Though the social trend is in confusion, the children of elementary and middle schools are all care-free. They are engaged in studies, make the results thereof public and are getting on quite freely. It is, however, a pity that the teachers are devoid of ability for carrying out the new educational method. It is necessary to turn out without delay as many capable teachers as possible who are possessed of a true spirit of democracy. Our teachers are especially wanting in the basic principle for exerting influence on their pupils with all their character. The present day teachers are of too much poor an coarse quality for their pupils to be favorably influenced through the latter's contact with the former.

2. What are Young People Thinking About?

(1) On a Change in Occupation Policy
Young people of Japan have noticed that there was a great chance of the policy in occupation in the past six years, with a line drawn in about 1947, between the period of the punitive dismemberment of old Japan and that of the reconstruction of new Japan.

Surely old Japan, being impatient for gaining upon Europe and America, has committed many sins and errors since the Meiji era, consciously and unconsciously, internationally and internally. It seems that she was destined to dismemberment. Although, however, she has put forth a great number of buds of repentance, she has not necessarily produced its fruits to perfection. Nevertheless, the sudden change of the objective situation appears now to force up that Japan to the position of a co-operator in the middle of punishment.

It may be said that, for the Japanese to whom punishment has been dealt out, there is some feeling that a convicted person who has not reformed completely yet, being necessary as a second in a scrap, has been made a co-operator on parole. It seems that here are the causes for the misfortune of Japan from the eternal viewpoint and for her luck from the actual one. That is, viewed from the actual angle, thoughtful young people of Japan do not always think that the causes of the Pacific War lie entirely in evil acts on the side of Japan.

Accordingly, they are glad to admit this change in occupation policy, but throw doubt on the motives of this change. In other words, the Allied Power's, misunderstanding the history of the Far East, carried out a punitive dismemberment by censuring Japan for her past from an absolute criterion, but everyday history moves in relative actualities inclusive of the Allied Powers. Thereupon this change leaves doubtful points as the whether, as they cannot ignore the historic reality, they revised their previous censures from a relative standpoint, and mitigated the punishment anew on reflection of having pronounced too harsh a sentence on the faults of Japan, or whether, though the sentence is not too harsh, they have mitigated the punishment in view of the situation only to utilize Japanese for the convenience' sake.

Young people hate the 'taking-advantage-of the situation' principle, the opportunism, and the authoritarianism very much. In order to make true co-operators of the rising generation of Japan – that is, in order to give them moral courage – an exposition with a wide view of things formed in the light of the history of the Orient and movements of the world is required. And I am confident that the rising generation want it.

(2) On the Nationalism of Asia

The Japanese were the most conceited nation and had the shallowest brains in Asia; they were blessed with an insularity. Japan with backward capitalism was so silly that, as soon as she made a little progress by bending utmost efforts to come up with Europe and America, and marked greater advances than other Asian countries, she, in her turn, made a cat's paw of herself for countries in West Europe, taking advantage of their movements for safeguarding their rights and interests and their aggressive acts, and partook of repasts chiefly in China. What a shame upon the Japanese as Asians having common scripts and common color that these were the causes leading to defeat in war, and that it was the Americans having different scripts and different color that did their best to hold them in cheek!

The quickening of the nationalistic movements in Asia has now awaken vibrations in the hearts of young people in this insular country. The greater part of them has joined the colors in the Pacific War, and has lived with young people of India, Burma or Indonesia on the field.

The reason why these young people of Japan have an aversion to present diplomat-politicians with Prime Minister YOSHIDA first on the list is that the odor of these past shrewdness are strong on them.

It is a good thing to co-operate with the Occupation forces; that is a matter of course. But I fear that their spirit may have forgotten that they are the Japanese who have given trouble to neighboring countries, and that they are a member of Asia; it may wish to impress the Occupation forces favorably by obtaining as many marks as possible without mentioning what it should req
uest them, and to get up by forestalling others or to make greater advances.

Japan must absolutely renounce a nationalistic egoism.

It is the feeling of the young people of Japan that, by reflection of atonement, they wish to contract neighboring friendship with Asian countries; that, by services for Asian countries, they wish to be permitted to join the Asian family of nations; and that, in consequence, they wish to contribute to the reconstruction of Asia and the peace of the world.

In that sense, what young people of Japan expect most is the movement of Prime Minister Nehru, a humanist in India.

(3) On the treatment of the repatriation problem and the families of the deceased soldiers

Thanks, respect and love of the whole nation are centered on General MacArthur because of his exerting extraordinary efforts concerning repatriation of war prisoners detained in the Soviet area, that is, by what with seeing and encouraging representatives of awaiting families personally, and what with sending Japanese observers to the United Nations.

Demobilized young people are especially sensitive on this subject in the light of a love of comrades in arms. Another important problem that is being forgotten is the treatment of the wounded soldiers and the families of the deceased soldiers. I understand well that, on the principle that war does not pay, these people should not be treated especially with consideration. But the circumstances of these wounded soldiers and families of the deceased soldiers, after the termination of war have been terrible indeed. I was only moved to tears as a fellow countryman at the sight of old mothers and wives whose pillars of the home have been snatched away, going through hardships in the fields or in an itinerant trade under inflation or deflation. Although the Daily-life Security Law is applied for the maintenance of their minimum living, it is quite impossible to make a living with the amount they are supplied with.

It was a wrong war, but it is not their faults. I am told that in the United States the expenses of $1 billion are used for ex-service men. Young people have been grieved over the actual conditions of Japan after the war's end as a question affecting humanity above winners and losers.

In view of these realities, I fear that in future there may be no one who will offer his life for the defence of his country.

(4) *Concerning the Police Reserve Force*

It is now a prevalent idea of Japanese youths that the Police Reserve Force which is 75,000 strong is not under the Japanese operation but has fallen to a mercenary.

'It is the youth's faith too, that one's own country can be safeguarded only by one's own hand. Strengthened as its equipments are, the mercenary Police Reserve Force has been losing the national interest. The salaried-manlike position of the member of the Force which has nothing to do with one's soul nor the moral values is going to be deserted by the pure hearts of the youths. Alas, this sorrowful out comes!

(5) *Concerning a song which is widely sung by the youths*

Let me quote here a song written by a certain youngman and sun widely by the serious minded youths excepting the Communists and the decadents.

> The Peace Conference is at hand, the Peace is coming.
> On that morning, for which we have longed for,
> As for the daylight shining through icy clouds,
> Let us, eightly million brethren, drape in black with tears,
> Our national ensign which flies on every door.
> It's a day of big sorrow, rather smaller joy.
> It's a day for burial of our fatherland Japan.
>
> On June 3, 1853,
> A black ship came into peaceful Uraga Bay,
> An American Admiral named Perry was on board it.
> Naosuke Ii, our forerunner had concluded with him,
> The Ansei Treaty of Peace and Amity.
> Ninety-seven years have elapsed since then.
> On August 30, 1945,
> A super-foretress landed on Atsugi air base,
> And the American General MacArthur came out of it.
> The instrument of surrender signed on the Battleship Missouri,
> The Peace Treaty which is expected to come soon,
> All means the treaty of peace and amity in Showa era.
> Look at the advance in Meiji era brought by the Ansei Treaty.
> Had we missed the development in Showa at this moment,
> Brethren,
> We might well be laughed at by those born in Meiji era.
>
> Admiral Perry freed Japan of her material seclusion.
> General MacArthur liberated us from mental isolationism.
> Look, the Japanese people
> Cannot be overcome by mere actuality.
> We have acclimatized into our race the historical reality,

The Buddism, the Confucianism, and what not.
Let us dissolve the agony of defeat,
In the melting pot of Japanese history.
In the melting pot of Japanese history.
Unequal treaty concluded in Ansei era,
Had been revised in the 34th year of Meiji era.
Let us make it independent and equal,
The treaty of Amity to be concluded in the era of Showa.
Yest, we have a great task to be completed,
With half a century's time.

A country fallen by the political failure,
Could be restored with the oppositionist's policy.
The loss of people's independence by sin,
Could not be regained without the hero of atonement.
Jesus Christ in Israel and Ghandi in India;
On account of Christ, the ideas of Israel,
Glitters for the eternal future,
And, because of saint hero Ghandi, the dignity of Indian race,
Overcame the Anglican peoples.
The garment of Jesus was plundered by a guard,
Ghandi had left only a pair of glasses and a spinning wheel.
That poor are the heroes of salvation,
Casts a heartwarming hope over the mankind.
Oh, our fatherland, our brethren,
Standing up from this depth of sorrow,
Let us make a vow loudly.

3. What Does the Japanese Want?

Domestic Matters

(1) Concerning Patriotism and Idealism

What is most required in Japan today is patriotism in the right sense based on idealism. I don't say this because of the aggravated Korean situation. Today's Japan lacks one thing that should underlie the free community which is attributed to her constraint upon the existence of the Occupation Forces. Since as a result of defeat the pre-war faith was abandoned and socalled 'patriotic acts' were prohibited by the occupation policy, the Japanese has warned even against the use of the word 'patriotism'.

But it is a virtue, not a crime, to maintain the right creed of life and the peace order of the free community and to render some sacrifice by the constituent members in order to safeguard against aggression.

I cannot but express my sincere regret at the fact that the faith in justice has been lost and the Japanese has corrupted into the way of thinking 'which is stronger?' instead of 'what is right?'

In the pre-war days, Japan was not such a mean nation that took a neutral and 'wait and see' attitude toward aggression or expected help from the Occupation Forces before shedding up their blood for repelling an aggression.

If the basic occupation policy is changed without justification for the sake of convenience, it will be unavoidable that the defeated people in depaire is liable to take advantage of power.

Now is the time for Occupation forces to re-examine and reconfirm 'what is right?', tracing back to the basic Occupation regulations, nay, to the Potsdam Declaration.

At any rate, the most important problem of today is, what the Japanese nation, situated very close by a new red nation burned with fervent and vigorous intention to attain her acial independence, should be hereafter.

Now we must awake the whole Japanese people, especially the young men and women, to idealism which is required to protect our freedom. We must unite the patriotism which is sprung from such an idealism. These all arise from the moral courage. The moral courage emerges from a free individual and free community. It is from this viewpoint that we cry for the revival of the free will. In order to unite the Japanese people and make this country strong, there will be no other way except the withdrawal of the Occupation Forces from Japan.

The Kuominstang Government of China has fallen down itself, not been defeated by its enemy. Now the movements of revival of the Asiatic race have been launched both in China and India.

How can we Japanese attain rehabilitative of our country, if we have not such spirit and patience for our Japanese as shown by Pandit Jawaharlal Nehru and Mao Tse-Tung?

To a great regret, the Japanese are thoroughly effeminated to-day. The men of intelligence call for guidance based on the new point of view.

Concerning Peace Treaty

The Prime Minister of this country, who is on the wrong side of seventy, had the impudence to state that the present Government would conclude the peace treaty. It is nothing more ridiculous than to hear he stated it, if he uttered it from his heart, though it would be excusable that he did it for the political tactics.

Without distinction of age or sex, the Japanese people are all anxious about the problem of the peace treaty. Because we are responsible not only for the present Japan but also for our descendants and history in the future.

Accordingly, for the purpose of concluding the peace treaty, the Cabinet should be formed by representatives elected on the basis of ability from among each field of this country.

No matter how the present Government be outwardly supported by the majority of the Diet members, if the peace treaty is signed by the present Cabinet which has been formed by the Ministers nominated in favor of party interests, it is feared that such draft or treaty will cause the people's anger and the treaty will come to be not implemented in the long process of history in future.

I am confident that the peace treaty should be concluded by a Cabinet composed of the Ministers who must be, at the least, (as I know that this depends on the contents of the peace treaty), the ones representing the former soldiers with experiences of fighting at the front, laborers, farmers and young men, as well as the men of lofty character with the ability of persuading the people.

A peace treaty concluded by the present Cabinet that has no strong sense of responsibility for such kinds of people as mentioned above is merely a peace treaty with some part of the Japanese people, not one with the majority of the Japanese people.

Foreign Affairs:

(1) On Japan's position in the set-up of international democracy in Asia

I have stressed that the Japanese people should be given an ideal and moral courage in order to resuscitate Japan as a trustworthy colleague of the free world. From this viewpoint I would like to point out that the Japanese people will be greatly encouraged if they are to be instructed in what manner international democracy is to be established in Asia with collaboration of European and Asiatic countries, what is Japan's position in it and what role is to be demanded of her politically and economically.

(2) On immediate abolition of occupation and control, and independent self-defense

I have already referred to this point. But what I would like to call your attention to is the new situation caused by the Korean war. In view of the present conditions such as, for example, the mine-sweeping at the front by the sea-clearing party of the Maritime Safety Board, transportation of war supplies to the front by Japanese ships and the operation of the National Police Reserve Forces, when Japan's positive cooperation with the U.N. is required more positively than before as the Korean war grows more and more intensified, things will not go as desired under the formula of occupation, because it is anticipated that some of these cooperative activities will hardly be covered by the Potsdam Declaration or the basic regulations of occupation. Accordingly a new arrangement or cooperation will become their table. Viewing it from the international law and also from international morals, I hope you will agree with me on this point. In preparation for a possible situation in which enforced cooperation is impossible legally and morally, it is desired that occupation and control be speedily abolished, thus liberty of will returned to the Japanese, and new relationship for cooperation set-up on the basis of the free will of the majority.

It is also desired that keeping pace with the tempo of preparations for defense in the U.S. and U.N., completing of preparations in this country for self-defense independently by the Japanese themselves be approved. To give some counter-measures for defense for the time being, they are: a setup placing defensive forces such as the National Police Reserve Forces, Maritime Safety Board, National and Local Autonomous Polices, Special Examination Board of the Attorney-General's

Office, Fire-Fighting Units, and others, under a single command in an emergency: Completion of civil defense corps in each perfecture: Expediting preparations for control on electric power, communications, traffic and others:

(3) On a peace treaty to be concluded rapidly and fairly
With various requests already submitted from various quarters on this point, I have nothing to say except on the following points:

a) A declaration of end of war may possibly be very difficult to write off the occupation and control by the big four powers carried out on the basis of the Moscow Agreement. Speedy conclusion of a peace treaty effective positively and creatively and the much-desired termination of occupation and control is desired.
b) In view of the fact that most of the wars in the past had their causes in the peace treaties concluded to settle the previous wars, it is desired that stress be placed on this point and the sublime spirit as shown in the Marshall Plan and U.S. aid to Japan be allowed to run through the expected treaty. That is to say, the treaty is desired to be based on the principle of, not 'who is right?' or 'which is right?' but 'what is right?'

   We desire from the bottom of our heart that an epoch-making treaty be concluded in the latter half of the twentieth century as a product in the latter half of the twentieth century as a product of man's wisdom with the victor countries giving territories and natural resources to the defeated country, thus putting an end to the basic cause that gives rise to war.
c) If the treaty is based on the principle of 'What is right?' and also on all-out penitence of mankind, it will not be criticized by the countries that did not participate in the treaty, nor offer a pretext for non-participation, intervention or aggression to them.
d) It is desired that the treaty be such as bring about neighborly friendship with the countries ravaged by Japan, and in particular with the countries in the Far East, through the spirit of service on the part of Japan.
e) As for reversion of territories, a popular vote is desired with all respect for the will of inhabitants, giving up all unilateral decisions.
f) As for the formula of Japan's defense and politics, the matter is desired to be bas4ed on self-determination of the race, stipulating no restriction in the peace treaty and leaving the matter to the free will of the nation.

(4) On participation in the United Nations and establishment of collective security guarantee
he Japanese people are heartily desirous of participating in the United Nations Organization, and when our desire realizes, we are not going to shirk our duty only asserting our rights, for such an action would be against the true spirit of the world organization nor deserve be worth the name of a member of the international community, and no voice would be granted to him.

It is the will of a great majority of our people to assume their obligations with sincerity and also to assert their rights. In order to cope with such we are at any time quite ready for taking necessary domestic measures.

If, however, the admission of our country into U.N. to which we aspire so much should unfortunately become impossible of realization through same nation's exercise of veto, it will be a serious problem what is to be done for Japan's security. In such a case, the collective security set-up according to Article 51 of the U.N. Charter is desired to be established all over South-eastern Asia, so that Japan's safety may be guaranteed as a link of that security chain. There is really no other way, and I most emphatically add that such step is desired to be taken.

January, 1951

General MacArthur,

For the honour of the United Nations and the United States of America, I hereby make a representation of my opinion, with courage and sincerity. I beg you for your generosity and wisdom to lend your ear to one who makes and advice for the sake of America. The leaders in the occupied Japan are obsequious to the authority, and those who hanker after distinction and think of their own interest only flatter them. This is the reason why an anti-American influence increases in Japan. People who see incompetent members of parliament and so called 'apres-guerre' public officials have a spite against America, resulting in making the Communist Party influential. Japan has a snake in her bosom. That snake is namely flatterers. What led Japan to defeat is neither army nor government, but the snake in Japan's bosom, the flatterers. It cannot be overlooked that such people flatter the authority today. They made the Japanese army take a wrong course, and makes the Occupation Forces take a wrong course. Of course, they do not intend to ruin the country, but they do so without knowing it. If the Occupation Forces lend ears to their words and are satisfied with their doings, a historical failure will be made in Japan near future. It is said that unpleasant advice is a good medicine. If our unpleasant advice is accepted, the United Nations will be honored with one more glory in the history of the world.

1. The men of ability in Japan are not these flatterers, but are among those who fought against America and England. Without their co-operation, it would be impossible in Japan to knock down the communism. If the American army leave Japan, a riot will break out everywhere in Japan and a social disturbance will not be suppressed. Is it said a success that the disarmed Japan cannot exist without the arms of the American army.
2. It cannot but admit that the result of diplomatic intercourse between America and Soviet Russia was a minus to the United Nations both in Europe and Asia. If an atomic bomb is used in future, it cannot suppress the enemy with a limited number of bombs, if all the world except south and North America is communised. If America intends to relieve the human beings in the world, she must win a diplomatic policy of today. To win, she must make use of men of ability in every country. The weakest points of America are that she relies on

her experiences too much and that she has a self-conceit and dogmation to settle the problems of the world for herself. This was said by Dr. Leishower and Mr. Baldwin in your country before we recognise it. America must make use of Japan.

3. What did the United Nations receive as a reward of their having knocked down Japan in the second world war? They are communisation of Asia except Japan, unification of China by the Chinese communists, disturbance in Korea and East South Asia, and treachery of Soviet Russia that was once a friendly country of America.

2. LETTER FROM SENATOR ROBERT TAFT

February 6 1951

Dear Mr Nakasone,

Thank you for your letter of January 24 and the enclosed draft of your petition to General MacArthur.

I read your communication with great interest. Though I am by no means an authority on Japanese affairs, I am of the opinion that you are correct in what you write concerning a number of issues.

I have been in discussion with John Foster Dulles about this problem and I believe that his views are extremely close to my own on the matter of the situation in Japan. Since his return from his posting in Japan, he is very pleased to receive information on the views of individual Japanese on what is happening in Japan.

I am very glad that we could meet during your visit to America.

Yours truly
Robert Taft

NOTES

Chapter One

1 According to Satomimura records, before this time the region was the territory of the Nitta family and Nitta Yoshisada spent his early years here. It would seem that the Satomi family, immortalised in the Tale of the Eight knights of Satomi, [*Nansō Satomi hakkenden*] moved from here to the Bōsō peninsula in 1441.
2 Nakasone Yoshikazu.
3 Now Takasaki High School.
4 The position of post office chief was traditionally an inherited one and carried weight in local politics.
5 The nickname, an affectionate diminutive, was adopted as the name of Nakasone's support group magazine.
6 A recess, or alcove where a scroll may be hung and items of value are displayed.
7 Saigo Takamori (1827-7) a samurai and bureaucrat of the Satsuma Domain who played an important role in bringing down the Tokugawa shogunate and who later took his own life following the failure of an uprising he led against the central government.
8 *Izu no Odoriko* was made into a silent film by Gosho Heinosuke in 1933, two years after talking movies were introduced to Japan and when most Japanese films were talkies.

Chapter Two

1 The most senior bureaucratic position in each ministry.
2 The first officers or lowest ranking officers mess.
3 Japan was forced to cede the Liaotung Peninsula, won from China during the Sino-Japanese War, after intervention by Russia, France and Germany.
4 A well known country *samurai*.
5 1 shō=1.8 litres.
6 Nasuno Yoichi was a famous *samurai* archer.

Chapter Three

1 November 1982.

2 Yoshida Shigeru, Prime Minister 1946-47 and 1948-1954; Kishi Nobu-suke, Prime Minister 1958-1960; Sato Eisaku, Prime Minister 1964-1972.
3 Traditional rice straw floor mats.
4 *Yūgekisen.*
5 A village headman from Chiba who sacrificed himself on behalf of his villagers by criticising the high tax burden imposed by the *daimyō.*
6 Approximately equal to one U.S. pint.
7 Established on 8 March 1947; descended from the Japan Co-operative Party.
8 *Sensei* is a term of respect used for Diet members as well as doctors and teachers of all kinds.
9 Established on 9 November 1945.
10 Established on 31 March 1947, descended from the *Nihon Shinpōtō*, Japan Progressive party.
11 The Imperial Rule Assistance Association [Taisei-Yokusan Kai], which replaced the political parties after their dissolution in 1940, was perhaps the clearest expression of totalitarianism in Japan.
12 *Kinsei Nihon Kokuminshi.*
13 Tsukahara Bokuden was the foremost fencing master of his time (1490-1572).
14 Yoshida Shigeru was the leader of the Democratic Liberal Party, formed in March 1948 from the Liberal Party and a faction of the Democratic Party.

Chapter Four

1 These words, and subsequent quotes from the petition, are reproduced as they appear in the original English text, without correction.
2 See appendix p. 253.
3 See appendix pp. 236-252.
4 When Yoshida was heard to mutter 'damned fool' in response to an opposition attack on the floor of the Diet, the opposition led first a vote of censure and then a vote of no-confidence. Yoshida responded by dissolving the Diet.
5 Article 9 of the Constitution reads: Aspiring sincerely to an international peace based on justice and order, the Japanese people forever renounce war as a sovereign right of the nation and the threat or use of force as a means of settling international disputes.

In order to achieve the aim of the preceding paragraph, land, sea and air forces, as well as other war potential, will never be maintained. The right of belligerency of the state will not be recognised.
6 Taira no Kiyomori always wore a monk's habit over his armour in an effort to present himself as peace-loving.

Chapter Five

1 *Minshushugi Kagakusha Kyokai [Minka].*

Chapter Six

1 Faction leader, appointed second vice president by Ikeda on the death of Ōno Banboku 29 May 1964.
2 The equivalent in Japanese of 'to fight like cat and dog', is 'to fight like dog and monkey'.
3 Government Account for Relief in Occupied Areas: aid monies made available by America during the Occupation.

Chapter Seven

1 Zengakuren, National Student Federation; Sōhyo, General Council of Japanese Trade Unions.
2 *Kokubo no Kihon Hoshin*
3 Cross-factional groups of LDP Diet members with expertise in particular areas of policy making.

Chapter Nine

1 The most serious of these incidents was the Kyōwa Sugar-Refining scandal which involved donations to both LDP and Socialist Party members.
2 Written with different characters 'satō' can also mean sugar.
3 A play on words: tara = cod; fugu = blow-fish; tarafuku = to eat heartily.
4 When, for example, the Chief Secretary of the Chinese delegation expressed a desire to invite the American table tennis team to China, the leader of the American group, Harrison, immediately accepted and left from Haneda for China.
5 A frequent post-war guest of Yoshida, who often travelled to the continent and to Hong Kong.

Chapter Ten

1 Known as the three 'k's for the initial letter of the words in Japanese: *kokutetsu, kenko hoken, kome.*

Chapter Eleven

1 First bulletin published in 1989.
2 A term used to refer to the suicide of an attendant on the death of his lord.
3 Hakuin was a Rinzai Zen master; Dōgen was founder of the Sōhō sect.
4 *Ketsuen,* a Buddhist term pronounced Kechien, implies 'to form a connection', or 'establish a relationship with other beings'. *Sonen* does not appear as a term in Buddhist dictionaries but implies a prayer for longevity or the elimination of difficulties, whist *Zuien* means to act in accordance with conditions or according to ability.

Postscript

1 St Matthew 26–42; Authorised King James version.

For Product Safety Concerns and Information please contact our EU
representative GPSR@taylorandfrancis.com Taylor & Francis Verlag GmbH,
Kaufingerstraße 24, 80331 München, Germany

Batch number: 08153795

Printed by Printforce, the Netherlands